I'LL NEVER
CHANGE MY NAME

I'LL NEVER CHANGE MY NAME

AN IMMIGRANT'S AMERICAN DREAM
FROM UKRAINE TO THE U.S.A. TO
DANCING WITH THE STARS

VALENTIN CHMERKOVSKIY

DEY ST.
An Imprint of WILLIAM MORROW

I'LL NEVER CHANGE MY NAME. Copyright © 2018 by Valentin Chmerkovskiy. All rights reserved. Printed in the United States of America. No part of this book may be used or reproduced in any manner whatsoever without written permission except in the case of brief quotations embodied in critical articles and reviews. For information, address HarperCollins Publishers, 195 Broadway, New York, NY 10007.

HarperCollins books may be purchased for educational, business, or sales promotional use. For information, please email the Special Markets Department at SPsales@harpercollins.com.

FIRST EDITION

Designed by Renata De Oliveira

Library of Congress Cataloging-in-Publication Data has been applied for.

ISBN 978-0-06-282047-1 (hardcover)
ISBN 978-0-06-287122-0 (B&N MD signed edition)
ISBN 978-0-06-287123-7 (BAM signed edition)

18 19 20 21 22 LSC 10 9 8 7 6 5 4 3 2 1

This book is dedicated to my mother, who made me the man I am today.
And to my father, for setting an example every single day.

CONTENTS

FOREWORD

Val told me that he is writing a book and asked if I would write a Foreword. I knew nothing about what that even means, but obviously I said "yes" and have been thinking about it ever since. He semi-insisted that I read a few chapters before writing this, but I declined, because while this is one book I myself have been waiting for, I really don't need to read it to know that everyone else definitely should. I can imagine what you all are thinking: "Obviously! You're his brother and you should say only nice things, blah, blah, blah." But if you really know me, you'd know how I refer to myself as "nothing but a traffic light." I just say it how it is.

Val became my brother at age zero (I was only six) and became my student at around age ten (I was only sixteen, obviously). So you have to understand that our time spent being brothers was limited to sometime before Val's puberty until sometime after he turned twenty-five. At that point he had a talk with me about how "he wasn't my student anymore" and that I needed to recognize "the grown-ass, accomplished, proud man standing in front of me." I will never forget that day. It's the day Val "officially relieved me of my duty."

I never asked to be anyone's coach. It just sort of made sense. I would take a lesson for fifty bucks and then teach Val what I had learned. Simple and cost effective. Fifty bucks for a dance lesson at that time for our family was like stabbing yourself in the thigh with a fork. No permanent damage, but it hurts like hell. Again, I know what you're thinking: "Okay, Maks, that is *so* dramatic!" But I assure you that every immigrant like us at some point had to part ways with fifty bucks for some "cha-cha lessons" and felt extreme pain, because that was like a tenth of the family's net worth!

I was a tough coach. I had very limited time, no finances, and lots of personal crap to deal with because I was still a freakin' child myself, but I loved Val so much and with so much passion that I wanted so much good for him. I did my best and coached the shit out of him and his partners! I will let Val tell you about his life as a competitive ballroom dancer, but I will only say that in our debut as a student/coach duo we managed to whoop some serious Juvenile Blackpool Champion ass (sorry, Mark Ballas, you know it's all love, but it's also all true).

Our parents' favorite saying while we were growing up was, "When we die, you'll only have each other, so you can never fight." And we never fought. I may have, one time, sorta shoved him, but I wouldn't remember and I would have to have been super pissed about something, because I could never inflict pain on him. We weren't twins, but we were so close that I felt his pain every time he hurt. Which happened a lot. I mean, this kid could not stop either falling on his face, or getting elbowed in the face, or getting his bottom lip stuck in the wheels of a skateboard (I will let that marinate with you for a second, but it really happened). I also always had a near–heart attack experience whenever Val and his partner were waiting for a result of a just-finished competition. In hindsight I was a fool, because my guy almost never lost.

Vicariously through my brother I too am a multiple-time World Ballroom Latin Dance Champion and a whooping seventeen-time

United States National Latin and Ballroom Dance Champion, I too am a Concertmaster Violinist in the Manhattan Music Symphonic Orchestra, I too am a poet, a rapper, an amazing point guard with a Shawn Marion shot, the bowler with the highest average that one summer, a rock-paper-scissors legend, and an impromptu-speech-giving god, but what you will find in the ensuing pages is that Valentin Aleksandrovich Chmerkovskiy is also a rare breed of a person due to an almost magical collection of life experiences.

I assure you that while you're coming to an end of my Foreword, I too am coming to an end of reading it. Probably not my first time, either, half because I'm making sure I don't sound stupid and half because I've probably read a billion Forewords by now and just want to compare "mine to theirs," LOL. I'm sure Val will be diligent in explaining where our competitive nature and pursuit of perfectionism is coming from. I too am about to turn the page and read something fresh, creative, empowering, educational, without a doubt extremely well written, and definitely profound AF. So, without further ado, do yourself a favor and read this book.

P.S. You're welcome ;).
—*Maksim Chmerkovskiy*

I AM VALENTIN ALEKSANDROVICH CHMERKOVSKIY

In the summer of 2016 I had just come off a national dance tour and was heading into my eleventh season as a professional dancer on the reality TV talent show *Dancing with the Stars*. The tour took me all over the United States with my older brother Maks, the two of us dramatizing the story of our lives. "Maks & Val: Our Way" told the saga of the Chmerkovskiy brothers, immigrating to the States from Ukraine and conquering the international world of ballroom dancing.

We had written and choreographed the show ourselves, and bringing it to towns in almost every one of the fifty states changed the lives of all those involved. Maks and I celebrated our adopted home of America through imagination and dance, and there was laughter at every performance, and tears, too, both on our faces and on the faces we saw out in the audience. We were welcomed beautifully and managed to connect with people from all corners of the country.

That summer politics dominated the American landscape.

Hillary Clinton and Bernie Sanders battled it out, and Donald Trump completely turned the political world on its head. Dancing in a show that honored love of our country, told through the eyes of two immigrant brothers from South Brooklyn, I traveled across the heartland during the full heat of the primaries, through the perfect storm of the party conventions, and amid competing barrages of partisan rhetoric. I felt like I was getting a crash course on democracy.

As if the news cycle wasn't loaded down enough, that was also the summer of the Rio Olympics. Even there, politics and patriotism entered into the mix. Because of the European migrant crisis, refugee participants were given special status to compete. Some pretty astonishing figures broke through during that Olympiad, and among the most prominent were the U.S. women's gymnastic team, the "Final Five" who brought home the team gold and collected a dozen medals in all. They were real-life superheroes—I was going to say they were like Powerpuff Girls on steroids, but in the sports world maybe that's not the best way to put it.

The dance tour I was on with Maks took its final bow in San Jose, California. I flew back to the New York area, where my parents lived, where I grew up, and where I considered my true home to be. A friend of mine used to say that people should either travel the world or live in New York City, because it amounts to the same thing. After two months of total immersion in America, the urban streets felt alive and electric, and I just wanted to plug myself in again to the big-city vibe.

Dancing down the crowded sidewalks of Manhattan (actually, I walked like everyone else), I ducked into a corner bodega for a coffee, the kind that if you order "regular" comes with milk and sugar, served in an iconic blue "We Are Happy to Serve You" cup. The Olympics were winding down by that time, but on the flat screen behind the cash registers, the climactic moments of the women's gymnastic events were playing out.

The team that year represented the best of America, the same incredibly diverse country that I had witnessed while out on tour. Laurie Hernandez, Simone Biles, Gabby Douglas, Aly Raisman, and Madison Kocian offered a rainbow of colors, backgrounds, and styles. They were in the midst of becoming the most dominant Olympic gymnasts ever, a lineup of super athletes that everyone in a politically divided country could get behind.

All the customers in the bodega, at least, were behind them, gazing transfixed at the TV screen. I've been a fan of gymnastics, an amateur fan if you will, my entire life. I glanced up and saw something that immediately caught my eye: a small-statured girl, very young, super charming. Beyond an obvious incredible athleticism, she had a special quality about her, a calmness in the middle of a pressure-packed situation.

The hard-to-put-your-finger-on-it essence came through in the way that she handled herself. She wasn't just an Olympic athlete, but a little star. A lot of athletes want to be celebrities and celebrities were always trying to be athletes, but here was someone who combined the best of both worlds in one compact package.

"Damn, who is this girl?" I thought to myself. She was in the middle of a tumbling routine, and on one of her passes she did something I thought was amazing.

She found the camera. That's how we say it "in the biz" when someone on TV breaks the fourth wall and looks straight into the lens. It makes for an instant connection. My mentor, Mandy Moore (the legendary choreographer, not the pop singer), had to work really hard to teach me the mechanics of finding the camera, because the move can easily look crazy and intrusive if overdone or done tastelessly. Well, this girl nailed it perfectly.

I vividly remember the moment I fell under her spell. She stuck the landing, raised her arms, and gave a wild, triumphant smile. From my time on *Dancing with the Stars* I knew the ability to find the camera was an essential skill for any performer. In one so young, that single move signaled some badass sass, as well as confidence and experience way beyond her years. It was as though she had winked at the whole scene, having fun with it.

I laughed out loud, shaking my head in appreciation. "Who does this lil' girl think she is?" I was blown away. I couldn't hear the commentary because it was a New York corner deli with a lot of noise going on, orders flying back and forth and sirens screaming by outside. But I remember the graphic coming up to identify the athlete.

"Lauren Hernandez, Old Bridge, New Jersey."

I couldn't help it, I called out, "Let's go, Jersey!" New Jersey, my second home state behind New York. I knew Old Bridge, and had spent my teenage years in Saddle Brook. I felt a swell of pride. I wasn't that deeply familiar with the world of gymnastics, but I had never seen many Hispanics among the ranks, so Lauren—everyone called her "Laurie"—was a revelation in that respect, too. This sassy Puerto Rican girl from New Jersey who could find the camera—well, all she was missing were the big hoop earrings and her boyfriend's name on her necklace and she'd be singing, "I'm still Laurie from the block."

"All right, Laurie Hernandez from Old Bridge, New Jersey," I said to myself, "you got my attention, little star."

Then I grabbed my coffee, left the store, and didn't think anything more about it.

Dancing with the Stars matched professional dancers like me and my brother with celebrity contestants who were singers, actors, media personalities, entertainers, or sports figures. I had only a few days before the scheduled announcement about which couples would be paired off to compete on Season 23 of the show, which would premier in September.

As is the case in real life, on *Dancing with the Stars* no one tells you beforehand who your partner is going to be. The choice of dance partner had been made for me, and going into the season I remained in the dark.

In the days leading up to the announcement, the buzz among the professional dancers rose to new heights, with multiple texts flying daily, almost hourly. Everybody thought they had the inside scoop. The burning topic? Who was matched with which celebrity contestant.

"Who do you got? What do you know? I got this person, and I heard you got that person."

I tried to stay out of the crossfire of gossip. I actually didn't want to know who my partner was going to be. I preferred to be truly surprised when the revealing moment was taped, and if I knew beforehand I would have to fake my reaction. I'd rather be honestly disappointed than be dishonest with how I felt.

Whomever she was, I would be spending a very intense three months of my life with this person. We would be diving in deep—physically, emotionally, and even, yeah, spiritually deep, maybe as deep as two human beings can possibly get over the course of ninety days. Pretty damn deep, let me tell you.

The "first meeting" segments were like mash-ups of a blind date and an arranged marriage, with a little bit of a shotgun wedding thrown in, too. Normally they took place in Los Angeles, organized by Deena Katz, the show's casting director, but at times they were shot elsewhere, for the convenience of the celebrity involved. The meetings were all done on camera. The producers liked to spring the news on the contestants with the videotape rolling in order to increase the drama. When we were finally introduced, our reactions were shot in close-up, to be broadcast so that thirty million people could dissect and debate every nuance of the match.

What partner I was assigned made all the difference. Would we be simpatico? Was she passionate about dance? Would there be chemistry between us? Season after season the first meetings made for a crazy, only-in-show-business challenge, but one that kept me coming back to the show every year. Not knowing made the process sweeter and more intriguing to me.

So I didn't want to be told, but my dear brother Maks was determined to tell me. After more than twenty seasons on *Dancing with the Stars*, he was totally dialed in to all the backstage chatter.

"Deena gave me an address in New Jersey for my partner first meeting," I told him.

"New Jersey, really? Hey, I know who that has to be. Bro, you got matched up with that Muslim chick, the fencer who competed in the Olympics, remember her? She made a big splash by competing in a head scarf."

I did a quick Google search. "Ibtihaj Muhammad?" I said, mangling the name as I pronounced it.

"Yeah, Muhammad, that girl." Maks laughed, considering the whole situation to be comical. "A Chmerkovskiy and a Muhammad doing the salsa—only in Hollywood!"

Deena took care of casting for the show, and wore a lot of other hats, too, acting as the liaison between celebrities and dancers whenever friction arose. She was the one who settled the dust and made sure everything ran smoothly.

On my way to the meet, she again got on the phone with me. "Listen, you're meeting your partner later today and we're really excited. Please call me right afterward and tell me how it goes. Oh, and stop in the parking lot when you get there and wait for the camera crew, because we don't want to ruin the surprise."

I followed the GPS directions through the wilds of New Jersey. Just before arriving at the address Deena gave me, I received a text from Shawn Johnson, the Olympic gold medalist who had been a winner on Season 8 of our show and then returned for Season 15. Even though we had never been paired up as dance partners, we built a solid friendship and kept in touch from time to time.

"Oh my God, I'm so excited. You better be nice to her or I'll kill you. She's like a sister to me."

"Shawn," I texted back, "I don't know what you're talking about. I mean, Hi. How was your summer? I hope you're doing well."

"Oh my God—you mean you don't know?"

"No."

"Oh my God, please don't tell Deena. She's going to kill me." Shawn tended to kick off all her texts with "Oh my God." I think she had the words programmed into her cell phone so they just automatically came up.

"All right," I texted back. I was conflicted. I didn't want to know, but I wanted to know. "I'm not going to blow the secret, but just tell me who it is."

"No, no, I can't," Shawn replied.

At that moment I pulled into the parking lot at the address, a huge pole-barn-style gym in Monmouth, New Jersey. Maks had gotten the sport wrong. It wasn't fencing, it was gymnastics. A big banner hung across the façade of the facility.

CONGRATULATIONS TO OUR LAURIE HERNANDEZ ON HER AMAZING JOURNEY IN THE OLYMPICS!

I took out my cell and texted a photo of the banner to Deena.

"Way to be discreet about the whole thing, but I promise to act surprised."

That banner might have given me a hard-to-miss hint about who I'd be matched up with that season, but I would still be a surprise to Laurie. I had to sit in the parking lot for a half hour, waiting for the crew to mic me up. I thought back to the week before, recalling that epiphany moment in the New York corner deli where I saw her for the first time.

During the course of the Olympics, Laurie Hernandez had become the quintessential American girl. She *was* America, the way America looked right then. In my eyes, she was the spirit of the new reality in the country, the beautiful one I had encountered in towns all over the United States that summer while on tour with my brother. Laurie Hernandez, a new American heroine—or rather, a heroine for a new America.

I was about to embark on a journey with this superhero, and

I thought, "Damn, that's a huge responsibility. I better do a good job." Laurie clearly possessed everything necessary to be a champion. At the same time, she was still young, just turned sixteen that summer. She had a maturity about her, for sure, but she still displayed a youthful presence. I thought it might be her eyes, so large, so full of energy, brimming with life and curiosity.

I would find out that Laurie could look down from her towering height of four eleven—or look up, rather—and those eyes, man, you would just sink into them. They spoke of innocence yet strength, pure humility through and through. Whenever I encountered a personality like that, I felt an overwhelming sense of wanting the best for the person, a need to help and protect her. I wanted to do all I could to communicate whatever knowledge I had accumulated, to provide her with all the tools from the huge toolkit that by then I'd been lugging around for over thirty years.

With every partner I had on *Dancing with the Stars*, women from varied backgrounds and wildly different paths in life, I tried to discover the overlap in our lives, attempting to plant our shared flag on common ground. What did I have in common with a sixteen-year-old Hispanic girl from New Jersey?

I thought of the journey Laurie Hernandez had experienced breaking into a world that in the past had never welcomed people who looked like her. Gymnastics remained very white, three-quarters white by a recent survey, with Latinos making up less than four percent of all participants.

"*Si Dios lo quiere*, to represent the U.S. as the only Latina gymnast would be such an honor," she told the press before the games. "I feel I could be a role model to other Hispanic gymnasts interested in the sport, but I also want them to understand the importance of being focused, determined, and not giving up, despite all the struggles."

Laurie must have had a hard time busting out of the box people wanted to put her in, perfectly symbolized by the white-black-

Hispanic choices on the U.S. census questionnaires or the SATs. Going through the public school system, I had to fill out similar forms myself, with neat boxes for "White," "Asian," "Hispanic," etc. For a long time I checked "Other," because as a recent immigrant that's how I saw myself. I wasn't the white that I thought of as American white, I wasn't black, I wasn't Hispanic.

I was an "other," an outsider, and maybe Laurie felt that way, too. In a lot of ways she was the most American kid I had ever met. She loved her church, her family, and her country, and she served all three very well. As brilliant as her achievements had been, I could hardly imagine the obstacles she overcame along the way, the folks stepping up to tell her that no, little Laurie from the block could not possibly do what she dreamed of doing.

In an odd way, we seemed to share similar battles of identity. She was a Hernandez, I was a Chmerkovskiy, but we had both carried the country's flag with pride, standing on a champion's platform to hear our national anthem. Not the national anthem of dozens of other potential countries that could have had their victories honored—no, it was *our* anthem, played for the whole world to hear because of our personal efforts on our country's behalf. Her road to the honor was through gymnastics, while mine was by way of championships I won representing my country on the parquet floors of international dance competitions. But that was my past, and presently I was looking to the future.

Dancing with the Stars was a show all about renewal, about busting down barriers, breaking out of assigned roles, forging new identities. The celebrity athletes, singers, and actors who came on weren't known for their dancing ability. They wanted to demonstrate that they weren't just a football player, a pop star, or a face on a hit TV series. They were human beings capable of embracing a lot of different roles and fulfilling themselves as people in a lot of different ways.

Over the course of our season together, I would come to find out that Laurie and I had more in common than people might think. But at that moment in the parking lot, our time on *Dancing with the Stars*—an intense, wonderful, and rewarding period—still lay ahead of us. The sound techs signaled to me that they were ready to go, so I climbed out of the car and headed in to meet my new dance partner.

I'VE THOUGHT A LOT ABOUT MY EXPERIENCE WITH LAURIE HERnandez recently, because I've been increasingly feeling restless over being labeled, boxed in, and pigeonholed.

I might be a Russian immigrant and Maks Chmerkovskiy's little brother, and she might be Laurie Hernandez and an Olympic champion, but when we danced we were just us, just Val and Laurie. We blew up the assumptions people made about us, dismantled the boxes they shoved us into, and just generally had a blast, changing the world one dance step at a time.

If someone says of me, "Oh, he's the *Dancing with the Stars* guy," I have every reason to be proud. I've built a great relationship with the show, a relationship that first of all is about gratitude. It's given me so many friends and so many opportunities that before anything else I have to say, "Thank you!"

But there's a small voice inside me eager to disagree: "Hey, wait—I'm *not just* the *Dancing with the Stars* guy." That can sound ungrateful, and believe me, I don't mean it that way. Just like when I hear, "Oh, that's the dancer dude." Yes, I'm happy for anyone to say that, but there's that same voice that rises up to shout, "No, I'm not just a dancer!"

I'm so many other things, too. I'm a poet, a boxer with a passable left jab, a classical violinist, a killer basketball player who loves hip-hop. I never want to be cornered by a description, never want to be boxed in, limited, defined. I'm proud of the variety, proud of the paradoxes, the weirdness, and the fact that everything I'm not is exactly what makes me who I am.

Oh yeah, that guy, he's the ballroom dance guy on TV. When someone labels you, it means that they can stop thinking about you as a human being.

That's why I'm writing this book. I want to show you the whole me, the real me, the one beyond all the preconceptions and stereotypes. We've all experienced being labeled and dismissed, and we've all felt the frustration of not being appreciated as a fully-rounded, independent individual. Who hasn't peered out at society and muttered, "There's more to me than meets the eye?" I knew that Laurie had told herself that, and then went out and proved it to the world.

Whenever someone typecasts me, my first impulse is to shrug it off, not to dwell on it, to keep it moving. In Ukraine, where I spent the first eight years of my life, I was stereotyped as a Russian because I spoke the language. But in Russia I was considered to be Ukrainian because I was born in Odessa. Later on, when I moved to America, Russians judged me as a person who left the home country, while to others I was stereotyped as a refugee, an immigrant. Not Val, not an individual who is complex, and who like all of us, has as many aspects to him as a mirrorball has mirrors—no, just another immigrant.

I am Valentin Aleksandrovich Chmerkovskiy, and I will never change my name, thank you very much. No matter how many times I say it, Chmerkovskiy will never sound less foreign, but that doesn't make me less American. And it definitely doesn't make me less proud to be one.

This book is about a different kind of patriotism, the kind that comes from the gratitude of the immigrant who pledged his allegiance to this incredible flag. It's about all the steps I've taken to make it to where I am now, dance steps and other kinds of steps, and about all the connections I've created and bonds that I've forged on and off the dance floor, people who taught me more than I could ever teach them. It's also about the promises that I've made along the way, many of them unspoken, pledges to family, teachers, mentors, and friends that their efforts on my behalf would never be taken for granted.

So that's the journey I invite you to take with me in these pages. We will erase a few labels, explode some boxes, and have some fun in the process. With stories of love and family, and with insights such as how pride ultimately saved my life, I'll seek to inspire you by showing how I was inspired. It's a journey of fulfillment, exploration, and celebration. It just might help you on your own journey, or at the very least entertain you along the way.

Come dance with me.

PART 1

A JOURNEY IN
DANCE

DWTS

In the summer of 2005, when the first season of *Dancing with the Stars* dropped, I remember that my initial reaction was simple and immediate. I rejected the whole idea. The formula of pairing professional dancers with celebrity partners, which was imported from a British program called *Strictly Come Dancing*, struck me as gimmicky and false. I feared the new show would do damage to the ballroom dance world that I loved, but which had always struggled with being taken seriously.

Ballroom wasn't a goof for me. It wasn't a game. I had been at it practically my whole life, and the art form as I knew it was as deep and powerful as that of more prestigious forms such as ballet, painting, sculpture, and drama. I had also been trained as a classical violinist, so I understood the aesthetic possibilities of a Mozart sonata, say, when compared with a finely executed paso doble, and I knew they could both tap into passion and humanity at the very highest levels.

Purely on a physical basis, I also knew the kind of dancing I was doing was an athletic activity as demanding and intense as anything else out there. All the common elements of athletics were present in ballroom—requirements of skill, competition, and fitness, as well as the real possibility of injury. Over the years an alliance of dance organizations lobbied to get our competitions officially classified as a sport. I was part of that movement, which rebranded ballroom as "dancesport."

My dad, my brother, and I helped in the push to get dancesport into the Olympics. That was the level of respect I thought it deserved. By no means was I a revolutionary, but when it came to dancesport my family and I were certainly among the founding fathers. We felt that the combination of aesthetics and athletics was precisely what made ballroom dance special and exciting. In figure skating, perhaps, or ballet, you had a similar kind of artistic physicality, but ballroom enjoyed nowhere near a status comparable to those disciplines. Meanwhile, rhythmic gymnastics had been in the Olympics since 1984.

My father saw his sons as athletes first and artists second. Matching dance professionals with celebrities? Somehow it didn't ring true. I doubt if anyone had ever considered doing a show with Michael Jordan teaching Michael Jackson how to do a layup. As a small community on the rise, ballroom dancers worked hard to give our art form a better reputation. Within that context, *Dancing with the Stars* seemed like selling out.

In the summer of 2005 I had just turned nineteen, and you have to understand where my mind was at that point in time. With my partner, Valeriya Kozharinova, I was dancing in ballroom competitions at national and international meets, and we were absolutely killing it. We had just won at the Blackpool Dance Festival, which was the oldest and in some ways the most prestigious ballroom competition on the international circuit, our version of Wimbledon. We also landed in the semifinals of the World Amateur Latin Dance Championship, and we were winning everything in the States that we could possibly win.

On the business front, too, the various Chmerkovskiy family enterprises were booming. There were four of us: me, Maks, and our parents. Our Rising Stars Dance Academy maintained its standing as the top children's dance studio in America. The dance competition we hosted in Brooklyn, the Grand Dancesports Cup, was fast becoming the premiere competition on the youth dancesport scene.

Finally, our chain of Dance With Me studios—which was just starting up at the time—looked to be a wave of the future, both for the family and for the dance world in general. Right from the start, our Dance With Me social dancing schools offered the best of both worlds, featuring the heart of a family business combined with the execution of a Fortune 500 company. Under my father's leadership, and in alliance with a powerhouse businesswoman named Jhanna Volynets, Dance With Me was proving to be ragingly successful, helping to put our family on a firm financial footing for the first time since we had arrived in America a decade before.

With all this happening, why would we bother ourselves with an upstart reality TV show on the West Coast? We were fighting the good fight on our own, and were too proud and too busy to drop everything in order to babysit celebrities in Hollywood.

But there was someone in our family who might have benefited from a little away time. During this period, my brother Maks appeared sullen and exhausted. He had to watch from the sidelines as a partner he had declined to dance with, Joanna Leunis from Belgium, rose to the top of the ballroom world. She had completely changed the life of the man she wound up dancing with, making Michael Malitowski one of the leading dancers in ballroom and winning the World Latin Dance Championship with him.

That could have been Maks. His opportunities with other partners dwindled away. My brother played all this over in his mind, not feeling a great sense of regret, necessarily, but definitely questioning where his life was headed.

Such was the situation within the Chmerkovskiy family that summer when the telephone rang.

Hello, Hollywood calling. They reached out to my brother first.

Hey, Maksim Aleksandrovich! Come on down!

It was like an invitation on *The Price Is Right,* a game show that was actually taped on the same lot as *Dancing with the Stars.* Later on, my parking spot at the studio would be two slots away from Drew Carey's.

A gig on a popular TV talent show offered Maks an opportunity to shake off the blues, change his environment, knock down a solid paycheck, leave behind the responsibilities that had boxed him in for so long as a dance instructor and provider for the family—in short, he would be able to get away from the headaches plaguing him in our home base of New Jersey.

So of course he said no.

From his perspective, the decision was a no-brainer. Naturally he was going to turn down a project that paired up dance professionals with celebrities, because it might make a mockery of all that we had invested our energies promoting. He would not go Hollywood just for a bigger paycheck and a bigger audience. That's the kind of move the Chmerkovskiy family considered a compromise, and we weren't going to do that.

So thank you, but no thank you. We're flattered, but we'd rather starve than eat a five-course meal on our knees. Righteous? Yeah, right—righteously idiotic! But very Chmerkovskiy-like. We thought we knew what we were giving up, and believed in our hearts that we were making the right choice.

I remember going over to a friend's house on June 1, 2005, and watching the first episode of *Dancing with the Stars,* airing back then on Wednesdays on ABC in the 9 P.M. time slot. I was a boxing fan, and as I watched former heavyweight champion Evander Holyfield massacre a fox-trot, I almost had to cover my eyes. The survivor of the infamous "Bite Fight" against Mike Tyson barely survived with his dignity intact. He left the show with no bite marks but potentially with a bruised ego.

I shouldn't be too tough on Evander, though, because I found out later that he was the reason *Dancing with the Stars* wound up on the air in the first place. At the last minute—at the *very* last minute, according to what I've been told—Evander signed on, and ABC gave the program the green light. If Evander had said "No" to the show I'd still be back in Saddle Brook right now, teaching kids to cha-cha.

There were only six couples in competition that first ramshackle season, with soap star Kelly Monaco teamed up with a Belarusian-born dancer named Alec Mazo to win the first Mirrorball Trophy.

While there was some great dancing on the show, watching back then I wasn't too impressed overall. I was still immersed in the more serious world of dance competition. As far as I was concerned, ballroom was a respectable sport, not something for the entire world to giggle about, witnessing some punch-drunk, one-eared palooka stumble around on the floor. Firmly seated upon my high horse, I could do nothing but look down on this new entry onto the ballroom stage.

In retrospect my reaction seems a little ridiculous. But we as a family made our decisions on an idealistic basis rather than on coolheaded cost-benefit analysis, and that strategy had always served us well. People were always tugging on my father's sleeve with opportunities, wanting to use our success to further theirs. *Dancing with the Stars* represented only a minor blip on the radar screen. We were right to turn our backs on it, weren't we?

How were we to know that the little reality TV import from Britain would blow up to be one of the biggest phenomena in American entertainment?

Success changes everything, and success in America, the land of success, sends an especially powerful message. Whatever the highfalutin, high-flying Chmerkovskiy brothers thought about the show, the rest of the country embraced it with full-hearted enthusiasm. The finale that first season brought in twenty-two million viewers, an incredible number for a broadcast television program that was just starting out.

Suddenly the picture swam into sharper focus. Did the *Dancing with the Stars* producers hold it against my brother for refusing them the first time around? Oh, when we were nothing but a summer replacement show, you turned up your nose, but now when our viewership is in the millions, you want to change your mind? No, the showrunners weren't proud. They again invited my brother to come on the show as a professional.

"Hey, Maks!" said the producer on the other end of the phone call. "We're interested in casting you for the second season. It's going to be a ten-week gig this time around. Here's the pay. [Insert the sound of a ringing cash register here.] We will put you up. We'll take care of everything for you. We're very interested in having you participate on our show."

I would love to say that my brother politely declined, but his response wasn't as polite as you would probably think.

Right at that moment we had a lot on our plate, operating both Rising Stars Dance Academy and our chain of Dance With Me studios. We had entered into the world of promoting ballroom dancing to an older generation, a nostalgic generation, people who could benefit from a physical, therapeutic, and mental perspective. *Treat yourself to a dance lesson!* was our message.

Strangely enough, we didn't put two and two together right away. We failed to realize that the people we were trying to reach with our Dance With Me promotions were the same people who watched *Dancing with the Stars*. "Synergy" wasn't a word that occurred to us, but what did mean something was that our beloved Maks remained down in the dumps. It didn't make sense to us that he would decline a chance for a fresh start on a hit Hollywood show, doing what he had done at the highest level in competition.

Seen from that perspective, *Dancing with the Stars* was a natural fit for Maks.

My father, mother, and I got together and staged something like an intervention. We didn't call it that, but that's what it was, because we were trying to blast Maks out of his funk.

"Maks, you've got to do it," I said. "You've got to go out there, you've got to try this. Switch it up a little, you know? You only have to do one season. You'll make a little money, enjoy a little bit of L.A., experience a change of scenery. Then you can turn around and come back home, you know?"

"No one will hold you hostage out there in Hollywood, will they?" asked my mother in Russian. "If the television show is not for you, then you do some other thing."

"Yes, you can always come back," my dad added. "You could come back and continue to dance in competition, but for now, you don't have a partner, am I right?"

"It's only three months," I reminded him. "Actually two months, or two and a half."

Not really realizing the impact it would have on our lives, the three of us kicked Maks out the door, onto the plane, and into a role on *Dancing with the Stars*. The move would come back to haunt us, because it immediately became clear that Rising Stars Dance Academy, for one, would never be the same without Maks as head instructor. He was the heart of that studio, with my father acting as the brain, and me and the other student-dancers serving as the soul.

I would take over the lead instructor's role as best I could, but Maks's pulling up stakes for the West Coast would have serious repercussions for all of the Chmerkovskiy family enterprises.

MY BROTHER WENT OUT TO L.A., AND A STAR WAS BORN. HE came, he danced, he conquered. In the winter of 2006, performing on Season 2 of *Dancing with the Stars*, Maks demonstrated that he had the ballroom chops, for sure, but he also exhibited another quality that made him a vital addition to the show's cast of professionals—a ready-made masculine image that translated very well on TV.

Ladies and gentlemen, introducing the Russian bad boy of ballroom, Maks Chmerkovskiy! The cameras loved him. He came across as cool, impossibly handsome, and slightly dangerous, the kind of charismatic figure that viewers could spin fantasies around.

Now that we had an excellent reason to, my parents and I tuned in for every episode of the new season. As we watched, we fell in love with the show and came to admire the whole pro-celebrity concept. The production itself smoothed out the first-season kinks and became sleeker, better, and more professional. The number of competing couples increased from six to ten. The shakedown run was over. ABC had a smash hit on its hands.

Sitting in front of the tube in New Jersey, a continent away from the action in L.A., I looked on with amazement, pride, and a slight pang of jealousy as my brother came into his own. As a family, we had trouble believing what was happening, because for the first time our unpronounceable, ridiculously difficult last name crept into the vocabulary of the average American household. Emergency room visits for sprained tongues increased noticeably.

For his first season on the show Maks was paired with actress, singer, and celebrated beauty Tia Carrere. They made for a dazzling couple, combining the exotic and erotic in an explosive mix. When they danced, it was difficult to take your eyes off them. Tia gave off the vibe of a new, modern kind of woman, eager to regain her prematernity form after the recent birth of a child. She just happened to be matched up with a seething, strutting Russian-American stud, like a gazelle in the embrace of a panther.

Maks managed to make a hot show hotter.

On *Dancing with the Stars*, contestants lived with the constant presence of the camera. Early on that season, an incident occurred, caught on camera during rehearsal, that ignited controversy and at

the same time cemented Maks's badass reputation. Tia had just performed a move that Maks had taught her. After completing it, she
looked over at her pro teacher in excitement and a sort of girlish pride.

"Hey, so how was it?" she chirped.

Maks looked lazily back at her, cynicism in his eyes and tough
love in his veins, and with a slight tinge of sarcasm uttered a phrase
that would be linked to him forever afterward, helping to define
his character on the show.

"Well, you know what?" he said. "That wasn't disgusting."

The odd thing about the whole tempest-in-a-teapot affair was
that for me and my parents, watching back in Saddle Brook, the
moment passed by without us thinking anything about it. We
didn't even twitch, because that demeanor, that voice, and that
attitude were all eminently familiar to us.

But to America at large, Maks's behavior was such a shocking
revelation, and it lacked political correctness to such a degree, that
it came off like a slap in the face. He suddenly became "Maks the
Knife." Blunt honesty made for great viewing, especially when it
was combined with my brother's aesthetic. And of course his dance
aesthetic was absolutely riveting, if I do say so myself—after all,
we are related.

Along with everyone in our Rising Stars circle, my parents and
I understood Maks so well, and his cold-hearted approach was so
notorious among us, that the dismissive, offhand comment to Tia
seemed to be part of just another day in the life of our favorite dance
instructor. But the internet had come into its own at the time, and it
didn't take long for us to realize that the rest of the world didn't see
Maks in the same way that we did.

Well, that wasn't disgusting.

What? Who in the hell treats a new mother that way? Poor Tia!
Some viewers got *angry*. A few wept tears over the unfairness of it
all. Others grasped the real truth of the moment, and reacted with
comments along the lines of "If you can't stand the heat, get off the

dance floor." The show's website portrayed an audience split fairly evenly between those who were appalled by what they considered to be my brother's vanity and bad manners, and those who applauded his tough-love approach to teaching.

Those were the days of chat rooms and discussion boards, before Instagram, Snapchat, or Twitter. Commentary about the show was pretty much limited to the ABC website. Visitors to the network's web page had to choose *Dancing with the Stars* from the menu of ABC programs, then click on "Forums" to access the discussion boards. Digging into all the commentary from back in New Jersey, when I was still in college, I became aware of my brother's popularity—or rather his notoriety.

I felt an overwhelming urge to demonstrate my loyalty. I didn't limit myself to voting, either, nor to soliciting votes back home or getting my friends to call. I set up anonymous accounts on the boards so I could defend my man. I'd check the list of all the chats starting up. Invariably, they spelled his name wrong.

Max is so rude. Max is hot. Max is an asshole.

Whenever "Max is an asshole" comments started to outweigh "Max is so hot" comments, I would come up with subject threads to balance the negative with the positive. Trying to fit in and not blow my cover, I spelled his name wrong, too.

Max is so cool. Max is actually really nice. Max is special. Look at this picture of Max with puppies.

It's not something I exactly brag about today, but bent over my funky Compaq computer in Jersey, I made the effort. I figured it was the least a brother could do.

Controversy was TV gold, controversy brought discussion board attention, controversy made the fans tune in. Love it or hate it, that's just the way things were. So whatever else happened between him and Tia (they were eliminated sixth that season), Maks had proved that he was what they used to call "good copy." All this arose from him simply being himself, doing what he had done every day at Rising Stars Dance Academy.

But then something occurred to temper the outrage and give the discussion board trolls a deeper understanding of my brother. For each contestant, producers on *Dancing with the Stars* created a "package," short pretaped pieces about a dancer's background, edited into miniature biographies. A package ran on Maks and his activities as a teacher at Rising Stars, showing him interacting with students. The collection of kids came off as absolute darlings, little men and little women who were accomplished pint-size *terpsichoreans* (I swore I would never use that comical, ancient-Greek term for dancer in this book, but there it is), and they charmed the pants off everyone out there in TV land.

Aw, maybe the bad boy wasn't so bad after all. Just look at how his kids respect Maks and thrive under his guidance! Viewers saw another side of Tia Carrere's tormentor, injecting a little Mother Teresa flavor into the mix. The package effectively rocketed Maks to star status, elevating his visibility among the corps of dance professionals on the show. He became a force to be reckoned with, not only as a dancer but as a personality, if not as an actual complicated, flesh-and-blood human being—which after all might be asking too much of reality TV.

The package on the Risings Stars kids lent Maks credibility that he wouldn't otherwise have enjoyed. As much of a stud as he was, his arrogance would have never been accepted if viewers hadn't been introduced to his heart, because arrogance without heart is just plain old obnoxious, which couldn't be farther from what the Chmerkovskiy household was all about.

All of a sudden, this brash sex symbol who had been eliciting comments along the lines of "Who the fuck does this dude think he is?" instead showcased qualities of humility, leadership, and sacrifice. Maks's genuine love for his young students was obviously reciprocated, producing an intense camaraderie that viewers could sense right through the TV screen. That same passion for teaching his students translated to how he taught his partners on the show, a fresh, unique, and above all genuine approach that people at home wanted to see.

I TURNED TWENTY THAT YEAR, AWARE OF A FEELING THAT things were snowballing. Because my brother's life changed, my life changed, too. From the enthusiastic viewer response to Maks's video package, the producers knew they had tapped into something special. They quickly reached out and asked if a select few students from Rising Stars Dance Academy could come out to California and dance on the show.

I made my first appearance on *Dancing with the Stars*, not as a pro dancer matched with a celebrity contestant, but as one of Maks's former pupils.

In our little New Jersey studio, the invitation to come on the show hit us like a bomb. We sorted out three couples to make the appearance: including my partner, the feisty Valeriya and me; plus four others—Nicole matched with Boris, and Sergey paired with Michelle. We weren't your typical Hollywood marquee names, but everyone involved had appeared in the package footage, representing the cream of the crop at the dance school.

The producers wanted us to come in with our dance numbers all set and ready to go. FedEx delivered tapes of two songs, Michael Jackson's "Billy Jean" and the perennial favorite "Mambo Number 5." We prepped routines for each, made recordings of them, and sent the videotapes out to L.A., so the producers could work out such details as blocking (positioning of the dancers) and camera placement.

When it came time to travel, the actual experience took on a slightly surreal flavor. The JFK-to-LAX flight was in itself a revelation to some of us: exciting, foreign, and fresh. We came away from the transcontinental journey thinking how immense America really was, because after six and a half hours on the plane, it would have made sense to us if we had landed in a different country. What? This is still the U.S.A.?

The beautiful weather and overall Southern California vibe sure made it seem as if we had entered into another world, a magical land where a car service picked you up at the airport and whisked through traffic. The producers put us into rooms at a boutique hotel right across from CBS Television City, the home studio of the show even though it aired on ABC. The studio has a long history, and everything from *American Idol* to *Three's Company* and *The Twilight Zone* has been shot there.

The journey from Saddle Brook to West Hollywood ought to be measured in light-years. I grabbed on to anything that felt even vaguely familiar to my Brooklyn-raised senses. A block up Fairfax Avenue was Canter's, the best New York–style deli in Los Angeles. In fact the whole neighborhood had something of a Jewish atmosphere, with places where I could get a good bagel, the old-fashioned food stalls of the Farmers Market, and—more sobering—the nearby Los Angeles Museum of the Holocaust.

We had an early call the next morning. The six of us walked across the street, received our ID badges, and made our way to the soundstage. Suddenly the exotic vibe of the experience totally dropped away for me, because the pros who were on the set that day were all dancers I knew well, people such as Tony Dovolani, Cheryl Burke, and Louis Van Amstel. These were colleagues who had history with me totally outside of any Hollywood bullshit that was going down. Being with them was like slipping into a warm bath of friendship, with my peers celebrating my arrival. I took my rightful place as a member of the extended family of ballroom dance.

And of course Maks was there, too. As he had my whole life, my brother bulldozed a path for me to follow on *Dancing with the Stars*. His presence was a huge blessing and at the same time something of a minor curse. I felt his love and protection, yeah, but I also saw myself slotted into the "kid brother of" pigeonhole that even back then was starting to feel confining.

I experienced a stab of envy and couldn't wait until I entered that glittering world myself. I glanced around at the lineup of professional dancers, and a childish, petulant voice inside me spoke up.

"These guys are not even close to my level, but here they are enjoying an incredible level of exposure. More people see them in a single night than have watched me dance during my whole competitive career. What the fuck is that all about? Two years ago they might have been ranked maybe forty-eighth in the world, while I was out there winning every competition. Now I'm coming in as a sideshow? What am I, a worn-out shoe?"

Etc., etc.

It was an exciting time, with big changes afoot, and I, too, had to change with my circumstances. When you feel everything around you changing, you have a choice. You either try to cling to what you know best and stay put, or you sense the changing tide, feel the flow, realize the dynamic, and grasp the bigger picture. Then you can begin making decisions to grow and build, and continue your efforts to thrive, to function as an alpha in a new environment. "Keep it moving" was always a phrase I kept foremost in my mind.

I started to make adjustments starting from that first guest appearance in Season 2. The key to my success on *Dancing with the Stars* was not my brother's advice, not anyone else's advice, not my dancing ability or competitive experience, not my looks—though all that helped. I made a simple but crucial decision early on. The tool that helped most on the show was my ability to see myself as a student and have a complete lack of self-consciousness about it.

I've been a student my whole life. From violin, poetry, and dance to plain, old-fashioned education in school, I loved learning. My previous experience in ballroom taught me to check my ego at the door, and also allowed me to feel comfortable on the set. I kept myself open, and thankfully was secure enough that pride didn't prevent me from being schooled in the finer points of producing great content.

I was able to say, "I don't know anything about this business of staging dance on television, but I'm ready, willing, and able to learn." My appreciative attitude toward those able to teach me went a long way to helping me fit in.

I was impressed, but I wasn't intimidated. As I stepped onstage at Television City, of course I was somewhat nervous, but by that time I had a ridiculous amount of experience performing—though obviously none of the competitions could compete with a million-dollar production in the heart of Hollywood. But certainly the nerves I had going into my debut appearance on *Dancing with the Stars* didn't come close to the nerves I felt at a world championship or a Blackpool championship, or even at the Russian restaurants in Brighton Beach where I performed when I was thirteen.

I'd been tested. I had endured my trial runs already. So for me the main emotion was not nervousness but excitement. *The brighter the spotlight*, I told myself, *the brighter I'll shine*. I felt completely at home on that stage in West Hollywood. Mostly I simply enjoyed the time spent with my friends dancing before an audience of millions.

Among those in the audience were two people who would change all our lives. The actor George Hamilton, he of the perpetual tan, competed on *Dancing with the Stars* that season, paired with a professional dancer whom I knew well, Edyta Śliwińska. Hamilton was dear friends with Steve and Elaine Wynn, the casino moguls who together had founded an empire based on real estate, hotels, fine-art collecting, and gambling.

The Wynns watched the show to root for their friend George, and Elaine especially was charmed by the package on Maks and the kids from Rising Stars. Like a lot of people, she was inspired, but unlike a lot of people she had plenty of resources to act on her inspiration. After she saw the troupe perform, she reached out to my brother.

"We have a charity event coming up in New York City at Sotheby's auction house, and we'd like to have your kids dance, perhaps something like a thirty-minute number."

Of course we said yes. We put a show together and had our whole fam at the event, performing for an audience of heavy hitters, not only the Wynns but Italian fashion designer Roberto Cavalli and Donald Trump (then just a real estate magnate). Steve Wynn fell in love just as his wife had. They ended up hiring us to do New Year's Eve showcases at the Wynn casinos in Las Vegas for the next three years.

The Rising Stars troupe swelled in number. New Jerseyans Cole Mills, from Oceanside; Kiki Nyemchek, from Teaneck; and Vlad Kvartin, from Fair Lawn, whose immigrant status was an open question, all got put up in luxury rooms at the Wynn Las Vegas. They did charity events and met such humble folks as Bill Gates and Warren Buffett.

The cherry on top of the sundae was when Steve hired the whole troupe for the 2006 grand opening of Wynn Macau, a new casino on the southern coast of China. The Rising Stars kids were the whole show. Wynn flew fifty teenage dancers from New York to Hong fucking Kong. These kids had never seen anything like it. The closest they might have gotten was an order of sesame chicken at their local Chinese takeout, and they would be disappointed to discover that the dish wasn't normally offered in the actual nation of China.

During this period, having Maks in my corner meant everything for me. No longer forced to put up with the misery of being a brokester working his butt off and being only poorly compensated, he could now afford to toss a few coins my way. Because I was still a broke-ass dancer scratching out an existence in the competition world, I appreciated the favor.

More impressive than the money, though, was having doors open to him in the incredible, weird, over-the-top vanity fair of show business. Maks was twenty-six years old, a stud, and on the biggest TV show in the country. He ran through Hollywood like a kid through a candy store. *Dancing with the Stars* had suddenly blown up into such a huge phenomenon that when Maks showed up at a party he was bigger than half—90 percent!—of the celebs in attendance.

Man, it was a crazy time. Overnight, my brother went from being a fucking nobody ballroom dancer in New Jersey to becoming the hot new face in entertainment. Everybody wanted a piece of him.

Through all of this I experienced the first small beginnings of an upheaval in my relationship with my brother. It was nothing too pronounced, but I could feel a tremor as the earth shifted beneath our feet. Maks and I were now living a continent apart. He had always been my rock, and the thing about a rock is it isn't supposed to change. I was so busy changing myself that I never stopped to imagine that my brother could become someone different than the person who had been at my side for so many years. At that point I was only faintly aware of what was starting to happen, but the real sea change would wash over our lives soon enough.

FIRST SEASON

It took me a while to join the cast of *Dancing with the Stars*. I had a couple of appearances here and there, some more memorable than others, but I was in my own world and had my own thing going on. Though the show became a huge phenomenon, it wasn't central to my life, since I was heavily involved in the world of ballroom dance competition, and that's where my focus was. But it was a nice treat to get away and spend some time in the weird, wonderful realm of Hollywood. As it turned out, I didn't sign on to the show as a professional dancer until 2011, for Season 13—at age twenty-five, the same age Maks was when he started.

I have nothing but the deepest love for my older brother. He means more to me than I can express. When anyone refers to me as "Maks Chmerkovskiy's kid brother," wow, I feel a surge of happiness and respect. But again, that small inside voice kicks in. *Hey!* I want to call out, *I'm not anyone's kid brother.* Well, I am, but that's not *all* I am.

I'm not some sidekick and I never set out to be Robin. I am Batman.

And yet my first sound bite on my first season as a pro, the first time the audience encountered me as a member of the cast, set the snarky, stammering tone.

"I'm Valentin Chmerkovskiy . . . no, wait . . . I'm Val—no, no . . . I'm Val Chmerkovskiy and it took my brother twelve seasons to try to win this thing and he still hasn't done so, so I'm here to redeem the family name." It was probably one of the most obnoxious things I've ever said, and I've said a lot of obnoxious things in my life. As a green-as-grass rookie, I was not aware that sarcasm didn't play well on TV. The show wanted sound bites, punch lines, and catch phrases, so I went ahead and made my first impression on the show, coming off like a snotty little douchbag.

Maks's fans jumped all over my trash talk. What they were reacting to was banter, nothing more, just playful sarcasm. The simple fact that there was now a pair of brothers dancing as professionals seemed to challenge some people. A tiny fraction of the commentators were off-the-hook fanatical, and they were extremely active in the show's forums and on other social media, posting comments daily. They were not always the nicest comments, either, and at times strayed into bullshit slander and totally whack opinion.

A few of the online posters came off as rancid little trolls, more interested in tearing other contestants down than building their candidate up. It was a losing propostion, but there were times when I could not resist baiting them back. "Hey, yo," I would post, attempting to give the crazies a reality check. "I'm standing right here with your main man, your hero, and we're laughing at you together, at how truly insane extreme your comments are."

Unfair and silly as it was, the fan base broke down into rival camps, the true-blue Americans versus the foreign immigrants, and I'll let you guess who led the list of the outsiders. The Russians were coming! The dark and deadly Chmerkovskiy clan! The show will turn into *Dancing with the Czars!*

My celebrity partner that debut season, Elisabetta Canalis, had a career in Italy as an actress, spokeswoman, and model. Elisabetta was a beautiful person, stunningly pretty, who spoke English with a sweet and sultry Italian accent. She had long served as a muse for fashion designer Roberto Cavalli, but in 2011 she was most well known for going through a very public breakup with superstar actor George Clooney.

Talk about being labeled: none of Elisabetta's credits, nothing about her sophisticated, statuesque European aura mattered, because all people saw when they looked at her was *Clooney's ex.*

A season on *Dancing with the Stars* was actually an excellent way for celebrities to push the reset button. Athletes, actors, singers, and media personalities could come on the show and display sides of themselves that the public never saw.

The producers participated in the same stereotyping as the rest of society, but the smartest celebrity contestants found a way around that, playing ball to some extent while at the same time not taking their public images too seriously. A sense of playfulness was required. Elisabetta found herself with an awesome opportunity to slip out from underneath her ex-girlfriend label and present herself as herself.

Unfortunately for her, she drew me as a professional partner.

I walked into the first meeting with my celebrity partner to find a drop-dead beautiful Italian woman. Elisabetta Canalis obviously didn't know me from a hole in the wall, and I came to understand that she had never really watched the show before committing to appear. And I repeat: Elisabetta signed up for *Dancing with the Stars* without having ever watched the show.

It was the blind leading the blind. I had zero experience as a *Dancing with the Stars* professional partner. My brother's advice and opinions could guide me, but for better or worse I was determined to make my own choices. Even so, I always felt Maks's presence, as if he was looking over my shoulder at everything I did.

There were four people in the rehearsal room, two flesh-and-blood humans, me and Elisabetta, and two ghosts, Maks and George.

Feeling the need to prove myself, I shifted immediately into alpha mode. I was coming in totally energized, not arrogant—I mean, I was grateful to be there—but maybe a little bit too cocky. I carried my experience in the competitive dance world as a badge of honor. I might not have spoken my attitude in words, but to the other professional dancers it must have come through loud and clear.

"Look, you little fuckers haven't been on a real dance floor in years. I'm an athlete! [insert chest thump] at the peak of my physique! [and another] I can dance ten dances in a row and not break a sweat. Y'all can probably not do two routines without wheezing and puking!"

I was ready to teach whoever I got as a partner how to become a world champion ballroom dancer, while in front of me stood a woman who had no idea what she was getting into. Elisabetta was certainly cool, smart, and pleasant enough, but as far as she was concerned, we could have been doing *Nunchucks with the Stars*.

"I'm excited to learn how to dance," she said, in a cool European tone that indicated Elisabetta never got excited about much of anything. People got excited about her, not the other way around.

We were at completely different stages in our lives. She was shell-shocked after being dragged through the media muck for a few months, and I was this peppy little upstart puppy nipping at her heels. We started working together and, yes, she was without a doubt an awesome chick, but dancing was hard for her.

In fact, dancing was really, *really* hard for Elisabetta Canalis.

I'll take the blame, all right? My style of teaching wasn't making the process easier. I should have told myself that with only three weeks to teach her how to dance, I had to accept how vulnerable she seemed and acknowledge what she could and couldn't do. I had no patience for insecurity and was so driven to succeed that

I overplayed my role a bit. I still had the competition perspective in my blood. I thought I was back teaching at Rising Stars Dance Academy, where tough love was the order of the day and no coddling was allowed.

I went into the rehearsal period full steam, and my attitude caught Elisabetta off guard. So about a week and a half in we had a little moment, she and I, caught on camera and pretty much summing up the state of our relationship.

We were rehearsing the quickstep, a fast dance that was really difficult to learn and even harder to get right. I mean, it's called the quickstep, right, so I think the difficulty should be pretty self-explanatory right from the start. Elisabetta might have noticed that my fashion sense was way off. I dressed like the sixty-year-old ballroom dance teacher I had worked with two years before in London—shout out to Alan Fletcher! Elisabetta's fashion guru, Roberto Cavalli would have shuddered and hid his eyes.

"Quick, quick, slow!" I called out. We were already halfway through the rehearsal process, dancing wasn't getting any easier for her, and my tone wasn't getting any brighter. I wasn't gloomy and I never belittled anybody, but at that point in time, I didn't place as much value on uplifting rhetoric, because I was so accustomed to using challenging rhetoric. I thought that if I pushed my students, they would know that I cared, because I was challenging them to surpass their expectations. The people in the world that I came from, the world of dancesport, knew never to take it personally.

But George Clooney had never talked to Elisabetta like I was talking to her. Nobody in their right mind would have dared to talk to this woman that way. She was a big star in Italy, where people walked on eggshells around her, the way they behave toward A-list celebrities in the States.

"Quick, quick, slow! Quick, quick, slow!"

"Hey, hey," she muttered, rolling her big, beautiful runway-model eyes at me. She didn't understand what I was doing, and didn't feel it either. At that point, she didn't even *want* to feel it. Instead of trying to make her understand, I should have focused on an easier dance step that would maybe help her enjoy dance in general. At least that would have represented progress, after which she might gradually come to understand what we were trying to do.

I spun around, demonstrating. "Quick, quick, slow. Quick, quick, slow."

"I still don't understand," she wailed.

"Quick, quick, slow. Quick, quick, slow. Quick—"

"Show me again," she ordered, cutting me off. "Show it to me again."

Those were her words, but what I heard in my head was something different:

Dance, monkey, dance!

I had an image of me as a Blackpool champion, standing there in front of a woman who's, what? George Clooney's ex? Someone who'd had a bit part in *Deuce Bigalow: European Gigolo*?

I turned to her and said, "You know I'm not your bitch, right?"

Whoa, whoa, double whoa.

She rolled her eyes and said, "What?" She was appalled. "What did you say?"

"I'm out here trying to make you look good," I said, trying to justify myself. "I'm here for you."

"Not for me!" she responded, then started gathering up her things, all the while muttering curses in street-slang Italian.

The camera caught it all, and even though the producers wound up editing out my "not your bitch" line, viewers got the idea. Obviously, we made up after that day and let bygones be bygones. But the damage had been done. Our rehearsal package aired in week two and not too coincidentally we got eliminated from the show that week, also.

Like I said, I'll take the blame. I wasn't good at communicating within what was a new environment for me. I had a lot of learning to do.

But actually, that early elimination might have been the best thing that ever happened to me on *Dancing with the Stars*. It not only ended the agony, but it meant producers could assign me to perform as a solo dancer on featured pro numbers. I was able to demonstrate what I was actually good at, which at that point was dancing. What I wasn't good at (not yet) was guiding a celebrity partner.

I busted my ass showing what I could do. I was already looking ahead to the next season, and knew I had to find a way to stand out. On the basis of my miserable showing with Elisabetta, I wasn't sure that I would be asked back. So I pulled out all the stops as a dancer.

Some of the pros allowed their feelings to get hurt when they were eliminated. Their egos kicked in and they would turn their backs on the remaining episodes of the show. They didn't want to perform in the precommercial "bumper," they didn't want to do the thirty-second filler, and they didn't want to do a performance for a visiting guest artist.

I had a different attitude. "Yo, I just left my whole world to be on this show! Give me as much camera time as possible!"

Unlucky Season 13 of *Dancing with the Stars* featured celebrity contestants such as Ricki Lake, Rob Kardashian, and J. R. Martinez, who won with an overwhelming number of viewer votes. Chaz Bono's appearance triggered protests from conservatives because he was transgender. NBA forward Metta World Peace partnered with my brother's future wife, Peta Murgatroyd, who was taking her first turn as a pro dancer, but Metta and Peta were the first couple to be eliminated.

Season 13 also featured a week-six exchange between my brother and the judges for which I might have been at least partly to blame. He and I stood together watching the couple going on before him, and it bothered us both when their routine received extravagant praise from the judges, totally overblown for what Maks and I considered was at best a mediocre performance. So he vented to me a little about the cluelessness of the judges.

Bitching about the adjudicators was a time-honored ballroom tradition, so I joined in on the trash talk. Instead of calming him down, I acted as a catalyst for his outrage, getting him even more hyped up than he was to begin with. He went out and did his number with his partner, Hope Solo, the famously fiery goalkeeper for the U.S. women's soccer team. It was "Broadway Week" on *Dancing with the Stars*, so they performed a rumba to "Seasons of Love" from the Broadway show *Rent*.

When judge Len Goodman came down hard on Solo ("This was your worst dance of the season, in my opinion"), Maks reacted. Waving his arms over his head, he encouraged the crowd to boo Goodman's comment—which they did, enthusiastically.

> *Goodman:* Don't start all that, Maks, because half the fault is yours.
> *Maks:* As long as the audience likes our journey, we're good.
> *Goodman:* Let me tell you, Maks, the audience likes the effect. They judge on efficacity. I've been in this business for over fifty years—
> *Maks (under his breath):* Maybe it's time to get out.

Judge Carrie Ann Inaba spanked Maks for his dis of Goodman ("Have some respect!"), so there was plenty of leftover tension when host Brooke Burke did the post-routine interview. She asked my brother how he felt about the scoring. He voiced his disappointment, then added a comment heard around the *Dancing with the Stars* world.

"With all due respect, this is my show," Maks said.

All microphones should come with a warning label, "Use of this device by Maksim Chmerkovskiy could result in injury or death." He was notorious for his "that wasn't disgusting" style of off-the-cuff comments. I knew exactly what he was trying to say— that the dancers were responsible for the show right alongside the hosts, judges, and producers. It was indeed "Maks's show" as much as anyone else's.

But that's not what America heard. Viewers misconstrued the comment as typical "Maks the Knife" arrogance. The discussion boards and commentary threads lit up. No one wanted to cut this well-meaning, English-as-a-second-language dancer a break. Maybe he couldn't express himself perfectly, but his heart was always in the right place. In protecting Hope he was only expressing his loyalty to a teammate.

It wasn't much, but within the closed system of *Dancing with the Stars*, the whole business qualified as a major dustup. I felt bad, because I had fired my brother up, and he said things he probably wouldn't have said otherwise. We were like kids on a playground. You act a little differently—and talk a little trashier—when you have your boy backing you up.

DURING MY DEBUT SEASON I EXPERIENCED THE BACKSTAGE chatter at *Dancing with the Stars* for the first time. I knew a lot of the professional dancers, so I wasn't a total outsider. Not much that was being said surprised me, since the talk was the familiar routine about aches and pains, the opinions of judges, and who was an item and who wasn't. I thought I was back in the sweaty changing rooms of the competition circuit, or in the cafeteria at high school. The environment may be different but people were the same all over.

I did get introduced to something that was new to me, though, an ongoing discussion among the *Dancing with the Stars* pros—not a debate, really, more like a sore topic that everyone kept revisiting. The question centered on who had it easier, the female professionals who were teaching male celebrities, or the male dancers, like me, who taught female partners?

That there was any question on the subject took me by surprise. To me, the answer was ragingly obvious. *Of course* the male pro had a bigger challenge, simply due to the nature of ballroom dancing.

In the pure, original, authentic tradition of ballroom, the dynamic between male and female partners was extremely well defined. The woman was the work of art, while the man served as the frame for that work of art. The man's job was to present his partner in the most ideal manner possible. The female carried the heaviest load and was the focus of the spotlight. The role of the male in the ballroom dance world, the authentic ballroom world, was to complete her in every way.

The woman had much more work to do, much more business to attend to, than the man ever would. There's the famous line about the difference: "Ginger Rogers did everything that Fred Astaire did, but backward and in high heels."

I would be the first to tell you it was a lot easier to learn how to be a male ballroom dancer than it was to be an effective female ballroom dancer. I didn't think anyone could seriously deny that, but I got plenty of pushback from the women pros on the show. With the celebrity contestants, they said, the assumption was that a man couldn't dance and that a female could. Plus men were clumsier than women, men were awkward, and men were harder to teach because their egos got in the way. I could see the women's point, but I wasn't buying their argument.

Look, I can furnish a simple example of the double standard in ballroom. A male celebrity dancer could spend four-eighths of a bar of cha-cha music—a bar being one, two, three, four, five, six, seven, and . . . eight!—just unbuttoning his shirt, then spend another half bar taking his shirt off.

Afterward he could throw in a pelvic thrust and maybe, depending on the song, whip that shirt around his head and throw it at the audience, ending up with a "New Yorker," posed with an arm raised high. The judges would score the male dancer's routine, the audience would love it, and people watching at home would praise the energy and excitement, with comments such as, "Oh my God, that was my uncle's move at the wedding!"

Meanwhile, what was the female of the couple up to? She couldn't just stand there and watch the male take four-eighths of a bar stripping his shirt off. I knew I could never leave my partner stationary, have her stand there smiling like a mannequin while I ronde around her, do two spins by myself, hold onto her, and then do a dip while she does her New Yorker. For a female to do what a male did simply wouldn't make sense.

In authentic ballroom the woman dancer is always absorbed in movement. She has much more to do than the man. Girl pros on the show did incredible moves by themselves and finished by themselves, only to have the male celebrity next to them strike a pose and shout, "Yeah!" The camera zoomed in for the guy's triumphant moment. Take the same choreography and reverse the gender, and we would have the male celebrity flying around doing crazy spins, stopping, and hitting the line, with the female pro doing the "Yeah!" moment.

The whole essence of ballroom dancing—as opposed to, say, solo tap—is that men and women dance *together*. We are creating with each other.

Who has it easier? The question reminds me of Zeus and Hera in Greek mythology, debating over who took more pleasure from sex, males or females. Zeus said women did, while Hera said men. Luckily they had someone who could settle the question with authority. The prophet Tiresias had spent some years as a male and then other years as a female (don't ask me to explain how, even though I do live in West Hollywood), and he answered that it was women who had the better time of it.

Did that end the debate? Nope. The conversation continued, just like ours did about whether male or female pros had the harder time on the show. I had my own opinion, but no one was interested in the new guy on the show putting in his two cents. So I just kept it moving and agreed to disagree.

AS THE SEASON PROGRESSED I REALIZED I HAD TWO JOBS, dancing well on the show and slipping out from the shadow of my big brother. During the period when he was toiling away season after season on *Dancing with the Stars* and I was killing it on the competition circuit, our dynamics had shifted, and I wasn't sure Maks was aware of that fact. I had become a different person from the one he had known so well before, and he had changed, too.

The years he had been in Los Angeles had affected us deeply. While I concentrated on competing, our lives took separate tracks, his on the West Coast, mine on the East. We saw each other often, but not as much as we used to. In his absence, I stepped up to be the man of the household whenever my dad was away. I had the impossible job of trying to fill my brother's shoes coaching kids at Rising Stars.

Now, signing on to *Dancing with the Stars* and entering into what had been Maks's exclusive arena, I didn't want to give up my newfound independence. I couldn't change the fact that Maks had been introduced to the show long before me. I couldn't help that audience members saw him first. I had to demonstrate to them that appreciation was not a zero-sum game, that people could appreciate me for being me, while still leaving enough space in their hearts to appreciate him for being him. My brother and I had to coexist and not lose our individuality, which took a lot of effort for a long, long time.

By the time I joined *Dancing with the Stars*, Maks had become jaded. He was more or less over it. He was a veteran of eleven seasons. Never once did Maks not give his all in a performance for the show, but I detected some of the old Russian gloom beneath the surface, a bitterness and tension. Something was bothering him. Perhaps his agitation was warranted, but I didn't see addressing it as my battle.

From the beginning I filtered his advice on how to survive on the show, separating the good from the bad. There was good, productive advice that I could use, unproductive advice that I couldn't use, and there was also productive advice that I chose not to use.

Ultimately, as much as you learn, as much information as you take in, and as much influence as you allow to shape you, you're the decision maker. "I'm the decider," as President George W. Bush said. Owning your decisions is the only way you fully insulate yourself from regret. When you allow someone else to make your decisions for you, that's when things can go south in a hurry. Maks had a different attitude toward the show, one that I didn't want to adopt just yet. I needed to go through my own growing pains, my own honeymoon period, and my own fed-up, disappointed period, too. I had to find my own gray clouds and my own silver linings. I didn't need him to hold my hand the way he had done in Odessa, in Brooklyn, and beyond.

They say you become an adult the instant you forgive your parents for whatever wrongs you imagine they've done to you. There was nothing for me to forgive with Maks, but I still had to fight my way out from his shadow.

I don't know if people realize how addictive the spotlight is, especially when you work so hard for it. Then it's the sweetest piece of cake you've ever tasted. The more you have to divide that piece, the harder it gets to share, and you find yourself wanting the whole thing. Being forced to split it with eleven other diva dancers creates a lot of intrigue and tension. Sharing the spotlight with a sibling has its own tricky challenges, working out to be great and awkward at the same time.

On *Dancing with the Stars*, everybody was a star. Hollywood itself was a town of big fish coming out of small ponds, and a few of the biggest fish gobbled up all the attention. But I was determined to get my head on straight, forget about my past success on the competition circuit, and consciously became the humblest pro dancer that had ever appeared on the show.

I had bombed out with Elisabetta, so I had nowhere to go but up. To get there, first I had to get myself invited back for the next season.

STEPS

Dancing with the Stars has spring and fall seasons every year, and the period of time in between them is called the "midseason." What people may not realize is that none of the professional dancers are guaranteed a spot on the show. The producers like to keep us in suspense until the very last minute. We find out we've been picked up only the day before we have to pack our bags and head back to work.

In defense of the producers, they are simply real people wrestling with the monumental task of coming up with the perfect mix of dancers for a million-dollar show. I came to see such last-minute dramatics not as an example of the cruelty of the world, necessarily, but simply as an indication of how show business worked. All the pro dancers signed a deal that gave the show priority in their lives, but it didn't work the other way around—the professionals weren't the main priority for the producers. Ratings were.

Us dancers were mere cogs in a machine run by the higher-ups. I didn't hate the players even though I might have disliked the way the game was played. I tried to keep my mind off the drama of whether I'd be re-signed and spent the midseason going about my business.

At that point, I wasn't reaping the fruits of my labor. I had stopped competing and came onto the show, only to receive a slap-in-the-face reality check. After that first season I returned to New York down but not defeated. I told myself that even a faltering move forward is still a step in the right direction.

I discovered my situation at home had changed a little. I couldn't go back to my work at Dance With Me studios and do it anonymously as I had in the past. Without realizing it I had become something like a D-list—no, not even a D-list—I had become a G-list celebrity. I wasn't a B, a C, a D, an E, or an F. I was stuck farther down the alphabet.

To my surprise I found that even G-list celebrity status translated pretty well in the suburbs. In America, television made things real. I now had a wider audience appeal than I had enjoyed before, and when I did a seminar at our Dance With Me studio in Fort Lee, New Jersey, for example, I'd attract not just the school regulars, but also some outside fans who wanted to stop in for a sniff. G-list was A-list in Fort Lee.

All the talk about the big payoff for joining a hit TV show was great, but it wasn't the money that was inspiring me. I'd been broke for years before that, and had always been happy as hell. I was after something else in Hollywood. I never wanted to be a little G-list bitch for anybody. That just wasn't my style. I came off the competition circuit as an alpha individual who had gained not just notoriety but respect. I wanted the same result from *Dancing with the Stars*.

And then a development came along that crystallized everything, allowing me a crucial bit of insight into myself. That midseason in 2013, at an event held in an Irish pub on Long Island, I was introduced to the concept of the meet and greet. The bar had dark wooden paneling and smelled of sweat and beer. I showed up to find a crowd of people who really, really wanted to hang out with me. I was astounded. G-list or not, I was able to attract a group of strangers willing to pay money to stand in line, have a picture taken, and engage in a five-second conversation.

I was about to turn twenty-six, and that first humble meet and greet represented a "Holy fuck!" moment for me. At first, it came off like every other meet and greet in the world, with the fans herded along one by one. Step up, take a picture with me, move out. In, photo, out. The arrangement felt impersonal, so I turned to the organizers.

"These people have dedicated their time to coming out here," I said, stating the obvious.

"Yes?" one of the handlers asked, not getting my point. "Keep it going!"

"Forget what they paid for this, that's on them," I said. "But what about their time?"

The expression on the faces of the organizers said it all: *What about it?*

Step up, take a photo, move out.

The fans were giving up moments of their life to stand and wait for an opportunity to speak to me. I wasn't going to give them a fake hug, a frozen smile, and send them off from my perch in the land of not-giving-a-fuck. Faced with actual flesh-and-blood human beings, I found that I couldn't treat them as mere *units*. How many units did you do today? Oh, I did two hundred units. At $50 a unit, that's . . .

I just couldn't behave that way. Right then and there, I felt myself changing, starting to care about people more now that I saw them caring about me. Some of their concern might be shallow— "That's the dude on TV! I want to get a shot with him!"—but others showed a deep appreciation. They could cite chapter and verse of what I had done on the show.

"Bro, that number you did, the quickstep to the Pretenders doing 'Don't Get Me Wrong,' that made my day, made my evening, and I went to bed that night dreaming about dancing." "Hey, my mom and I had a couple of years of watching the show together and it brought us a lot closer." "My grandma passed a month ago, and your season was the last thing we shared—I always remember she loved your cha-cha to Katy Perry."

Connection. That was what was happening in that smelly pub on Long Island, and I came to realize that connection was what I'd been searching for my entire life. Suddenly I understood what I was really doing on *Dancing with the Stars*. I had been given this opportunity to have an impact on people, simply by virtue of (a) doing what I loved, but also (b) just by showing a little bit of care.

The agents and meet-and-greet organizers failed to understand that connection took time. They wanted the usual process of stepping up, taking the photo, moving out. They looked at me with pity in their eyes, as if I wasn't grasping an essential truth about my place in the world.

For me, the process was different: Step up—*connect!*—take a picture, say thanks and goodbye with a smile. We're both human beings, I thought, justifying the process to myself. This was one area where my usual motto of "keep it moving" did not apply. The ratio of effort to happiness seemed to be mathematically magical. I was a superhero with a superpower, where I could affect so many people in such a positive way. It was the best thing ever.

From that point on, *Dancing with the Stars* took on a different meaning for me. I still wanted the glitz, the glamour, and the status—I mean, I was still a performer—but now I understood the incredible power of connecting to people. I had always believed I had to act in keeping with my moral compass. I was raised that way, and it was still as if I was representing my parents with my actions. But I never really cared about strangers before, or what strangers' perception of me might be.

In that moment my attitude changed completely. Ah, so *this* was what I had been doing that first season on prime-time television. It wasn't about hauling down a big payday (though that was nice), or beating out my fellow competitors (or, as in my case that season, *not* beating them out). No, I was in the business of connecting with people.

All of which made me desperately want to get re-signed for a second season, because that would allow me the opportunity to embark upon a similar trajectory with hundreds of thousands of new people. It didn't matter who the audience member was, or what their situation in life might be. The exchange worked both ways, inspiring and being inspired. It was always possible that I could inspire somebody else, and that fact inspired me to stay inspired myself. Now *that's* a lot of inspiration.

There were three tiers of producers in charge of *Dancing with the Stars*. First there were my employers, the production company that worked with me, the in-the-studio, boots-on-the-ground team. They were hired by BBC Worldwide, the folks who held the rights to the program's original concept, first used by a popular show in the UK called *Strictly Come Dancing*. The BBC execs had the power to say, "Hey, we like this guy and we don't like this guy." They in turn had been contracted by the show's distributor, ABC, and execs at the network could also weigh in: "We don't like this gal, but we really like this gal."

The production company, the BBC, and ABC. That was a lot of people I had to answer to—me, who had never had to answer to anyone but my father before. I could not possibly question his love, and though his discipline was hard, I knew his intention was to give me the best shot at success. So this was a new situation, interestingly different and really terrifying at the same time. All told there were maybe forty people who were making the ultimate decision on my life, and I didn't even know a lot of their names—never looked them in the eye or shook their hands.

Given my less-than-stellar showing in my first season, the thread I was hanging from was probably a lot thinner than most of the other pro dancers. But maybe the producers heard about what was going on at those meet and greets during the midseason break. Perhaps the people I met with and greeted had been inspired to post positive stuff about me on the show's discussion boards. Or the harsh reality could have been that I was still simply riding on Maks's coattails.

Whatever the reason, the thread didn't snap. I found myself on the receiving end of a Hollywood phone call, inviting me to join *Dancing with the Stars* for the upcoming fall season. It felt like a reprieve, as though I had dodged a bullet.

MY SEASON 14 PARTNER WAS SHERRI SHEPHERD, WHO AT THE time was a host on *The View*. Super smart, super bubbly, she was a comedian in her forties who had just had a kid, and was a woman who had been through a lot in her life. I always think that the funnier a comedian is, the darker her journey to that laughter must have been. And this turned out to be the case with Sherri. Her strength came through in her personality, which had a lightness to it, yet at the same time a gritty drive. She had a generous energy despite her past experiences, from poverty in Chicago and homelessness in L.A. She made the arduous climb up comedy's ladder in little clubs around the country, and for her to wind up where she was represented a huge accomplishment. Now she had a beautiful son as well.

Sherri rose super early every morning and took her place alongside ABC powerhouse Barbara Walters and one of my all-time favorites, Whoopi Goldberg. She had her hands full with *The View* and being a new mom, but she was so much in love with *Dancing with the Stars* that competing on the show had been her longtime dream. Every year, she had requested time off from *The View*, and every year, she was told no. It didn't seem to matter that ABC broadcast both programs.

Finally, in time for Season 14, Barbara changed her tune. "Fine, Sherri, you can do it," she said (and I'm paraphrasing the conversation I got secondhand from Sherri). "We're going to arrange for you to be in L.A. on Monday and Tuesday, and on those days you'll be on *The View* via satellite. Then you'll take the red-eye Wednesday to be on the show in person Wednesday and Thursday, and for Fridays' taped show."

Got it? Okay. A midforties new mother, flying back and forth across the country for weeks. But Sherri's passion for *Dancing with the Stars* made it happen. It was her dream come true. I had a private thought of "Fuck! What a responsibility!" I didn't want to be the one who shattered the dream. How could I not want to give this woman an awesome chance to grow? I wanted her to be the star, because she deserved it.

She kept to her regular schedule on *The View* during our three-week rehearsal period, which I loved because we were in New York City, not in West Hollywood or in some kind of windowless sound-stage bunker somewhere in the Valley. I was working two blocks from Lincoln Center, with a dream gig in my dream city. I could be a human being with some resemblance of a normal life. I could have dinner with my parents, act irresponsibly with my friends, or hang out with a local artist over a big lunch in the Village—and at the same time still be part of an incredible television phenomenon. The best of both worlds.

Even though I wasn't exactly a pro at being a pro quite yet, we had a great season, and I was able to give Sherri a lot more than I had given Elisabetta. I discovered the skill of patience, which could work wonders with a partner new to the ballroom world, and which was a revelation for me at the time. I kicked myself for being such a little Hitler with Elisabetta, and resolved to be more forgiving this time around.

Sherri wound up with a collection of amazing appearances to treasure, a string of killer routines, as well as smaller moments of serene reflection. She was a memorable contestant on *Dancing with the Stars*, which was no small feat amid the dozens upon dozens of contestants spread over twenty-five seasons, some of whom were not memorable at all. We were eliminated after week four, so again, I wasn't able to bring my partner to the halfway point in the show. But by that time Sherri was exhausted and ready to leave.

I idly formulated a half-assed conspiracy theory, speculating that Barbara Walters had a hand in what happened. She got fed up with Sherri flying back and forth, with half her heart on the dance floor in West Hollywood, the other on the set of a talk show in New York City. Barbara was powerful enough in the network hierarchy to get the word to the judges: Sherri Shepherd must be eliminated!

"You did a little dancing," I imagined Barbara telling her co-host, "but you're finished out there." I couldn't blame Barbara a bit if she had been thinking that way. Sherri was an essential element on *The View*. When there were awkward moments between the other hosts, between Barbara and Whoopi Goldberg, say, it would always be Sherri's voice sounding a comical "dun-dun-dun" that cut the tension and made everything okay.

She contributed at least one great punch line every time she was on *Dancing with the Stars*. She might not have been the best dancer, but she was the highlight of each episode she was in, just due to her effervescent personality. On the level of pure entertainment, on the level of lasting inspiration, she was awesome.

Peta Murgatroyd won that season as a pro dancer with her celebrity partner, Green Bay Packers wide receiver Donald Driver. She and I had both joined the show the season before, when she was eliminated first and I was eliminated second. Now I was eliminated fourth with Sherri, and Peta won the whole thing, taking home the Mirrorball Trophy with Donald. I loved Peta and was happy for her, but my inner competitor took a cold-eyed view of the situation.

"Well, Peta's moving at a faster pace than me," I couldn't help telling myself. "That means I'm probably doing something wrong." I needed to evaluate what I could do differently in the next season, but I wasn't totally sure how to make the adjustment.

BY SOME SECRET CALCULUS OF PUBLIC TASTE, AFTER THAT second season I moved up from being a G-list celebrity to taking my place on the F-list. I managed to get invited onto *The View* and shake hands with Barbara Walters, which made me feel a little bit full of myself. I took a picture with Whoopi Goldberg. I mean, come on! Whoopi Goldberg! I was moving on up!

At the same time I was still the same old Val, the local kid, teaching lessons and holding seminars at the Dance With Me studios in the New York metropolitan area. I was the same dude that students had sessions with for $60 an hour a year ago. I was on a TV show, but nothing had changed apart from that. Who cared about Hollywood?

Doing the hard work on the dance floor was where all my credibility had come from. I wouldn't have been able to preach what I did if I didn't have follow-through in the studio. It wasn't any kind of a miracle, and I wasn't there exactly doing God's work—I was doing Val's work. I wanted to help people feel good and help them sense their innate self-worth.

Heavily involved in the Dance With Me studios and hitting every meet and greet I possibly could, I nevertheless kept my ear to the ground for word from West Hollywood. Through the grapevine I heard that the next season, Season 15, would be an all-star affair, bringing back champions and fan favorites from the show's entire run.

Okay, I thought, *I'm out of a job*. I had been on for only two seasons at that point, and neither of them had achieved an all-star result by any stretch of the imagination. It seemed I would never make it past eighth place. I was simply doing the math, being not pessimistic but rather realistic about my prospects of getting called back for this special season. My life hung in suspension.

But finally the call came.

First some British guy came on the line and screamed, "Hello! Hello! Hello!" several times over. Then he handed the call over to the American producers, Joe and Ashley.

"Hey, how are you?" Ashley burbled. "We're very excited because you're back on!"

"Oh, wow, thank you so much."

"No, thank *you* so much," Joe chimed in. "We're excited about your partner."

Next the celebrity cast got announced, headlined by popular champions Emmitt Smith and Drew Lachey. Then there was Apolo Ohno, who was, you know, Apolo fucking Ohno, wearer of the sickest soul patch, possessor of possibly the coolest name ever, and winner of eight Olympic medals. Gilles Marini, probably one of the best celebrity male dancers the show had seen, came back for a second turn. Peta got paired with him, making her the clear front-runner among the pros. Actress Kirstie Alley was again matched with Maks, forming the same couple who were runners-up on the show's highest-rated season.

Victim number three for me would ultimately be the one who helped me turn a corner on the show. My partner, Kelly Monaco, had won the Mirrorball six years before, in the first season, when *Dancing with the Stars* was just a six-couple, six-week show. She represented probably my last best chance. If I didn't prove myself this time around, paired with a former champion, how could the showrunners possibly justify bringing me back again?

Kelly and I vibed right away. She was a chick from Philly, and I was a boy from Brooklyn, so we had growing-up-in-the-hood stories to share. Hanging together meant a blast of big-city East Coast nostalgia. I was twenty-six, Kelly was thirty-six and had been through a lot of experiences in her life. On my part, I was happy AF teaching rumba walks to a former *Playboy* Playmate.

She had broken out at age twenty-one as a centerfold and worked her way into a starring role on the long-running ABC soap, *General Hospital*. During the years after her first *Dancing with the Stars* season in 2005, she had become increasingly connected with A-list Hollywood, a world that was totally beyond my scope. She knew everyone in town and had all the heaviest hitters on her speed dial.

She was also an extraordinary beauty, and as a dance couple we looked perfect together. When we interacted during our rehearsal spots we displayed a great sense of banter, indulging in smart-mouthed urban patter. We simply had good chemistry, the kind that translated perfectly onto the TV screen.

That season was the first time that I felt the fans marked me for a big dose of romantic melodrama. Viewers played up my intimate relationship with Kelly, which took me somewhat by surprise.

Maybe it was naive of me, but I never could understand why people are so obsessed with other people's chemistry. Getting swept up in the tempest of gossip, as I did with Kelly, I found the fixation was a little over the top, not to mention annoying. Interviewers and columnists wanted to know *everything*. But when you've got something really special, you're not talking about it publicly 24/7. You're too busy living it. The curious public pried into every corner, marking everything we had together like a dog marks its territory. And, yes, I just drew a comparison between gossip and a dog pissing on a tree.

I didn't want the negative energy of other people's opinions to infiltrate my life. I never read the tabloids or checked into the gossip shows on TV, but just knowing that they were talking about us became an intrusive influence. Whether Kelly and I were an item wasn't why I wanted to be the focus of conversations around the office water cooler. I wanted my efforts, my accomplishments, my moments of impact to be the center of attention, not what I did or did not do off the set.

This is where you might look at me and say, "Really, Val? Hollywood is obsessed with romance? You're so damned smart, but you didn't know *that?*"

Yeah, I'll cop to it. For all my experience, I was naive. I didn't know that people in general and Hollywood in particular had become absurdly fixated upon other people's relationships, to the point where it sometimes seemed as though it was *the only fucking thing in existence*. I'd gaze longingly out of my bedroom window and wish upon a star: "Oh gee, I wish people were this concerned with a single-payer health care option." Yes, well, not really, but you get the idea.

With Kelly I experienced for the first time being the focal point of the public eye. As a couple, Elisabetta Canalis and I had been nonstarters. Even though we had great chemistry, Sherri Shepherd and I didn't exactly look like we were messing around—fooling around, maybe, joking like crazy, yes, but not hopping into bed together.

I can't completely play ignorance over the situation, because to some degree I participated in it. There was a reason for that. I had gone two-episodes-and-out with Elisabetta and four-and-out with Sherri. Honestly, I was down for whatever would earn me another week to produce an awesome dance number for Kelly, even if it meant taping a package crammed full of cheeky innuendos and romantic nuance, and even though it meant being unable to watch a package without cringing at least once.

It wasn't as if what Kelly and I had together was some kind of artificial charade. I was young and single, she was amazing, and we had a natural attraction for each other. But I was never a person who kissed and told, and I was raised to keep personal lives private, with flamboyant PDA's considered low-class. So the season might have been cringeworthy at times, but at least I did get a lot of airtime, and the internet went crazy with Kelly and Val.

For the first time, I had a fully adult season. The producers promoted me as the new sex symbol on the show. It worked because Kelly was so feminine and confident that she was a model for every woman. When a woman looks happy, fulfilled, empowered, and strong, the man standing next to her suddenly becomes a sex symbol.

Yes, we played into it, okay? By week ten Kelly and I were just laughing at the whole melodrama. Since I was already committed, I pushed my chips into the center of the table and went all in. During a "Wet, Wild, and Skimpy" flamenco routine, Kelly flung off her top like a challenge, stripping down to a feathered bikini. As if in response, I ripped off my pants and went near-commando in a black Speedo. Then we climbed onto a platform with a pool of inch-deep water and dance-splashed around in that for a while.

Off the hook, out of control, but way, way popular. The audience went nuts. For a quick minute "Speedo flamenco" became a thing. I had pushed the trademark Chmerkovskiy move of taking my shirt off to a whole new level.

"*Well that happened,*" I tweeted afterward. "*#sorrymom.*"

The routine was a testament to our relationship, how I made Kelly feel, how I was able to present her to the world. On the discussion boards, the comments came fast and furious. "Damn, so it's real, not just made for TV, and he's not just the little brother." I started enjoying a bigger presence on the show, a bigger voice, and made it farther and farther into the season, all the way to the finals. But romance-for-ratings represented a deal with the devil, one that would come back to haunt me on future seasons.

My partner mentored me in ways that I desperately needed back then. I didn't have that many friends who were truly entertainment industry insiders, and I lucked out with Kelly. My brother had a very different kind of relationship with Hollywood, and a different relationship with the show, so while much of his counsel helped me out, some definitely did not work for me.

Kelly knew the town backward and forward. She was friends with people who had made it to a very high level, and now she was in love with a person who had just pulled himself up from G-list status and clawed his way onto the F-List. She was able to give me invaluable insight on how the wacky world of Hollywood worked.

To cite just one example, I had always struggled at press events, especially the sort of round-robins with multiple reporters that were commonplace in entertainment. I would get upset over questions that seemed shallow and absolutely brain-dead, centered on some kind of nothing issue that I didn't care about. In my mind I pictured myself as a talk show hero, on *Larry King Live* or *Real Time with Bill Maher*, deep into meaningful and incisive political exchanges. I'd be ready for complex discussions, but the journalists would toss me softball question after softball question, and I always wound up feeling as though my intelligence had been insulted.

Kelly set me straight.

"The key in all situations, Val, is always to know your audience," she told me, an example of the kind of memorable advice that's helped me forever afterward.

"It's not about what you know or what you want to say," she went on. "It's about doing all of those things at the right time for the right audience. There's a time to preach about changing the world and a time to just lightheartedly discuss your cha-cha."

If you know that the audience was there for a specific reason, in other words, speak to your audience and speak to that reason. Don't just blurt out opinions, and don't just share your weighty thoughts with everyone equally.

Know your audience—a good rule of thumb in show business, and since the entire world is a stage, a good idea in life as a whole, too.

Reflecting on the events of my childhood, I realized that I had understood the concept from the very first, even if I was too young to put it into words. One way or another, I had always been playing to the audience.

To explain better what I mean, let me go back to the beginning, not to my start on *Dancing with the Stars*, but back to the real beginning, in a decayed Soviet harbor town known as the Pearl of the Black Sea.

PART 2

A JOURNEY IN
LIFE

FAMILY

The most important thing to know about me is family.

In fact, very nearly the *only* thing to know about me is family. Ours was a household of two sons and two parents, and as a team we worked together better than the 1998 championship Chicago Bulls, better than a NASA astronaut crew, better than any other family I know. We were like a circus act, "The Flying Chmerkovskiys & Sons."

At the head of the clan stood my father, Aleksandr Chmerkovskiy, nicknamed Sasha, and my mother, Larisa Chmerkovskaya. My older brother, Maks, beat me into existence by six years, seventy-six days, and a few spare-change hours and minutes. He might have had a head start, but I've been catching up ever since.

Whenever I spoke as a kid, everything tended to come out in terms of "we." *We* have a dance school. I might have won a dance competition, but it was really we, we, we. I was afraid people couldn't understand that. I began to censor myself, because it sounded as though I was using the royal "we," that obnoxious, high-handed, regal style of speaking, as in the British Queen's "We are not amused." But for a long time, my reality was limited to a core gang of four: me, my brother, my mom, and my pops.

My whole life was "we."

Only recently, as I grew out of my twenties and into my thirties, have I felt any degree of separation from the family unit—not much, but some. When I was growing up, my parents were always nearby, always with me, and my whole world was right there in front of my nose. Courtesy of my mom's cooking, the Chmerkovskiy family was a movable feast. It didn't really matter where we'd park our gypsy caravan, whether living in Ukraine or experiencing life as immigrants in New York City, I'd always be chilling with the fam. We could be chilling in Antarctica and we'd still be together.

Odessa, Ukraine, was where my father was born and grew up, where he met and married my mother, and where my parents raised Maks and me. Moms and Pops had what could be jokingly described as a mixed marriage. My mother's parents were both Eastern Orthodox and raised their daughter in that religion, while my father's people were Jewish. The truth was, our household was secular, and everyone was too caught up in keeping hearth and home together to attend church or temple services.

I grew up in a Communist country where the weight of history was almost crushing. My paternal grandmother watched as her entire family was executed by the Nazis. Then she raised her children, my father included, in Soviet Ukraine, an atheist environment where the official party line portrayed religion as the poison of humanity. Comrade citizens could be sent to prison for any overt display of a religious symbol, whether it was a cross or Star of David. My family's roots might have reached deep into Judaism and Christianity, but that background had to be kept buried, out of sight, when my father was young.

When my father was twenty-three, he lost his own father, whom he adored, who was his hero, who represented the only person on earth for whom he had any sort of filial love. He died three years before I was born, and so I was named after him, my paternal grandfather, Valentin Chmerkovskiy.

Even my mother spoke about him with reverence. "This was the greatest man," she would say, with a faraway look in her eyes. "I married your father because I was in love with your grandfather."

Throughout my childhood, I was always more intimate with my mother, but more influenced by my dad. Just as my dad's father was his hero, my father was mine. Honestly, even today I have a hard time with people telling me, "When I was growing up, Michael Jackson was my idol." Or LeBron James, Fred Astaire, or Steve Jobs or whoever else they say, anyone in the world. *Really?* I'd think. Did you have a father growing up? How can your idol be anybody besides your father? I have to check myself, because not everybody has been fortunate enough to have the type of father that I have, or to benefit from the kind of relationship that I enjoy with my parents.

In Russian there's a phrase that translates to "hands of gold" in English, and as applied to my grandfather it meant that everything he put his mind to turned out to be a great success. His passing was a blow that my dad never really recovered from—an emotional and spiritual blow, yes, definitely, but also a financial one. From that moment on, my father had to make his way on his own.

We were Russians in Ukraine, we spoke the Russian language at home, and I think that a little of the philosophical Russian sadness invaded all our souls. The citizens of Eastern Europe were well known for their brand of weary cynicism, and there were many Russian phrases that foretell the future as a disaster waiting to happen. Doomsday was always just around the corner. In the unlikely event that anything positive occurred, the standard response was to say, "*tfoo, tfoo, tfoo,*" spit over the shoulder, and knock on wood three times, just so as not to jinx it. I don't think of it as superstition as much as paranoia. Every silver cloud had a gray lining and a slight sense of pessimism afflicted us all.

My dad's answer to his father's untimely death was to step into a phone booth and come back out as Superman. He did what everyone else in Ukraine was doing, which was to hustle relentlessly for the smallest scrap of advantage, the most minuscule amount of gain, but he did it in a supercharged way. When you're just scraping by, life very quickly becomes a Darwinian game of survival of the fittest. Aleksandr Chmerkovskiy was fiercely determined to be the fittest of the fit. Desperate times called for desperate measures.

Among countless tales of borderline danger and risk of legal consequences, one stood out in particular. My father probably would not want me to tell this story, but I have to portray the extremes he went to in order to keep our family afloat. Somehow Pops and his cousin found out that in Poland there was a shortage of big industrial scales, the kind that weigh slabs of beef at meat packing plants. The contraptions were going for the equivalent of a hundred dollars a pop in Warsaw. That's where the demand was, and my father looked around Odessa and discovered a source of supply close at hand.

He and his cousin went to the town's central market after it closed for the night, bribed the sole security guard with a bottle of vodka, and grabbed all the scales they could, ten of them, as many as they could squeeze into a borrowed compact car. They drove the stolen trove to Poland and sold it off for a thousand bucks. They then bought as many Levi jeans as they could and drove back to Odessa to flip the merchandise.

From very early on, that kind of hustle was in me. It was like a heritage passed down from my father and grandfather. I was not scared. I would not back down. The hustle was in me because my father was in me, and I sure didn't want to apologize for that.

I refused to judge him. It was never my place within the family to question anything my parents did. When I was a kid their favorite phrase was "Who asked you?"—which in Russian was, "*Kto tebya sprashivayet?*" The phrase had pretty much the same nuances in Russian as it did in English, and it would haunt me every time I sat down at the table.

"Mom, I don't wanna eat this borscht."

"Oh?" she would say. "*Kto tevya sprashivayet?*"

"Mom, I don't wanna practice the violin."

"*Kto tevya sprashivayet?*"

"I don't wanna wear these hand-me-down clothes."

"*Kto tevya sprashivayet?*"

Or whatever the issue in question, there was an automatic, universal response to any complaint.

"*Kto tevya sprashivayet?*" Who asked you, little one?

My folks have never understood the common American practice of parents becoming pals with their children. There was a distance between us that was filled with love, a distance that basically turned into bottomless respect as I grew older. The distance might have been based a little bit on fear, but it also bred a rock-hard sense of accountability. I was held responsible. I never wanted to disappoint or hurt my parents, who had given so much to me. I didn't want to disappoint my father, didn't want to anger my mother. That's why, later in life, one of the greatest moments came when I realized I had become friends with my dad. It's when I finally knew I was an adult.

My mom had just as much steel in her as my dad, but she hid it under a warmer, softer exterior. She was the quiet storm in our household. I have her borscht in my blood. She doesn't get credit for anything when she should get credit for everything, literally everything. But my mom is the type of person who never made it about her. She was never front and center. That was her complexity and that was her insecurity. But she was always there for us, the steadfast anchor that my father, Maks, and I depended upon.

Her biggest fear was that the shadowy, illegal world of the Odessa hustle would somehow take over our lives. That, and the army. Somebody once said that the time not to become a parent was eighteen years before a war, and in Ukraine the prospect of war lurked everywhere, all the time. The authorities required all males to register for military service at age sixteen. The possibility of her sons being gobbled up by the army in Ukraine really frightened my mom. Her youngest brother had served in Afghanistan when the Soviets were there. He saw his best friend die in his arms and he returned to civilian life a shattered man.

My parents might have been the twin suns of the family, but there was another planet orbiting around them, a big one, a Jupiter to my Mars: my brother, Maksim.

We are different. That is what people fail to understand when they lump Maks and me together as the "Chmerkovskiy brothers." Our differences do not diminish our deep love and loyalty, or interfere in any way with the crazy-ass level of respect I have for my older sibling. In fact, our differences probably only serve to emphasize our brotherly feelings. If we were exactly alike it would be no big deal to love each other, because it would be like loving a version of ourselves. But to love someone totally different from yourself, that takes strength.

Maybe it was because he spent six more years growing up in Ukraine than I did, and the experience left a deeper stamp on him, but it is not too much to say that darker currents run through my brother's soul than run through mine, Russian currents, Odessa currents. He was Shakespeare's Hamlet while I was more like Prince Hal. Or to put it more into Russian terms, he was Andrei and I was Pierre in Tolstoy's *War and Peace*. Later on, when they labeled Maks as "the bad boy of ballroom dance," he didn't object to the "bad" as much as he did to the "boy."

We're both alphas, and at times having two of us in the same household was like putting two wolverines in a cage. He's a Capricorn, which is a goat, and I'm an Aries, which is a ram, so my parents had to watch this sheep and goat going at it time and time again. But when we weren't fighting, our efforts were channeled in the same direction. Together we were unstoppable. We bulldozed through things. When the direction got muddy and we found ourselves bumping heads . . . Well, it still made for a pretty epic moment. When it comes to the two of us, it has only ever been extremes.

Once we moved to the States, I developed a level of American optimism that Maks could never fully embrace. My father had a personal brand optimism, too, not so much hopefulness but confidence that consistency and hard work would pay off. He believed that as long as you show up and work hard, your minuses would turn into pluses and success was just around the corner.

My brother had a very different kind of optimism that came from a very different place. It was less about entitlement and more of a fundamental demand for fairness. That things should be fair was his only rule. There might have been a little more arrogance involved in Maks's kind of confidence, a brashness and a sense of pride. He was fair but firm, very firm in his expectations. The good life for him represented a delayed payment for the sacrifices he had endured, and he believed he had endured many. But the luxuries that my brother dreamed of simply gave me anxiety.

Maks's attitude: "I paid my motherfucking dues, I deserve whatever I go after, and I deserve it more than the guy next to me because I've worked harder than the guy next to me."

All this is probably Val-style overanalyzing. Really, the main emotion I feel for Maks is a ferocious form of gratitude. He blazed my path. I watched him power through life's heartaches and disappointments while I marched behind him, benefiting from the wisdom of hindsight. I was spared a lot of trouble because of all the things I learned from my brother's experience.

Then again, I proved from a very early age that I was quite capable of creating trouble all by myself.

ODESSA

My earliest memories of Odessa, the city in Ukraine where I was born, are of a courtyard. The crumbling old estate house where my family lived had been broken up into apartments after the Russian Revolution, but it featured a central space where kids played and adults gathered to smoke and gossip.

We were in Courtyard 27, on the corner of Baranova and Artema streets in the center of Odessa. Except for a brief moment when the sun passed over at noon, the courtyard was always in the shade, and I remember it being bathed in a weak, green light. Although in reality it was usually overflowing with life, for some reason in my mind's eye I always see the big courtyard as deserted, a very romanticized Chernobyl-like scene, straight out of the post-apocalyptic world of *Mad Max*.

In the middle of the space was an abandoned car, a rusted-out Zaporozhets that no one ever drove. It was just *there*. The Zaporozhets was the Soviet version of an economy compact, a "car of the people." Manufactured in Ukraine, the "Zapo" was a notoriously shitty automobile, a "soap box on wheels." Even so, people had a lot of affection for this poor man's Lamborghini.

That broken-down car in the courtyard served as a fitting symbol for the permanently stalled Ukraine economy, in a country that seemed to be just rusting away. But the folks around me growing up were still very much vibrant and alive, and when a car stopped working it was typical of them to use it as a decoration or a jungle gym for kids.

The courtyard represented a real community, where my neighbors simply laughed at bad luck and trouble. People are what made my young life brighter, not the possessions that they did or didn't have. The surroundings weren't lavish, in fact they were pretty shitty, but I loved my home and was proud of it. I wouldn't want to have grown up in any other place in the world. That paradox— bleak surroundings coupled with a ridiculous sense of pride—is the essence of my childhood. It taught me that circumstances can't break your spirit.

In retrospect I can paint you a picture of a really great time in my life. The world of Odessa might be difficult to grasp for anyone who hasn't experienced it. What outsiders see first is the bleak economic landscape. There was little money around, no jobs, zero opportunity. The streets of Odessa were like a series of dead ends, one after another, and if you traveled down enough of them, cynicism started flowing through your veins.

My dad was always hustling, finding any way he could to support his family. For a while he shuttled back and forth to Turkey, buying Levi denims and leather goods there to sell at the central street market back home. I grew up in a country where you had to stand on line for five hours to purchase a piece of chicken, where you were given little ration tickets to pick up a loaf of bread once a week, and where stores would run out of everyday basics all the time.

But a child sees life through a different lens. What I saw didn't break me, but simply led me to appreciate my family. I grew up much more preoccupied with people than with possessions. I didn't need a big-ass front yard with a picket fence, because I could play with my friends Yura and Andrei. We used our imagination to make the best of what we had. A shitty courtyard? No! A realm of games and magic and joy. The skill of using imagination to transform reality is still incredibly useful to me today.

Odessa is "The Pearl of the Black Sea," a kind of St. Tropez made not for billionaires but for commoners, with a beautiful seaside atmosphere and gorgeous women everywhere. Paris might be a city where you fall in love, and New York is capital of the world, but Odessa is the most charming city in Eastern Europe, with St. Petersburg maybe a close second. The natives know that and believe that, and the pride of Odessans can be intense. In my heart, I have zero loyalty to Ukraine or to Russia. But I was born in an incredible fairy tale of a place, and that's where I'm proud of being from, and not a foot outside of the city boundaries.

Everyone I have ever met who came from Odessa turned out to be vibrant and interesting. Natives affectionately refer to the place as "Odessa Mama," which is also the title of a popular song. In conversation, they will always ask, "Have you been there? Oh, you have to go. You have to go! Odessa is the most wonderful place in the world!"

In the presence of a native don't ever pronounce it like the town in Texas, don't say it as though it rhymes with "Vanessa." Put a little soulful James Brown spin to the middle syllable. "Ohd-yeah-sah."

Various streets and neighborhoods in the city have completely different flavors—Romanian, Bulgarian, and Turkish influences from the south, Russian or the Caucasus from the north and west. You might even run into a vampire or two from nearby Transylvania. Much of the architecture has a French influence, which gives off a classic, stately vibe. Romance is always in the air. The seaside setting adds to the charm—and it is a sea, not an ocean, the Black Sea, locals are very definite about that.

Back then, unless you were some privileged political refugee like Angela Davis, the whole Russian empire wasn't a popular place to *move to* as much as a place to *escape from*. The constant threat of war was one reason. In the past Odessa had been overrun by Turkish armies, Russian Cossacks, and Nazi stormtroopers—you name it. To this day the whole area remains in the middle of a tug of war between Russia and Ukraine.

Amid all this history and atmosphere I took my tiny place in the world on March 24, 1986, officially becoming my parents' problem to deal with. Whether I'm remembering it through the rose-colored glasses of nostalgia or because it really was the Pearl of the Black Sea, growing up in Odessa seemed like paradise to me. I guess that unless you've spent your early years abused or starving, all childhood days appear golden in hindsight.

The first specific incident I remember took place in Courtyard 27 when I was five. My brother was playing a Ukrainian kid's game similar to Pogs, the bottle cap game that was so popular in the United States in the mid-1990s. Instead of cardboard milk bottle caps, we played with the wrappers of Turbo, a particular brand of gum. The packaging unfolded into little pictures of a Ferrari, a Lamborghini, or some other high-end sports car—anything but a Zaporozhets! In our eyes, anything foreign was way cooler than anything home-grown.

The game was to flatten the gum wrappers out, stack them, then hit the stack with the edge of your palm. As long as your own "car" landed right-side up, you got to collect all the other wrappers that flipped over. We kept going until one player had won all the cars. A simple, mindless game, but one that held endless fascination for us as kids. We were so poor that we couldn't afford to pay attention, as the phrase goes, so we had to make do with what we had, which was countless collections of discarded gum wrappers. But everything is relative, and Turbo was like currency to us. I played as if the stakes were life and death, a little competitor even as a young kid, already determined to win any contest that came my way.

That day I hung on a railing watching my brother play, and this being Ukraine naturally the railing was broken. On the other side was a one-story drop into a concrete basement entranceway, where trash got stacked up to be collected. Maks made a sudden move and backed into the broken railing. Like the action in a TV cartoon, the metal railing rebounded and catapulted me into the air. I went sailing, flying headfirst down into a pile of garbage, where I crashed onto a box that had a nail sticking out.

There was blood, a lot of it. It happened to be my mother's birthday. It's funny how you don't remember all the times of soft kisses, the empty hours, or the safe and secure moments you had as a kid, but the bloody ones always remain sharp in your memory.

Having an older brother might have allowed me a little more leeway in the world of mischief, a little larger field of action. In his early teens Maks was already a miniature adult, old beyond his years. I skipped along behind him, always acting out, always curious and outgoing, always tiptoeing on the edge of danger. I was the one who went sailing over the railing. He was the one who walked his bleeding little brother up to our mother's birth-day party.

I was ambitious and very social, while he was way more timid, way more shy. I was the kid who cut up books and set the pages on fire under the dinner table while the family sat eating. Maks was the one who was reading those books. He was introverted. I was an extrovert.

I was also the one who got kicked out of kindergarten after two weeks. Kindergarten! How in the fuck do you misbehave badly enough to be expelled from kindergarten?

I was guilty of multiple offenses, it turned out, a pretty long rap sheet for a five-year-old. I was a little kid decked out in denim head to toe, courtesy of my father's Turkey-to-Odessa Levi hustle. I thought I was hot shit. During recess one day a teacher found me swinging on the schoolyard gate, poking my hand out to adults passing by on the sidewalk.

"Spare change? Spare any change?"

The school authorities called my moms and pops. "Why is your kid begging during recess?"

Unfortunately for me, my parents had the same question, one that I'd eventually have to explain, either after the inevitable ass-whupping or before. Maybe I had once seen a panhandler on the street somewhere. Maybe it was a form of street art for me. At any rate, the incident represented an early introduction to the joys of paid performance.

It was also strike one according to the kindergarten authorities. Strike two came when they found me tying my schoolmates together with their own tights, the long stockings that Ukrainian youngsters traditionally wear. I would pull a kid's tights up from the waistband, stretch them out, and knot them to another kid's before anyone knew what was happening. My poor, innocent schoolmates had never been pranked precisely in that way before. There were tears.

Tears also came with strike three, the stunt that got me officially expelled from kindergarten, when I took to speeding on the merry-go-round and—potentially, allegedly, your honor, I reserve the right not to incriminate myself—I may or may not have pushed kids off at high velocity.

"Mr. Chmerkovskiy, we're afraid that your son Valentin plays too rough with the other children. We are going to have to send him home."

That was me. I was not the *Fast and Furious* but the fast and curious, and there was very little logical reason for anything I did. "Keep it moving," was always my motto. I wasn't a troublemaker, but I was a discoverer of trouble, a busy little man fascinated with adventure.

THERE WAS SOMETHING ELSE IN MY YOUNG LIFE BESIDES TROU-
ble, though, just a hint of light amid the doom-and-gloom back-
drop of the Russian soul, like a door cracked slightly open in a
prison. Opportunity entered my life around the same time I got
expelled from kindergarten. The scar from my fall into the garbage
pit probably wasn't yet fully healed.

I was riding in the family's beat-up Soviet truck with my father
and his cousin, Joseyk. Like every other adult male relative we always called him "uncle." My uncle Joseyk was just out of prison,
where he had served time for buying items overseas for a certain
price and then reselling them in the Soviet Union for a little bit
more—a seven-year stretch for embracing the simplest, most fundamental concept of capitalism. What America was built upon
landed him in prison.

To my young eyes Uncle Joseyk was as cool as Frank Sinatra.
Beyond the fact that he had spent time in prison—and prison in
the Soviet Union was no joke—he had a flair about him, a charisma that was infectious, a quality that in current slang would
be called "swag." Uncle Joseyk represented the first time I discovered swag in action. He had spent years in lockup but somehow knew his way around a jazz piano, and could wail out on an
accordion, too.

Riding in the backseat, I didn't have a thought in my head, I
was just idly singing along with whatever song was on the radio.
A popular Russian rock band, Lyube ("Любэ") played its hit
tune, "Батька Махно." It was the national reciprocal of U2's
"Sunday, Bloody Sunday," and like much of Soviet rock music those
days, the lyrics had a lot of military references. This was during the
Russian invasion of Afghanistan, the U.S.S.R.'s version of Vietnam,
where the army took a huge hit.

The song kicked off with an army trumpet and a gunshot, then
segued into a stomping melody that sounded like a group singalong

in a bar. The lead vocalist, Nikolay Rastorguyev, pronounced dark-shit sentiments somewhat along these lines:

In Afghanistan you die slowly alongside your friends . . .

I was humming along to lyrics I didn't understand. My uncle turned his head to look at me, listened for a beat, then nudged my dad.

"Hey, he's really got potential," my uncle said.

Pops snorted in disbelief. "What? Valya? Potential in singing? Based on what?"

In Russian culture, the knee-jerk response was to question everything, always with a slight hint of pessimism.

"Yeah, I can hear it," Joseyk said. "He has pitch. He was singing along in tune."

"All right, okay, he has pitch. So what?"

"You should try him out for music school."

My father shrugged him off, going back to worrying about the million other problems he had playing in his mind.

If you said "music school" in Odessa, everyone knew what you were talking about: the National Academy of Music, housed in a beautiful old Beaux Arts building in the center of town. I always consider Odessa to be the Eastern European equivalent of New Orleans. There was always a lot of music around, not only classical but also ethnic, pop, and especially jazz—the city was known as the "Jazz Capital of Russia." The families of George Gershwin and Bob Dylan both emigrated to America from there.

A couple of knockaround Odessa dudes driving in an old beater of a truck, fantasizing "you should try him out for music school"—that would be like two street guys who were living a poverty-stricken existence in the Bronx, say, thinking they could dash out and enroll a kid in a music program. Not just any music program, either, not something remotely possible, but rather something ultra-prestigious and wildly out of reach, like disdaining New York's *Fame* high school, LaGuardia, and instead aiming directly for Juilliard.

Why not? Why not upgrade your rust-bucket Zaporozhets, and not for a Ford but for a Bentley? Maybe because it's totally impossible?

My father broke his silence. "How would we do this?" he asked my uncle.

That moment changed my life. Whatever it is that gives somebody a fresh perspective, that's what makes things happen, that's what sends people on a unique path. Everybody has different perspectives at different times. My dad was a little more cynical in his outlook, maybe because he was preoccupied with scratching out a living for his family. So he didn't even hear my pitch-perfect humming in the backseat. But my uncle did, because he came to it from a perspective that was slightly different from my father's.

My father could be forgiven, since it wasn't as if his younger son was singing all day long. In fact, as a kid I rarely ever sang. From my dad's perspective, I wasn't musical. If anything, my parents were afraid that I was going to end up becoming some sort of extreme sports maniac, a BMX or motocross rider, something like that, because I hurt myself all the time as a kid, falling off shit, running into things.

In that moment, Uncle Joseyk could have heard me and said nothing. As rare as talent itself is, I think it's almost as rare for a person to recognize and encourage someone else's talent.

But my uncle called me out, and then it became a matter of the simple domino effect that happens whenever someone decides to believe in another person. It's why today I instinctively and consciously try to seize every opportunity to encourage someone else to feel as though they can do anything they want to do. Even if they don't wind up pursuing their dream, for a moment they'll feel good because someone else sees a possibility in them, just as Uncle Joseyk saw a possibility in me.

The next week, miracle of miracles, my father managed to sign me up for an audition at the Music Academy. My mom dressed me up in the nicest, most formal clothes I had, the outfit I wore whenever there was a formal occasion. I don't remember asking questions, and I don't remember getting any answers. That wasn't the way in our family. As a kid I was expected simply to show up and take care of business, with no input from yours truly required.

We went to the Music Academy as a family, but I had to head into the audition room alone. I'm sure there were plenty of stage parents who drilled and drilled their children for the perfect performance. Pops and my mom were more casual: *Here you are . . . Do your best . . . Let's see what happens!*

I met the instructor, a severe woman with hair wrapped so tightly in a bun that it pulled the features of her face backward. Some folks in Beverly Hills would pay top dollar for that kind of skin treatment.

She plunked out an "A" on a piano and nodded at me. I vocalized an A note as best I could, singing it at the top of my lungs. She sounded a few more notes for me to sing, then cupped her hands and clapped out a rhythm that I had to repeat, which I did precisely. For my grand audition finale, she asked me to sing a song of my choice. So I did the tune that I had hummed along with in the car with my uncle.

In Afghanistan the skies are black with smoke

There I was, belting out lyrics harsh enough to traumatize any kid, with so much heart and conviction that I won the room over and I knew it. The teacher conferred in whispers with a balding administrator who had come in while I was singing. Everyone on that faculty looked like what they were—Soviet-era music school teachers. I finished and stood there, with a normal six-year-old's empty expression on my face, like a motel with a neon "Vacancy" sign burning out front.

I don't know if they found me comedic, but charisma and a pair of little brass balls played a big role, since I definitely wasn't the most talented kid auditioning that day. Ms. Hair Bun spoke some more to Baldy, then turned to me.

"What instrument would you like to play?" she asked.

She caught me off guard. My mind rattled through the possibilities. Guitar? Nuh-uh. The Music Academy definitely wasn't a Jimi Hendrix sort of place. Something small and manageable, like a flute, maybe, but that was too girly.

"Violin," I said, unknowingly sealing my fate for the next decade or so.

Somehow out of nowhere I had just been accepted into a world-class music school. I believe it was the first time my parents discovered their kid was special.

Back at home, they asked me, "Why did you say you wanted to play the violin? None of us play it and you've never in your life ever held one."

To which I replied, "Can you see me carrying a piano to school every day?" *I don't think so,* I thought to myself, sarcasm that I would never say out loud to my parents.

I had chosen one of the smallest instruments, which ended up being one of the hardest to learn. My logic was to try to make my life easier, but instead I made it incredibly more difficult. Little did I know that the Academy required piano study for all students, because piano was how we learned *solfeggio,* otherwise known as music theory.

MY BEGINNING EFFORTS WERE PAINFUL, BOTH FOR ME AND FOR everyone else with ears in the vicinity. I've read that clinical physiologists have determined that out of all musical instruments the violin is the closest in sound to a human voice, which was why it has such an eerie ability to trigger extreme depths of emotion. Listeners can hear the violin crying, but when they are subjected to the attempts of a six-year-old beginner, innocent bystanders can feel like crying themselves. My sound fell somewhere between very bad singing and a cat being strangled.

The rule was that I had to practice for an hour every day after school. Scales repeated endlessly easily qualify as among the most annoying sounds in the world. We were crowded into a two-room apartment, where my parents slept on the foldout couch in the living room, and where Maks and I had our bunk beds in a tiny space nearby. So there was no place to run, no place to flee from my wretched practicing.

"Okay, you see where the clock is now?" my parents (usually my mom) would ask. "If you practice until three you can go out-side and play."

I could hear other kids in the courtyard having fun, and they could hear me inside playing scales. I kept one eye on the clock and one eye on the sheet music on the stand in front of me. To the T, to the minute, to the absolute second that three o'clock came I'd drop the violin as though it were on fire and rush my ass outside to be a regular kid again. It didn't matter if I was in mid-vibrato—when the big hand hit the twelve I was gone quicker than Usain Bolt at the 2016 Olympics. I wouldn't even bother to put the violin in its case, I'd just toss it on the bed and head right out.

So what happened next was really my fault. I was outside after practice one day when I heard a surprised shout from inside our apartment. Apparently Maks had been reading and was so focused on his book that he sat on my violin and crushed it. The instrument wasn't exactly a Stradivarius, but it was the local version of the best, costing a lot more than we could afford to spend. My parents were furious at the loss. Maks caught an ass whooping, and I tried my best to look as though I felt bad.

"Oh, damn," I said mournfully, while really, on the down-low, I was the happiest kid in the world, because the accident meant that practice would be put off indefinitely. But I underestimated my parents, because they came up with a new violin for me in two days. That's just the way they were. If you were their kid and you had committed to something, you had to live up to your responsibilities. Not only did I have to start practicing again after a too-short break, I was now sentenced to make up for the time I lost, practicing for two hours a day instead of one.

After years of study I finally came to believe that the ability to create music is almost a superpower. That's why I feel music education is so important for children. It doesn't matter whether they become a CEO, an insurance salesperson, or a garbage man, it's important for kids to develop their "passion palate"—enthusiasms that will further their individuality and help them find happiness and fulfillment.

There was music on the Academy's syllabus, obviously, but there were also classes in math, science, and language. It was a prestigious musical institution that still emphasized the fundamentals of learning. The glorious architectural monument of a building added a sense of romance to ordinary school days.

I entered when I was six and remained for two years, leaving only when our family immigrated to the States. This was the first time that my path diverged from Maks's, who attended a school focused mainly on math and science.

I loved being there. The Academy had classes for first grade through twelfth, and I would always hang out on the upper floors, where the older high school students studied. I was up there so often they adopted me as a kind of little brother.

Maks was walking me to school one day and we saw a pair of tough-looking tenth graders heading toward us. They looked menacing to him, and when he told the story later, my brother always emphasized how nervous he became.

"Look at these two," he muttered to me. "We're definitely going to get jumped here."

Before I could respond, the older kids broke out in smiles. "Hey, Val, what's up?"

They were my friends from the upper floors of the Music Academy. "This is my brother, Maks," I said.

"Nice to meet you!" they responded, slapping me five as they headed on past.

Walking away, I couldn't help teasing my brother. "I guess we didn't get a beatdown after all."

If I hadn't been such an empty-headed little kid during the incident, I might have realized that my relationship with Maks was beginning to change. We were moving in different directions. Though I was a solid ten inches shorter than my brother back then, I always packed a harder punch.

Those were golden days, and way before ballroom dance, hip-hop, or Hollywood came into my life, I had already been deeply and permanently influenced by "Odessa Mama," a city that served as a third parent to me.

When I finally got to America, no one understood where I was coming from. Friends I met in Brooklyn couldn't grasp it, in New Jersey no one knew, and in West Hollywood they definitely didn't know. People from Odessa are like people from New Orleans—we're proud of our heritage, and we speak differently, act differently, create differently. We infuse our conversation with comedy and sarcasm and jazz, and we carry our hometown with us wherever we go.

IMMIGRANT

The decision to leave Odessa didn't come easily for my family. In recent times there were essentially two waves of Russian immigration to America. The first came in the 1970s, when the government loosened the emigration rules for Jewish *"refuseniks"*—outcasts, poets, and activists who spoke out against the Soviet society. The second started when Mikhail Gorbachev opened the borders in the early 1990s officially ending totalitarian rule and giving independence to fourteen Soviet republics, Ukraine being one of them.

I hope that last development can help clear up how I could be a Russian coming from Ukraine. The U.S.S.R. was like the U.S., in that it was made up of numerous supposedly separate-but-united states. (Critics challenged that idea, saying, "The *Union* of *Soviet Socialist Republics*—four words, four lies.") In America, how many New Yorkers live in New Jersey, and how many New Jerseyans live in New York? In the same way, a lot of Russians lived in Ukraine. With the breakup of the Soviet Union, it was as if New Jersey had now been made a separate country.

My father was in his late teens in the 1970s, and at that time he saw those who left simply as traitors, betraying the ideals of national pride and loyalty. He was always an idealistic man, especially in his youth. For him, the sentiment back then was, *We're proud Russians,* so we are gonna stick it out no matter what.

Years later, with the Russian economy thoroughly in the toilet, things were different. It was time to leave. Now my dad was a parent of two and no longer a kid in his teens. He left behind that prideful, patriotic, kneejerk response in favor of a little more common sense. *There's no opportunity here, and it's not a safe environment to raise the children—it has to be better somewhere else.* That somewhere else was the United States of America.

There's heaven, and right next door is America, and that's how Eastern Europeans looked at it. For anyone to dream about going to the States was a laughable ambition. Contrary to popular belief, it's really hard to get to come to America. The immigration authorities don't just hand out visas like red roses.

My parents faced a tidal wave of doubt from others: "No, you can't do it!" and "You won't survive!" With the overwhelming odds against them, the chances appeared slim to none that they would be able to accomplish what they set out to do.

How does anyone even begin the process of leaving? Imagine picking up everything you know, your entire life, your children's lives, the lives of your loved ones, and moving it all to the other side of the world, the most exclusive side, the place hardest to get into. And once you manage that impossible task, then what do you do? You don't speak English, you don't have any friends, you don't have a job. What then?

How proud, how determined, how desperate, how strong did my parents have to be in order to look at that forty-foot tidal wave of negativity coming straight at them and just buckle down and do it anyway? It took a lot of courage. They made a decision for which I'm still being paid dividends, the investment they made in us, allowing our incredible family to grow and prosper in a new land.

So when you think about the person who is able to get up, drop everything that's comfortable, everything that they know and are used to, you have to understand that they face overwhelming odds. Once they're able to breathe out and settle in, the immigrant sure isn't feeling a sense of entitlement, but rather of immense gratitude. The Thanksgiving holiday in our household has become like the Fourth of July, observed more enthusiastically every single year.

I celebrate family and America. Those two things are what I'm most grateful for in my life. My name will never say that proudly for me, but if you're willing to go beyond my impossible-to-pronounce last name and lend me your ear for a five-minute conversation, you'll quickly realize that I'm as American as it comes. My pride for this country, which is ultimately reflected in my loyalty to it, is a prime example of what the flag stands for.

IN THE CLASSIC "WHO ASKED YOU?" STYLE OF OUR FAMILY, I don't recall being consulted about the decision to leave Odessa. I was seven years old and did have an opinion. The other family members could have asked me but they didn't. I do remember a huge family dinner—it must have been in the spring of 1993—when the idea was first announced.

Everything in our culture was a dinner thing, an hours-long combination feast, debate, and performance, with plenty of food and alcohol. The time spent around the dinner table was our Sunday church, our temple, synagogue, and mosque. We shared everything, all our thoughts and emotions, for better and for worse, accompanied by noisy interruptions and intense back and forths, all allowing us to wind up feeling united once again. The dinner table was where you made the big announcements, where the head of the house had to be the wise one, and where we learned the most, where we connected the most.

This particular dinner, there were a lot of raw sentiments and more than a few tears. My father found himself looking at the same people he had been preaching to years before about loyalty to Russia. Those teenage ideals had now caught up to him in the real world—not the imaginary world he had created for himself, influenced by Soviet propaganda. Now he was a grown man with a grown man's responsibilities. *We can't stick it out after all.*

My mom was different. She hadn't been preaching ideology in her teenage years. She had lifelong friendships, ones that she had always treasured and cared for.

"Oh my God, we're leaving Odessa," my mother moaned. But even with all those deep feelings, still she signed on to the move.

As an adult looking back, I stand in awe at my parents resolve. These two people essentially said, "We are all in on each other and our kids. This is it. I'm all in as a father and I'm all in as a husband. I'm all in as a mother and I'm all in as a wife."

I was sitting at the table, but I didn't have any chips to play. I was excited, but I had just turned eight and was always in a state of perpetual excitement about something, anything, everything.

Me: "Okay, wow, leaving—that sounds exciting. Where are we going? What's happening? I think we should go right now!"

The whole family, in unison: "Who? Asked? You?!?"

Before we could leave Russia, the four of us had to trek up to the United States Embassy in Moscow to get our official exit documents. From Odessa, Ukraine, we traveled by train to the Russian capital. This was a 25-hour trip, and let me tell you, Russian railroads never prioritize the comfort of their customers. The bottom line was getting from point A to point B in the most stripped-down way possible. The conditions were cramped and the trip seemed endless.

In Russia there's an expression, Спать Валетом, "*spat valetam*," which means "to sleep like jacks." When you are faced with the task of fitting a body on a single bed, say, or another piece of furniture that's obviously an impossible fit for two people, you "*spat valetam.*"

Valetam was a reference to "валет," the jack in a suit of cards, a figure which faces up or down depending which way the card was held. *Valetam* meant to imitate that, where one person would sleep one way and the other one would sleep opposite. I guess the English equivalent might be "69," but I like *spat valetam* better, even though it has no sexual connotation.

On that trip to Moscow Maks and I *spat valetam,* crammed onto a single bench seat, my face right next to his smelly feet. I found out that the process of emigrating wouldn't be so damn easy, at least not for me and my brother.

Meanwhile, the adults were left standing. For the whole day-long journey, one adult was always standing. My parents' sacrifice seemed to exist on a higher, finer level than the world of us kids. It might have been true everywhere, but I felt as though in the old country, my parents were always sacrificing, one day after another. Every day was about the struggle to survive. They were always symbolically standing on their feet in a crowded train. Unless you were a masochist who was in love with pain and struggle, sooner or later you were going to decide that enough was enough.

BY THE EARLY 1990S, OUR FAMILY HAD REACHED THAT SORT OF tipping point, and it put us on that train to Moscow, seeking official permission to leave for America. My grandmother, my father's mother, had contacts with groups that gave aid to Jewish people leaving Russia, headed mostly to Israel, the States, or Canada, with some others going elsewhere in Europe or to Australia. Though we weren't observant and were at best culturally Jewish, my father's passport had the word "Jewish" stamped across it, just like a yellow Star of David would have identified him in the past. The same religious classification that had held my father in so many ways was now going to allow us to leave Russia.

After that traumatic train journey, we arrived in Moscow to find the city locked in a civil war, not a full-scale one, but there was a level of unrest that definitely put troops in the streets. We had landed smack in the middle of a constitutional crisis, with President Boris Yeltsin facing off with hard-line Communists in Parliament. My parents couldn't believe it. We could see the smoke rising from where tanks were shelling the Parliament building. Of course, as a seven-year-old, I found the whole business terribly exciting.

We survived getting strangled by Russia's horrible bureaucratic red tape, received our precious exit visas, and returned to Ukraine to pack up. The move to America felt permanent, as though we were leaving for another planet, as if the airlines flew only one direction and there was no possible way to return.

We got rid of anything we could possibly sell, until our old apartment was bare to the walls. Everyone around me wept. Thank God I was too young to cry.

"My whole life I've lived here," my dad said. "My father's buried here. All of our friends are here. And I'm saying goodbye to all of that."

At the end of May 1994, two months after I turned eight, we boarded an American Airlines flight to the U.S. with a single stopover in Shannon, Ireland. As I stumbled off the airplane at JFK airport in New York City, I recall my first impression was that the air smelled different. Not only that, but the colors seemed sharper, with a greater variation of shades than I was used to, and the water from the water fountain tasted fresher than anything I had ever drank. It was a whole different level of life than what I'd experienced in Ukraine.

I had heard one magic word whispered over and over. I thought, *That must be what America smells and looks and tastes like.*

"Freedom."

FROM JFK WE WENT STRAIGHT TO BROOKLYN, NEW YORK, TO the home of relatives, the family of my grandmother's cousin, Garik, and his wife, Sveta. They had a son named Dima, who had two boys: an older stepson, Damian, who was around Maks's age, and a younger son, Brian, who was my age.

A time-honored immigrant tradition required that those who came before host families who arrived later. But it stung a little, to come to America, hat in hand, and join Dima, a sort-of cousin who in Odessa my father had always considered something of an insignificant little punk. Dima had left Russia with his parents in 1977 and was now a grown man, living in a forty-story building in the Brooklyn neighborhood of West Brighton, and enjoying an established life in the States. It wasn't like he was a gazillionaire—there were no one percenters walking around these streets—but Dima was solidly middle class.

I looked around and thought the whole arrangement was incredible—the towering apartment complex, the playground that was right on the grounds, the clean sidewalks, the green patches of lawn. And not a single broken-down Zaporozhets in sight.

But my life was about to get a whole lot better. In a little sort of ceremony over dinner on the evening of our arrival, my grandmother's cousin came forward.

"Sveta has now a gift for you boys," my father announced to us in Russian. I could hear a slight sense of embarassment in his tone, that a relative was about to give his sons something he was not able to afford. No one else would have detected that, but I knew my father better than most.

It didn't matter. Maks and I had entered into an American fairyland, where the surroundings seemed nicer, plusher, and richer than what we had back home. And here came Sveta with a wide smile on her face, holding out two large cardboard boxes. We couldn't believe it. A safe place to land was enough of a prize, and now we were going to get presents?

I eagerly opened my package with no expectation of what was inside. If the box had been empty I would have still used it proudly, and likewise if I had discovered gold bars I wouldn't have been surprised. Instead, there was something better than gold bars—a pair of beautiful inline skates, black Rollerblade Lightnings with dark purple laces and chrome fasteners.

The model had been introduced just a few years before and had effectively revolutionized the sport. Its invention was the greatest single engineering feat ever in the history of mankind. Or so I thought. My eight-year-old head exploded. This was America, right here, fresh off the boat and right out of the box. The molded plastic off the boot cuffs appeared to come directly from the future (or, as it turned out, from a factory in China). I was too stunned to speak.

"Do you have something to say to Sveta?" my father whispered, giving me a gentle cuff on the head.

"*Spasibo! Spasibo!*" I cried out to our hosts, thanking them in Russian. Maks got a pair, too.

Forget about the little booklets of cardboard with government stamps all over them. Those Rollerblade Lightnings were our true passports to the United States of America. In Ukraine we had had old-style roller skates, with four wooden wheels—well, we didn't have them in our family, of course, but a few well-off people did. These Rollerblades meant that Maks and I had somehow blown right past the clunky, old-fashioned roller skate and proceeded directly to the Rolls-Royce of inline locomotion.

The next morning we strapped on our blades and rumbled down the sidewalk to West Playground, a block-long recreational area that featured handball courts, exercise equipment, and swings. In other words, the place was typical local urban park, nothing big, nothing fancy, just a place for kids and adults to gather. I remember being excited to be abroad in Brooklyn without grown-up supervision. We were discovering new terrain.

Wobbling along like a pair of drunks, Maks and I entered the park. He mastered the skates a little more quickly than I did, and left me behind. We first passed an area where older people played chess, mostly Russian immigrants. We were going at a snail's pace but it felt like we were flying. Talk about a pair of rookies!

Beyond the chess players were the swings, hanging unused in the springtime sun, then up a bit further on the right were the handball courts. (I've since lived in several other cities in America, but Brooklyn is the only place where handball is a major, deadly serious street game.) After handball came the basketball courts.

Through the green chain-link fences of the courts, we could see a sidewalk and another, smaller set of swings, all neglected and broken, making for a place where no kids would ever venture unless they happened to be well-armed. It was as if the area had a sign posted in front of it: *Shady Shit Happens Here.* I could already catch a whiff of dark, violent street energy.

Maks was twenty yards ahead of me. Before I knew what was happening I saw five dudes surround him. They were shouting and although I didn't understand English I knew they were roughing him up for the Rollerblades. I remember seeing a pair of identical twins, heavyweight, Italian-American thugs, leading the assault.

I practically crapped myself, I was so terrified. I couldn't believe what was happening.

Back in Odessa I had been a devoted fan of an American television program called *Rescue 911.* Hosted by *Star Trek*'s Captain Kirk, William Shatner, the reality show portrayed police, fire, and paramedic units responding to real 911 emergency calls. The concept appeared magical to my young eyes. I had never witnessed anything remotely like it in Ukraine. Find yourself in trouble, dial 911, and instantly—instantly!—hordes of helpful, life-saving emergency personnel would descend upon the scene.

At that moment at West Playground, I didn't have a phone handy. *I gotta get our pops,* I told myself. I was too small and too far away to help my brother. The only thing I could think of to do was to turn around, wobble back up the street to the apartment building of my grandmother's cousin's son, and burst into the place bellowing out the familiar call I had seen on *Rescue 911*.

"Call 911! Maks is getting beat up! Call 911!"

My dad chose not to call 911, deciding instead on an immediate, more personal response, more Russian than American. He rushed outside wearing only his boxers and black socks, on a mission to save his fourteen-year-old son from getting mugged for a pair of brand-new Rollerblade Lightnings.

We met my brother at the gate of West Playground, walking back with his head in his hands, his T-shirt ripped, and no skates. After I left to get help, the situation in the shady area beyond the basketball courts turned serious. One of the twins busted a bottle and sliced Maks's shirt open. But by now the culprits were long gone.

Welcome to America, in the most real way possible. Welcome to Brooklyn.

Years later my brother and I would go back to the old neighborhood every once in a while. Our grandmother, who had also immigrated to America, still lived in East New York, we had friends in the area, and we'd go out to Russian restaurants in Brighton Beach. Sometimes we'd make a detour to Avenue X and West Street, to the apartment building that was our first stop after arriving in America. Taking a trip down memory lane was inspiring and humbling at the same time.

Growing up I always felt the nabe was Italian and the Chmerkovskiys were just visitors. For that reason, I felt more comfortable around black and Hispanic kids than I did around Italians and native Brooklynites. They were the ones who were always calling out, "Go back to fucking Russia!" They were the ones who had a sense of entitlement to any outdoor space they wanted to claim. The minority kids I knew were like me, a bit like strangers in a strange land.

On one of those nostalgia trips back to the hood, Maks and I could see how the place had changed from a mostly Italian enclave to a Russian one. The Russian immigrants were the alpha dogs now, the dominant ones. It was the old story of American transformation.

Visiting brought up a lot of emotions. I remembered that on our first Halloween, after we moved into our own apartment, we had our windows egged. It wasn't directed at us personally, but it was intimidating at first, until a couple years later we stepped out and started throwing eggs ourselves. When we came back from the mission, our mom was furious.

"You wasted all our eggs!" she wailed.

Nostalgia was a blade that cut both ways. Going back, remembering was always bittersweet.

We were living in New Jersey by the time of this particular visit back to Brooklyn, and on our way home Maks wanted a bottle of water. We pulled up at a Key Food supermarket on Avenue Z, a few blocks away from West Playground. I guess not all of the "fuhgeddaboudit" guys had moved out of the neighborhood, because there was one of the Italian twins, the former skate-thief, grown older and heavier.

He was bagging groceries in the checkout line.

I don't think the twin recognized us. If revenge is a dish best served cold, this one was frozen solid. But I have to wish for you the same kind of sweet payback, and hope that you encounter one of your childhood bullies later on in life, bagging groceries as a supermarket checkout boy.

Every family has its own library of stories, accounts of this or that incident, a funny response to what someone said, a shared memory to treasure. Maks and I bonded over our "welcome to America" stolen Rollerblades saga. You may have run across it before, because we've told it often enough on talk shows and in media interviews. At the time, what happened was traumatizing, but it's a very comfortable story by now. We grew up and carried it with us, a shared lesson learned from a childhood experience.

SCHOOL

Odessa to Brooklyn represented a huge, head-twisting transition for all of us in the family. Due to the Rollerblades incident, Maks and I had been put on notice that we had to watch our shit, step up our game a bit, figure out how to negotiate around the obstacles and pitfalls of the brave new world we had been dropped into. But my mom and pops had steep learning curves, too.

We had people in Milwaukee and could have moved out there. Nothing against Wisconsin and the Midwest, but I can't imagine how different my life would have been if my parents had taken that route. New York City is the life for me, my true home, full of energy and possibility and excitement. Even today, whenever I stay for long stretches in L.A., somewhere in my heart I rest easy with the knowledge that the City is just a plane ride away.

In Brooklyn, the Chmerkovskiy family was no longer surrounded by people who looked like us, sounded like us, and lived like us. We were now trying to survive amid huge numbers of other immigrants from all over the world. As much of a melting pot as Odessa had been, Brooklyn was on a whole different level. Just a walk down the block meant I'd hear maybe a half-dozen different languages, with countless heritages represented: African American, Italian, Puerto Rican, Dominican, Cuban, Russian, Polish, Indian, Pakistani, Arab, Muslim, Albanian. It was New York City, man!

To my young ears, all of the voices sounded Italian. Jewish, Russian, Latino, it didn't matter, everyone had an Italian accent, which meant excessive swearing, excessive fronting, and excessive displays of the alpha-dog survival instinct.

There was no place in the world with more tough guys than New York City. As a teenager I once wrote:

New York City, my concrete jungle
These streets make the proudest cat humble
Make the loudest dog mumble
On these streets you don't rumble
You get stomped on and fumbled

My brother had been fumbled right out of his Rollerblades by a virtual United Nations—six dudes, including the Italian twins, an Asian kid, and a Russian kid with a Rottweiler. Like I said, all of them sounded Italian to me, all of them seemed to be called Vinny, Anthony, or Mike. In that neighborhood, you could be a Jewish kid named Misha Guberg, but you'd very quickly become "Mike G" on the street.

The Rollerblade fiasco turned out to be a pretty cheap price to pay for a vital, life-saving lesson. The message came in loud and clear: we had to protect ourselves. In the States, we were now navigating in a completely different setting, and the rules from Ukraine didn't apply here.

When you're forced to survive, you find out a great deal about yourself and very quickly come to understand just exactly what you're capable of. We landed in Brooklyn and it was as though we had immediately stepped aboard a treadmill screaming along at two hundred miles per hour. Whiplash city. No breaks, no let up, no time outs.

From our crummy apartment on Avenue X, I remember hoping that somehow we'd be able to move up the alphabet in the future, because the lucky people on Avenues A, B, or C had to be leading better, wealthier, safer lives. My mom and dad enrolled me in second grade classes at P.S. 216. I had a two-block walk to school, and for the first few weeks my mother accompanied me, but eventually I fell in with other kids from the neighborhood who were heading there, too.

The streets could be brutal, and I saw a lot of shit I probably should not have. Living near West Playground and innocently heading past it as I went to and from school, several times I encountered scenes of spontaneous violence. Seared into my young memory was an incident when four attackers ganged up on a couple, the man getting bloodied in a vicious beating, the woman pleading for it to stop. A whole gang of dudes picking on a guy with his lady—I had never before been introduced to that level of aggression, certainly not in my neighborhood back in Odessa.

Did those early days in South Brooklyn shape my life? Absolutely. In witnessing violence I learned to look out for myself, for my own safety and well-being. I might have been all of eight or nine, but the city taught me that I had to get it together in order to make it through to the next day. Even the name of my neighborhood had a life-and-death ring to it: Gravesend. As much as my father, mother, and brother had my back at home, nobody was holding my hand when I ventured out into the streets. I had to figure it out on my own.

Odd as it sounds, the move to Brooklyn led us to connect to our Jewish roots much more than any experience we'd had in Ukraine. It all started with Maks's school. According to educational district boundaries, my brother was supposed to go to Abraham Lincoln High, which was pretty rough in those days, obviously a reflection of the neighborhood as a whole. My parents visited the school to check it out and meet with the administrators, but neither of them spoke much English so I'm not sure how they communicated. But from that initial visit they took away a stark picture of the school environment. In the hallway they encountered the Lincoln High football team clattering past on spikes. To the immigrant eyes of my parents, the boys looked like hulking gangbangers, all tattoos and fades.

"Um, I think Maks will go to yeshiva," my mother whispered to my father.

My brother wound up at Sinai Academy, a school heavily populated with Russian immigrants, many of them not particularly observant or religious. Like the Chmerkovskiy family, Maks's schoolmates weren't so much Jewish as Jew-ish, just trying to get themselves out of the public education environment. The yeshiva's administration devoted itself to correcting that state of affairs. This was the first time Maks was really exposed to religion on such an intense level. His school day no longer consisted only of chemistry, biology, math, and English, but also featured three to four hours of biblical studies and religious history.

Maks quickly realized that the program wasn't for him, and we as a family realized we were more cultural than religious Jews. Judaism was part of our heritage, for sure, but so were many other influences. Religion by no means took first place, especially not above our passion and commitment to family.

Please don't misunderstand me. I believe in God, I am faithful, and I do feel like there's something larger in the universe than little old individual Val. But did I ever have a formal, specific, ritualized relation to a higher being? No. Ultimately, what were we as a family looking for at the yeshiva? Shelter? Safety? We didn't want to choose shelter and safety at the expense of losing educational freedom and the ability to interact with a wide range of people, or being informed by more than just a single school of thought.

Maks left Sinai Academy after only a few months to enroll in Midwood High School in Flatbush, still a huge public school, but maybe a little less rough around the edges when compared with Lincoln.

Meanwhile, at P.S. 216 the fists were flying more than they ever had in Odessa, or so it seemed to me, although the unruliness was probably just normal grade-school stuff. The insults might have been a little rawer, the trash talk a little trashier. I got a lot of "go back to Russia." The only time I remember answering back, I said something that I regret to this day.

"You stinkin' immigrant!" yelled a black girl a little older than I was. "Go live in your own fucking country."

I responded in Russian with something terrible.

"What did you say?" she demanded. "What did he just say?"

A Russian kid translated it to her. "He said, 'Why don't you go back to Africa yourself?'"

She started crying and the whole incident blew up to the point where I almost got expelled. And absolutely, I should have gotten fucking expelled for the ugly thing I said, which no doubt I had picked up on the street somewhere, overhearing brute ignorance expressed out loud. I was eight years old and possessed zero sensitivity about what was coming out of my mouth. Before moving to the States, I had lived in a world where I never saw a single black person, so I had no context, no understanding. Understanding comes from experience, and tolerance comes from understanding, but I was a little idiot who just got his feelings hurt and lashed out with a stupid insult.

A year later, even six months later, I was a different person, because by that time I had built an almost dizzying number of friendships. By third grade I was becoming assimilated into an urban culture that I fell deeply in love with, and a lot of it was based on African American experience. As many hardships as I've been through, I could never claim a deep understanding of the hardships of being black in America. But I managed to shed at least some of my ignorance through a combination of education and friendship.

It helped that I loved history, so I learned about American history and African American history. I lived in a diverse neighborhood where everything I was doing involved all kinds of different people. Soon enough no one was a "black kid" to me, or a "Puerto Rican kid," they were simply my friends. Looking back it still seems an amazing process, this opening of the heart to people different from yourself.

"The enemy is fear," Gandhi said. "We think it is hate, but it is really fear."

Stereotyping was just another version of fear, fear of the other, probably based somewhere deep in the human character. In the past, cavemen distrusted the tribe from the next valley over. What's great is when we elevate ourselves beyond such a fearful, knee-jerk response to the world. That's a great gift New York City gave to me, the gift of an open heart. It forces you to evolve beyond the animalistic instincts that we all possess.

I wasn't exactly oblivious to the differences in the upbringing of my friends, but at the same time nobody around me looked at differences with hate. Emerging from that eight-year-old's fog of ignorance, I began to consider social differences mainly with interest and curiosity. I found myself not intimidated but *delighted* by people from other cultures.

Instinctively, like every other kid around me, I was trying to make do with whatever gifts I had. What did I have? From my experience at the Music Academy, I already knew that I could perform. I had a few barely remembered lessons in ballroom back in Odessa, so I knew I could dance. Did I go around advertising that fact? Are you kidding me? As an outsider desperately trying to fit in, I would have rather cut off my feet than admit that I was a dancer.

But I kept wishing that I could use my hidden skill somewhere, somehow. Then my teachers announced that the third graders would mount a play based on the *Happy Days* TV sitcom, which was probably the most deeply felt portrait of American pop culture at the time. Of course, I did not get cast as the lead, the cooler-than-cool Fonzie, or even All-American Richie Cunningham, both of whom were well beyond my reach. But I did land the role of Potsie Weber, Richie's best friend and sidekick, who was sort of dim and the butt of many jokes, but a likable kid nonetheless.

That little school show where I played Potsie was the first time I plugged into the thrill of public performance. I was playing a real American character, and I was saying lines in English, which was cool. In the middle of the show the cast had a dance number, a 1950s rock 'n' roll show-stopper. I fucking killed it. I was Potsie, but I was also James Brown, Elvis, and Bruce Springsteen.

In that moment, my ability to dance changed from being something I wanted to hide, and turned instead into my superpower. I went from being a weird kid with an accent, whose mom made him tuck in his shirt every day and who never wore Jordans or Nikes, to one of the cool kids. I might have been playing the nerdy Potsie, but I was a stud-ass little performer on that grade-school stage. I got laughs, I got applause. I could hear the buzz from parents and kids. "Who is that guy?"

What pumped me up was not the praise, but how much a change it was from the usual stereotyping that I had encountered. No one said, "Oh, there's a Russian kid—let's send him back to where he came from." I got none of that. It was more on the order of amused amazement: "Oh, dope. I like that kid!"

A few years ago, I went back and visited P.S. 216, invited by a teacher who amazingly enough remembered me and reconnected via Twitter. "Yes, my God, you were really talented," she recalled. "We all knew you were going to be somebody."

I almost started crying when I heard that, because it represented recognition by people who had known me and were invested in my early education. To be able to fulfill their expectations gave me an incredible lift. I even spoke at a P.S. 216 graduation ceremony, an experience that was like my Oscars, my Golden Globes, my Emmys, my everything. Returning to my elementary school, walking through those halls so alive with memories—I got chills right now just writing about it.

EVEN AT HOME, I WAS BECOMING THE GO-TO PERFORMER IN MY family. As newly arrived immigrants only gradually becoming comfortable with English, we loved any loose, physical, easy-to-understand comedy shows on television, and one of our favorites was always *Family Matters*. Jaleel White as Steve Urkel was a scream to us. Gathered around the dinner table, and especially if we had relatives over, my parents would often make the same request.

"Valya, Valya, show them the Steve Urkel."

I'd roll up my pants, put on my grandma's glasses, and repeat the character's signature riff.

"Did I do that? Did I do that?" *Snort, snort.*

It never ended there. I was the official party trick for the whole family.

"Valya, Valya, play that song. Play the violin. Play something on the violin."

I would get out my fiddle and riff on a Schubert melody. I always got applause and approval—and requests for more.

"Valya, Valya, something else, something else, please!"

Midperformance I'd glance over at Maks, sitting there with the others, looking on. My brother was shyer than I was, and because he didn't push himself forward, his presence was not really felt in the room.

When we first came to the States, Maks was at an awkward, in-between age, fourteen years old, a time objectively recognized as among the most horrendous periods of adolescence. Hormones were raging, voices were changing, acne erupted, and social graces were not yet fully developed. Hitting grade school as a newcomer, as I did, was a lot different from Maks's hitting high school, where the cliques and peer pressure could be vicious.

I don't want to take anything away from him. He would later fully grow into his height and his almost impossible handsomeness. Even back then he wasn't a pushover by any means, but he simply didn't have his legs underneath him in America yet. His immediate immigrant experience was totally unlike mine. The six years between us made all the difference. The worst that could happen to me was that I might be slapped around a little on the playground, while he had to make his way among youth gangs equipped with assorted lethal weaponry.

In fact, our emigration experience had also been totally different. When we left Odessa he was fourteen and had a circle of close friends, and he had a girl he liked a lot, too—his dance partner, with whom he was in love. In contrast, I was a little eight-year-old kid, excited to be going to the States.

But some of our differences lay in our personalities. I wasn't going to be bullied. Even if some kid attempted such an indignity, I had the energy to assimilate and to adjust and to politic my way out of pretty much any situation. If I ever got into a tough situation, I made sure I had five dudes who were even tougher next to me.

My brother didn't have the personality to marshal those five dudes as backup. At fourteen my brother lacked the social skills that I possessed at eight. He was at an age when kids have a lot more insecurities than when they're younger. Maks came in cold to a different country with no language skills in English, and all of a sudden there were girls involved in the equation. He was navigating a different terrain than I was, where the stakes were a bit higher and the possibilities for embarrassment were a bit more extreme.

Maks also happened to have quite literally shit his pants on the flight to America. Stuck in the middle seat in coach, maybe disoriented by the newness of the experience, he could not summon the balls to speak up, disturb his seat mates, and head to the toilet. There was a long line for the john, anyway, and at that point Maks didn't have it in him to say, "Hey, yo, I gotta cut the line." So he wound up landing in the United States with a pantload.

Whenever I tease him about this story, he always responds by bringing up how smelly I was as a baby. He was six when I was born, so I'm sure he encountered his share of my dirty diapers back then. One pantload story deserves another, I suppose.

We all had to hit the ground running when we arrived in Brooklyn. Maks was forced into a leadership role immediately. In fact, we were all forced to take on new responsibilities, but the others in the family were probably more comfortable than Maks, since the demands of his new country had effectively pushed him out of his comfort zone. I was younger and more carefree.

But even as a kid back in Ukraine, my brother hadn't exhibited a can-do, going-balls-out kind of personality. He was a bookworm. In America, he was a tall, awkward dude who couldn't immediately find his place. Entering high school in Flatbush, there was no older brother to tell him how to fit in. He had no friend or cousin or anybody to guide him: "Hey, try to make friends with this guy" or "Take those classes" or "You should join this team." He was on his own.

The two of us had some of the typical high school experiences, but we never joined school athletic teams, and we were never part of any clubs, so that interfered with opportunities to assimilate. We didn't do sports after school, we went to dance or music lessons. And we always quickly returned to home base, bringing back the fruits of our labor to share with the household.

My parents signed Maks up to teach at a local dance academy, and he made friends there, but they turned out to be kids who were not very nice to him. He also wasn't the best at choosing friends at Edward R. Murrow High, so he had a rough time all around. The truth of it was, his best friend during this time was his eight-year-old brother. He never really confided his troubles to me, and he never cried himself to sleep or anything like that, but I could clearly feel the intimidating energy that was blowing through his life.

I don't want to take anything away from me, either, because I was a cool-ass little kid. I was the dude who people reached out to. Even though he didn't unload his deepest secrets, Maks felt more comfortable trusting me than any of his friends. For the formative years of our lives, from when I was eight years old until I was, say, twelve or thirteen, we were as tight as two brothers could be. Those years established the bond that we have today. Maks will always be my oldest and most genuine friend. Not all siblings are close, but I've been best friends with that dude for a long time.

To his little brother, Maks was always the Man. His situation would change drastically over the course of the next few years, and he would come into his own in ways that neither of us could imagine. From being "the Man," he would grow into a real man. But for those first few years in America, I remember what he meant to me. He was my touchstone, my constant, a way to assure myself that even though everything else was changing around me, my brother would always be there.

MUSIC

Performing onstage as Potsie in the school play was a turning point for me, because it was the first time I allowed myself to speak out in public in my new home of America. I spoke not with words but through my movements and my energy, and managed to communicate on a very intimidating level. For the first time since Odessa I felt that I had the upper hand. I was connecting to people on my terms, and since my English wasn't up to speed yet, I got the message out via movement, displaying my personality and charm that way.

But I was forced to prove my talent over and over. My first ballroom teacher in America dismissed me immediately. He said something along the lines of "At best, you're only all right, kid." My unvoiced response? "I'll show you."

And I did. Three years later, when I was eleven and partnered with Inna Brayer, we won the U.S. Open dance competition at the Junior 1 level. That victory got us invited on *Sally*, a popular talk show in the mid-1990s, hosted by Sally Jessy Raphael.

All of a sudden I was the shit. I remember being super excited, obviously—just three years off the boat and already on American TV! If you knew me during that period you'd have caught me smack in the middle of an identity crisis, in my lil' gangsta phase, acting out, with an ego as big as the twin towers. You want me on your show? Oh, excuse me, I'm going to have to check with my imaginary agent first.

Sally's style was ragingly sensationalistic, since she competed head-to-head with TV schlock-meister Jerry Springer, whose own show once featured a transvestite who wanted to be an amputee so badly she cut off both of her legs with a chain saw. Compelling television.

Every once in a while *Sally* hosted an episode that did not involve warring spouses or doggie hypnosis, one that actually contributed something pleasant to society. "Age Is Just a Number" was one of those shows, and it represented my big television debut. As the host, Sally invited guests who were at the opposite ends of the age spectrum. Inna and I were the cute little couple doing ballroom, contrasted with a very sweet ninety-year-old from the Broadway show *Forever Tango*. There were a dozen people of different ages who were all being accused of doing extraordinary things—or being celebrated for them, it was hard to tell the difference.

I had actually seen *Forever Tango* on Broadway. A few years earlier my dad had scraped up some money somehow, enough to take his family on a classic New York outing.

"Hey, we're going to Manhattan to have dinner at a restaurant, then afterward I got tickets for a show." He could have been scheduling a flight to Mars for all the sense it made in the context of the Chmerkovskiy family finances.

We went to Olive Garden. I thought the place was the flyest shit on the planet. The waiter plopped a plate of marinara down in front of me and I had never seen anything like it. Red sauce? Really?

"Oh my God, 'pasta,' what is that?"

"It's like noodles, but better," my dad said. I didn't know what it was, but I dug in, and I quickly realized it was very different from mama's *macarone*. After the restaurant my father took us to *Forever Tango*. Dinner and a show. It was as if we were checking off a box on the list of what to do to become real New Yorkers.

A year later, Inna and I joined the *Forever Tango* ninety-year-old and the rest of the "Age Is Only a Number" guests on *Sally*. I entered into that holy of holies, that sacred inner sanctum, my very first green room—I didn't know what a green room was, but I thought it might be a synonym for "paradise." A table stood loaded with snacks and soft drinks.

"This food is free and I will have some," I told myself. My dad had always preached that there was no such thing as a free lunch, so the green room feast was kind of a guilty pleasure for me, really going against the grain of my upbringing.

For the performance I wore a blousy shirt featuring a zebra-print collage, with a big open slit in front. I thought I looked like John Travolta in *Saturday Night Fever*, when really I more resembled Spanky on *Our Gang*. I didn't have braces yet, and I shouldn't have smiled as much as I did, because the audience probably would have liked knowing a little less about my dental architecture. But I just couldn't resist. My smile was a check and I just kept on cashing it.

The producer gave us our call, and Inna and I went out under the bright studio lights and performed a paso doble, which is a march-style dance loosely depicting a bullfight. The explosiveness of the dance lay in the intensity of the movement across the floor. But it turned out that the *Sally* stage was tiny, tiny, tiny. Because there was no place to move, our paso doble that day just looked like a bunch of stomping around, as if Inna and I were crushing grapes for wine.

We did our best, making fierce faces to indicate our serious intent. We were just a couple of cute kids, and the audience loved us because kids can get away with anything, even when wearing the strangest outfits ever seen on *Sally*. I might have looked like a zebra making wine, but I was still getting applause.

The after-dance interview was worse. Sally sat us down on director-style chairs that were way too high. During this period of my life I was working hard to convince myself that I wasn't a child anymore, but being seated with my feet dangling in the air killed my confidence. I had stopped tucking in my shirt only half a year before—I was just that fresh. Any swagger I felt was very recently acquired, but now I was a television superstar.

"So which category do you dance in?" Sally asked.

I thought my answer was super intelligible, but in reality it made no fucking sense at all. My fractured English at age eleven should have made my appearance go viral, just like *Shit My Dad Says*. I was attempting to inform Sally that because the competition was so weak in my age bracket, I usually competed in an older age category.

"What age do you dance?" she repeated.

"We compete in Juniors," I said with an air of confidence. "But sometimes we're allowed to go higher."

Sally pulled a vaudeville-style double take. "You're allowed to get high?"

Ah, ha ha ha. The audience laughed and laughed at the gag.

Sally Jessy Raphael put on shows that capitalized on the worst of human nature, and here she was just goofing on me, playing to the cheap seats.

No amount of audience laughter could possibly faze this lil' gangsta, though. I've often wondered where the fearlessness of a child goes when it leaves during adolescence. Where does all our courage disappear to, the strength to be who we are, unapologetically and automatically? Back then I had no real idea of who I was, so what did I have to fear? What insecurities could I possibly have, when I didn't have anything to lose?

I loved the whole experience of being on TV and thought my zebra shirt looked fucking awesome. Thank the Lord *Sally* was a daytime show, because my classmates were in school when it aired.

There were no DVRs or YouTube back then for them to use to replay my humiliation. They missed it, that was it, and life went on.

Nowadays the opportunity to review experiences on a cell phone takes people right out of the moment. We see it all the time, folks at concerts or live events, holding up in front of them their "black mirrors," their little rectangular devices. Recording a moment gets in the way of being in the moment, and a replayed experience tends to be less sincere and more artificial than an actual one.

Did my classmates feel my new superstar status when I returned to school after being on *Sally?* Maybe not, but I'm sure I had a little added pep to my step.

I DON'T ACTUALLY REMEMBER MUCH ABOUT LEARNING EN-glish. I was enrolled in ESL—English as a Second Language—classes but for the life of me I can't remember a single teacher or classroom session. The only English I had before I emigrated was gleaned from American TV shows. As I demonstrated during the famous Rollerblade incident, I knew to say "nine-one-one," which sounded pretty cute in a Russian accent. I knew "hello," and also the two syllables that linguists have determined to be the most widely understood word in the world: "okay."

The truth was, I learned how to speak English from trash talking on the basketball court, and from the rapid-fire rhymes of rappers I idolized. If you encounter profanity in these pages, blame the streets of Brooklyn, where it is used as simple emotional seasoning in casual conversation. When people ask me how long it's been since I moved to the States, I can't help but hear the implication: "It hasn't been that long, has it?"

I always have a knee-jerk response: "I've been here twenty-three years! This is a Brooklyn accent, not a Russian one! And I'm proud of it!" For me, the thought and context behind the words is the priority, not how they're pronounced. Back then I didn't care that I was sounding like a rapper. That's how we spoke on the street. That's how everyone I knew spoke.

But it was an exciting time, because kids all around me, even native speakers, were learning new words and new ways to convey meaning. When you're deprived of the ability to communicate effectively through words, it's hard and demoralizing and a little like being imprisoned within yourself. Maybe that's why I'm so in love with words today. I love choreographing words even more than I love choreographing dance steps. When I'm able to phrase a thought in just the right way, with just the right tone and rhythm and just the right context, it's the most powerful feeling in the world.

I wasn't just learning a foreign language, I was also learning a foreign culture—humor, attitude, fashion, the whole package. We lived in the hood where everybody wore Air Jordans. I thought the local Payless shoe store was an absolute wonderland. That was my Saks Fifth Avenue. My parents were going to spend $40 on a pair of sneakers for me? I don't know how many people can relate to standing at the register absolutely quivering with anticipation.

"Oh my God, this is gonna be so cool!" At the same time, alongside a rush of gratitude, I would feel the most incredible load of guilt. *Forty dollars*, spent on me? I knew they didn't have the money. When you're broke, everything is expensive. Even then, at eight or nine years old, I was posing questions to myself. *How can I start contributing?* Those sneakers were great, but when would I start paying my dues to the family team?

Fast-forwarding a little, my first purchase with my own money came at age twelve. I remember it well. I had finally started making some bank for myself, working as a dancer alongside my brother at Russian restaurants. The first week I saved $75, the next week after that about the same amount, and on and on every week until I had put together a grand total of $250.

I headed off to the mall and for $200 I bought a pair of JNCO jeans. You cannot imagine how ridiculous teenage fashion was back then, but just Google JNCO and you'll get a hilarious whiff (the style is actually making a comeback now). With the red stripe down the side and the brand-name character on the back pocket, JNCOs were obnoxiously wide and humongously long, resembling parachutes more than pants.

Yeah, JNCO jeans were obnoxious and ugly and stupid, but all the cool kids wore them, and just for once in the course of my life in America, after all the tucked-in shirttails and dweeb outfits, I hungered to look like a cool kid.

During my early years I was convinced deep down inside that I was the coolest kid in the world. But as a native Russian speaker in America, I was like Charlie Chaplin trapped in Helen Keller's body. I couldn't shine. I couldn't entertain. I couldn't speak English that well. It was like hell on earth.

I wasn't the only one who was an immigrant in my school, and I wasn't the only one who had a weird-ass accent. There were Asian kids, Latinos, and countless other Eastern European immigrants. Simply as a matter of survival, I gravitated to my Russian peers. People naturally relate to somebody who sounds like them, and I also related to kids who understood what my mom was going to whup my ass for, because this Russian kid, he had his ass whupped for the exact same misdeeds as I did. Having things in common was how I built friendships that have lasted all my life.

Among my other baggage, I hauled around a tongue-twister of a last name. I always feel sorry for non-Russian-speaking Americans whenever they encounter it. They might be making introductions at a party, or reading a slip of paper to announce me onstage, and I see the puzzlement and fear come into their eyes when they realize they will have to try to pronounce the impossible. Right at the start, the first syllable represents an almost insurmountable obstacle.

"Chmer-"? Really?

The non-Russian mouth simply balks at following a "sh" sound with an "m" sound. In New York City, you might ask a deli person for "a bagel with a *schmear*," meaning a bagel with a smear of cream cheese. That Yiddish "sh"-followed-by-"m" phrase comes close.

"Shmer-." Spoken aloud, the first syllable of my name sounds like a Dr. Seuss character.

After mangling the hopeless first syllable, the nonnative speaker gratefully rolls into the "-kov-" only to discover that a "v" is to be pronounced like a "w," so it isn't "-kov-" it's "-kow-." The last challenge comes with the "Whoa! What's-that-'i'-doing-in-there?" final syllable, "-skiy." Is it "skee" or "sky?" What the hell? I give up!

"Shmer-KOW-skee."

If you think that's tough, try the Cyrillic alphabet version of Valentin Aleksandrovich Chmerkovskiy: Валентин Олекса́ндрович Чмерковський.

Oh, screw it, I sometimes think. Maybe I *should* change my name. Val Smith. Val Jones. Life would be so much easier. But I've always had way too much stubborn pride to do it. My name is my self. My name signals to the world that it has to take me as I am. Even if people shatter their teeth trying to say it, my name is me.

On the streets of South Brooklyn in the 1990s, I was a member of a little Russian immigrant crew that played a lot of basketball in the parks around the area. We'd do pickup games against black kids, Italians, and Puerto Ricans, and get respect because we were able to hold our own. Eventually we mixed up the teams, metaphorically displaying social assimilation right on the ball court. Slowly, by hearing kids talk trash to each other, I learned not only the language but the energy and culture of my new home. We were all different, and that was our similarity.

Popular music took on a larger and larger role in my life. I started listening to a lot of hip-hop, and that kind of music absolutely overflows with strings of densely packed rhymes and outrageous verbal play. In hip-hop, the words were choreographed in the most beautiful way to complement the coolest sounds and most stirring beats that I had ever heard. The songs seemed to echo my guiding principle, "Keep it moving."

One of the reasons I came to love hip-hop as a genre was because the songs told stories. I didn't have to read books because I listened to rap. Growing up I wasn't a bookworm like my brother. It's a lousy confession to make in a book, but I'd rather write, I'd rather create, and I'd rather express myself than read. Don't get me wrong. I'm super grateful that you're reading this book right now. But as a kid, I never cracked a book besides the texts that teachers assigned for school. Instead, I listened to Nas, to Biggie, to Tupac and the other elite poets of the street.

But that soon changed when I opened my mind and started reading literature after meeting two of the most important people outside of my immediate family circle, who entered my young life almost immediately after I came to America.

MY FAMILY WAS AS POOR AS THE DEAD, BUT MY PARENTS HAD simple basic requirements regarding their children. First off, we needed to find a dance academy for Maks, and naturally I would tag along with my brother to his lessons. But in the eyes of my parents violin was my calling, so I needed to have a music teacher as well.

We discovered a great one. Her name was Yulia, and she taught students in her little Bensonhurst apartment. As an added attraction her husband, Victor, worked as a tutor in Russian language and literature. While the members of the Chmerkovskiy family were Americans now, my parents didn't want us to leave behind the glories of Pushkin, Tolstoy, and Chekhov—the Russian author, not the character on *Star Trek*.

P.S. 216 didn't provide music lessons for students, and there was no school orchestra or band, but my parents were determined for me to continue my music education. I had been playing for three years at that point, and I guess they had endured all my strangled-cat early practice sessions and had suffered enough to finally earn the right to hear the Vivaldi.

Yulia became an instant influence on my life. She was hard as nails, stricter than any coach I ever had. She adored me and believed in me. I owe her and my parents so much for my life in music. My experience with Yulia emphasized my separation from the crowd of kids at school. The Chmerkovskiy family had different after-school activities, ones that would give us tools that were just not available at P.S. 216. I thought all of our extracurricular activities made us either strange or special, depending on how I was feeling at the moment.

My violin lessons cost $15 for an hour. Yulia would accept the money when we could afford to pay, and when we couldn't—well, we always came up with the fee eventually, because there was nothing more embarrassing to a Chmerkovskiy than debt. We were like the Lannisters from *The Game of Thrones* in that respect, because we always paid our debts.

Yulia would take the fee for an hour's lesson and then proceed to teach me for two and a half or three hours. I went to her straight from school, already totally exhausted from the day. I had a constant thought running through my head: *Screw these violin lessons, do I have to go through my whole life, man, with these frigging violin lessons?!* I went two or three times a week. She would teach for a while, then take a break midlesson to make me sandwiches.

I was always tired. I'd ask to go to the bathroom just to get a break from the lesson, several times literally falling asleep on the toilet. "Hey, hey," Yulia or Victor would call in to me. "Are you all right?"

Eventually, after I had worked with her for a year, Yulia invited me to play at the recitals she hosted at her apartment for three or four students and an audience of their parents. The monthly events offered me a chance to be a performer again. My green room might have been Yulia's tiny six-foot-by-six-foot kitchen, but stepping out from it still meant going onstage, grandly entering her living room, another small space crowded with damask-covered couches and leather easy chairs.

I had to exercise my ability to rise to the occasion, to appear in front of people and be able to pull through in the clutch. In that cramped little apartment with the odor of Russian food in the air, I first learned how to steel my nerves for performance.

Then Victor started tutoring me in Russian literature. On those days I would take two-hour lessons with Yulia and then spend an extra hour with Victor, three times a week. Victor introduced me to Pushkin, Nabokov, Tolstoy, and Dostoevsky. I sure wasn't reading anything like that in elementary school. I don't think I formally encountered Dostoevsky in English translation until years later, in high school.

This introduction of serious literature at such a young age, with analysis and explication demanded of me, helped develop new ways of thinking and expressing myself. The mash-up of classic Russian literature with the new sounds of hip-hop shaped me, giving me a unique perspective overall. I listened to Nas chronicle his life journey in Queensbridge at the same time I was reading about Pushkin in St. Petersburg. The two worldviews collided to make me who I was, something I'm incredibly grateful for to this day.

Victor favored a real Russian-style education, which meant plenty of memorization. I not only had to read poetry but learned to memorize and recite it, too. It was an old-world practice, since in American public school teachers never had us memorize any literature at all. For Yulia's recitals I had to learn by heart an entire Bach prelude, and then for Victor I had to memorize and recite passages from *Yefheny* by Pushkin.

These two wise, gentle, educated people changed my life. Yulia was one of those artists who preached the value of music over all other activities in life.

"Why are you dancing, young man?" she would demand of me. To my parents, she said, "Why does he need this *dancing*? He has the opportunity to be a soloist. Do you know what that means? There are only so many people in the whole world who make their living as violin soloists. There's Itzhak Perlman and there was Jascha Heifetz and—well, I can count them on the fingers of one hand! Valya could be that good. He has that type of potential."

But life had different plans for me.

PART 3

A JOURNEY IN
DANCE

ZENDAYA

In joining *Dancing with the Stars*, I had moved away from the competition world with the idea of enjoying the realm of Hollywood creativity, but my past kept catching up with me. I found myself immersed into the same intrigue, encountering the same faces, dealing with the same disappointments. The only thing that had changed was the set.

In my fourth season on the show I came within a hairbreadth of winning it all, but lost instead to one of my biggest rivals, Derek Hough. The defeat was difficult for me, as devastating as an earlier defeat in a ballroom dance competition at Blackpool, where I lost by a single mark to another longtime rival of mine, Mark Ballas.

I had often competed against Derek and Mark on the ballroom competition circuit. The universe then saw fit to play one of its little pranks, bringing both of these characters back into my life on *Dancing with the Stars*, where they turned up again like zombies back from the dead and quickly became fan favorites.

Do you know how many Derek Houghs I've gone through in my life? I've always liked to be tested against the best. More than that, I've absolutely loved to beat the best. Great rivals make for great competition. My mentality has always been, "How many spins can the champion Nino Langella do? Five?" Then I wanted to do six. I *had* to do six. If you want to be a great competitor, you have to be the best at what you do, and surpass what your competition does best, too.

That spring of 2013 I was happy to get the "Joe and Ashley" call, inviting me back for Season 16.

"This season's going to be a little different for you," Ashley promised.

"Awesome, thanks," I responded, intrigued and excited.

On the same day I was supposed to meet my partner, I flew into Los Angeles from the East Coast, landed, and grabbed a cab. I gave the driver the address Joe and Ashley had given me, which was located somewhere in downtown L.A. That was strange to begin with, because almost everyone on the show lived in the Hollywood Hills. It was like a thing with *Dancing with the Stars* people. West Hollywood especially was our turf. So why was I headed downtown?

On the ride from the airport, my phone lit up with texts. The dancers were gossiping and speculating about partners, texting back and forth like crazy. Everyone wanted to weigh in.

"Models live downtown," Maks texted. "You probably have a model."

"Bro, I already had a model, Elisabetta Canalis, and look how that turned out."

Models were as a rule tall drinks of water, which was fine on the runway but problematic on the parquet.

"She can't be taller than the frame," I texted. This was part of that ongoing discussion Maks and I had, about the male dancer acting as the picture frame and the female partner being the work of art.

"Bro, she's going to be taller than you," Maks texted, ever the optimist. "You'll just have to get creative."

I was coming off the season with Kelly Monaco, who was maybe five four in heels. On TV, height and everything else was relative. You could be six feet tall, but if you were standing next to Kareem Abdul Jabbar, you'd look like a leprechaun. Likewise, you could be five six, but next to someone four ten, you'd look like a beast. I listed my height as five eleven but that was on a really good day, if I had my high-tops on, if the humidity levels were just right, if my body somehow stretched.

It was a sunny morning in downtown L.A. The cab pulled up to the address and I got out, feeling as though I was reenacting Will Smith's performance in the title sequence of *The Fresh Prince of Bel-Air*. In top form coming off the midseason break, I was inspired, too, after making the finals with Kelly. Now for the follow-up, I told myself, ready to take home the Mirrorball trophy.

I paid the taxi driver and he drove off. I knew the cabbie had left me on the correct corner, but I had no idea where the actual building was, so when I saw a thirty-something woman crossing the street near me, I asked her for help. She was very noticeable because she was very tall.

"Excuse me, do you know where this address is?"

As I spoke to her, a younger girl, almost as tall, came out of a nearby building, walking alongside a big dude with dreds.

Later on, knowing Zendaya, I became really familiar with how she walked. She barely dragged herself from point A to point B. I've noticed that professional athletes tend to display that slow-moving roll, too. The girl was probably just tired, because since a very young age she had worked multiple jobs, doing Disney shows, getting her music career off the ground, and acting in movies. She slouched up to the corner with her pops just as I was finishing my question, and I discovered that the tall lady was Claire, Zendaya's mother.

"We're actually going to the same place," she said. "Just follow us."

The vibe was casual and slightly mysterious. I hadn't yet snapped to who they were. We headed inside and tried not to stare at each other while waiting for the elevator. We rode up to the second floor, the door opened, and the show's field producer greeted us there.

"Oh, you guys have met already?"

I was still a little slow on the uptake. "Huh? What?"

"Oh, so you're my partner," Zendaya said. I wasn't entirely caught up on my Disney show binge watching, so I didn't immediately recognize who she was.

While the sound techs were bustling around getting the microphones in place, I told this pleasant looking, very tall young lady that it was nice to meet her.

"Oh yeah, hi, I'm Zendaya."

I shook hands with her father, Kazembe, and chuckled along with Claire about how we met before meeting. I always take on the role of host and assistant to the producer, small-talking the families, helping to create a lighthearted atmosphere around the shoots. Once I felt that sort of vibe had been established, I stepped aside and called Deena Katz, the show's casting producer.

"Hey, Deena, do you know how tall I am?" I asked her, keeping my voice low.

"Yeah, you're like six feet one."

"On my Wikipedia bio, Deena, if you Google me, it'll say that I'm six feet tall. On Google I'm six feet tall, but in real life, I'm not six fucking feet tall." Lying on your résumé can sometimes backfire.

"Oh, you'll still be good," Deena assured me.

"Damn, plus she's like, what, sixteen years old?"

She sighed. "What's the problem now?"

"I've just had my best season on *Dancing with the Stars* partnered with a five-four thirty-six-year-old, and so the next season you follow that up with a sixteen-year-old who's six five? What are you trying to do to me, give me whiplash?"

"Oh, she's not six five, Val, not anywhere near," Deena said. She was very well accustomed to diva fits.

"Have you seen her parents?" I glanced over to the family. Claire had to be six six and Kazembe, Zendaya's father, stood at least six four.

The most important fact for me about the previous season, besides my friendship with Kelly, was that I finally got to experience the entire run of the show. I gained insight about what it takes, how to pace it, what mistakes I made in the past, what things I did right. It was easy to second-guess. *Maybe I shouldn't have done that dance at the beginning, it would have been better at the end. Maybe I shouldn't have done all my best moves in week four.*

But at least I ran the entire race, so I now knew how it could be run, how to ace the course, where before I had only seen it from the sidelines, which was not the same. I knew what to expect, and felt primed and ready to get started. So what if I drew a teenage Amazonian as my partner? I would just have to get creative, as Maks had suggested.

Dancing with the Stars came loaded down with intrigue and drama that on sheer principle I didn't want any part of, and which largely centered on who got what partner. A casual watcher of the show might see nothing except a huge happy family. But a few fans like to play up rivalries, even some that aren't there. It all became a spectator sport for the committed home viewer: keeping tabs on who was siding with whom, where the fault lines were, what was going down behind the scenes.

My impulse was always to set the record straight, and tell folks that I wasn't a member of any faction. I sided with me, I sided with reason, I sided with loyalty, I sided with positivity. I felt as though there needed to be a healthy, arm's-reach separation between me and all the back chatter. I didn't want other people's intrigue to influence my process or my relationship with the show.

The commentary on the discussion boards was insistent. "Why does this one guy always get assigned to the most awesome partners?" Inquiring minds wanted to know, and they weren't talking about me. But I didn't care about which guy had what partner. Why? You want me to keep it real? Because all the dancers on the show are awesome, that's why. This amazing pro rival of mine might keep getting amazing partners, but I wasn't going to bother myself with the injustice of the world. My response was more along the lines of "Hey, how can I become awesome, too, so I too can get awesome partners every time?"

The real fans of the show will understand exactly what I'm talking about, and hopefully I can satisfy their worries about animosity or friendships, cliques or outsiders. Never assume that there was any hatred or dislike on my part, because I can assure you that there was none. Don't mistake my indifference to the show's melodramatic subplots for a negative attitude. I just tried not to pay that business any mind, because involving myself in it turned out not to be a healthy choice for me.

The notion of adjusting to a role and really committing to a role held true no matter what the show threw at me. From the perfect grown-ass woman in Kelly Monaco I had to transition to a 16-year-old Disney star, Zendaya. My range was truly being tested, both as a teacher and a dancer. I couldn't imagine any two partners more different. Who was going to be next? Betty White?

"Hi, I'm Val," I said to my new partner.

"Zendaya," she said.

"Yeah, Zendaya, this is going to be a lot of fun."

"Cool," she said. "You know, we all watch the show." She pointed to her moms and pops. "I'm on this series, *Shake It Up*."

"All right, cool, a Disney show, right? How old are you?" I just wanted to make sure.

"Sixteen."

"Oh, sixteen? Okay. Let's get started. Why do you want to learn ballroom?"

We didn't do too much dancing that afternoon, just a little talking and then a few basic steps. The cameras shut down after they got whatever they needed, and I had an informal conversation with her parents. They had done their research, and they had seen my season with Kelly.

"You have a contemporary for week one?" Claire asked. "I saw your contemporary last season."

She used a casual, smiling tone, but I almost winced at the reference to my contemporary dance with Kelly, which had emphasized adult romance and heated passion.

"Well, we're going to have a different type of contemporary, Claire, I promise."

In the car heading back from the meeting, I thought over my predicament. How was I supposed to transition to teaching a Disney princess after an ex–*Playboy* Playmate turned soap star? My role on the show had developed into this sex symbol, and suddenly all that business felt totally out of context. Beyond that, it was borderline creepy for an adult my age to act in that way with a young lady like Zendaya.

I immediately understood that I had to rethink my entire approach. Luckily I knew what viewers might not have realized, that the sex symbol business had been largely a creation of the producers. Sure, they had a little help from me, but basically being a player was foreign to my nature. My natural approach to other people in general and women in particular had been trained into me by my parents, a polite, chivalrous attitude that represented a deeply felt cultural inheritance. If I'm courteous and warm, I'm not trying to be a smooth operator, but rather simply behaving how my mother raised me.

The role of mentor and teacher was much closer to my heart than the role of badass stud, which I had always considered pretty ridiculous even when I was playing at it. During my time at Rising Stars Dance Academy, I had interacted with many, many Zendayas before, teaching kids and functioning as a role model. Those close to me understood that it was a much more authentic side of me than Val the Lady-Killer would ever be.

I recalled Kelly's advice, *Know your audience*. I realized that the upcoming season would not be about creating as much as about educating and mentoring. I was paired up not only with a celebrity, but first and foremost with a young woman, a young girl, who obviously had potential and obviously had heart.

The presence of Claire and Kazembe in the mix would also be different from the last season. The two of them had looked me in the eye and tried to gauge what kind of influence I would have on their daughter. All of a sudden it was as if I was in the middle of a parent-teacher conference. But that situation also was something I was used to from Rising Stars. I had witnessed stage moms and dads who helped the process, and those who interfered to the point of sabotaging it. The lessons I learned back in New Jersey transferred to my work on *Dancing with the Stars*. I knew I had to enlist Zendaya's parents as allies.

As we started working together, I soon realized that Zendaya Maree Coleman had a beautiful perspective on the situation and definitely a mind of her own. Her intelligence turned out to be what I responded to the most about her. Because we both appreciated each other's wit and vibe, we were able not just to get along, but to build a real friendship based on respect, family, and love.

Sure, Zendaya was sixteen and I was twenty-seven, but it seemed like only yesterday when I was sixteen. I hadn't been just a dancer back then, because at sixteen I was still playing violin and traveling around the world. I might not have starred in a number one Disney show, but I was the number one young ballroom dancer in the world.

I found that I could tap into my previous experiences when teaching this particular sixteen-year-old girl, because I knew how to have a conversation with her. I was still down with hip-hop and familiar with the progressive political scene. I was from Brooklyn and she was from Oakland, both places with intense urban cultures.

When the show announced we would be partners, the comments on social media emphasized the discomfort some people had with the whole idea. They knew me as this racy younger brother guy who took his shirt off at the drop of a hat, and who last season didn't stop there.

"He stripped his pants off right on TV!" ran the commentary. "That's so weird. What is he going to do with a teenage girl?"

People wondered how it was going to work. *Well, haters,* I thought, silently responding to the negative comments, *you'll find out.* And you know what? You're weird for even letting those kinds of thoughts cross your mind.

I knew from my work at Rising Stars that it was often uncomfortable when parents attended a rehearsal, but that season I wasn't shy about it at all. Claire and Kazembe had an open invitation. Come on ahead, I thought, come and see how caring I am about the welfare of your child, how much I want for her this season on *Dancing with the Stars*. Come witness the process, because it's amazing.

I had to build their trust because I would be making a lot of demands on their precious child. They had to see my seriousness and passion so that they could be inspired to reciprocate. I needed them to support their daughter on this journey, to be as serious and passionate as I was. If I wasn't passionate about what I was doing, there was no way in hell that Zendaya, a sixteen-year-old superstar in the making, would become passionate about it. But from the outside, "passionate" can sometimes seem "over the top."

The deciding moment came early on, during the initial rehearsal period. Zendaya was returning from an appearance on the Teen Choice Awards, and we had rehearsal scheduled, and she made me wait. Twenty minutes late, then half an hour. I smoked cigarettes back then, so I was smoking outside the building when a car pulled up and out came Zendaya.

Again the lazy, tired-looking walk, the slow Oakland swagger combined with a teenage I-couldn't-care-less attitude. She passed me by with no apology, no acknowledgment even. I realized that Zendaya wasn't fully present in that moment.

Where was the sense of building camaraderie with your teammate? Where was the drive, where was the faith, where was the love? People signed up for the show for many different reasons, as a passion project, as a way to further their career, or because they were bored as fuck and their agent got them the gig.

Dancing with the Stars wasn't just business-as-usual for me, but a dream job for which I just happened to be compensated. It wasn't some paycheck that my agent landed me—I didn't *have* an agent, all right? I was committed to the process, not for the tabloid exposure or because it was prime-time television, but because it made me happy and gave me purpose.

In that first rehearsal, I didn't sense the same commitment from the Zendaya camp. That day as I was standing outside, Pops strolled past next, then a kid came along, a little boyfriend the young star was supposedly dating. At her age, the word "dating" didn't mean much of anything. The girl was dating her career. She was always supremely focused, but now there was a boyfriend, who didn't seem to notice me at all.

Claire was the only one who did. "Hey, Val!" she called out. Then came another manager, a tutor, and a few other members of a sixteen-year-old's entourage.

No "Hey, Val, I'm so sorry I'm late." Nothing like that. I put my cigarette out and headed back into the rehearsal room, where the group had set up shop around the music machine.

I shifted into teaching mode, which for me is like having tunnel vision. I tuned out absolutely every single thing in order to zero in on what we were doing. The assembled entourage disappeared and it was just me and her in a room, and I was teaching a sixteen-year-old girl how to dance the right way, full out, 100 percent of the time. Zendaya would do a step and I would weigh in with constant feedback, challenging her every move.

Again!

And again, and again, and again!

No! Again! No, you can do better!

Are we going for average or are we going for excellence?

Learning to dance was not about doing it superbly one time, but about being consistent. We weren't going for "okay" that afternoon, because Zendaya was a special talent, and special talents had a special, higher bar to clear. The standard was set not by the outside world, but by Zendaya herself, because of her talent. But it wasn't talent that would allow her to succeed, rather it was her desire to fulfill that talent to the best of her ability.

"You're going to give me ten of those steps perfectly," I told her. "Because it's not about greatness every once in a while, or only sometimes, but greatness every single time."

I clapped my hands for emphasis. EV-er-y-SING-le-TIME!

The room around us fell silent. Collectively, Zendaya and her people realized that this was not some silly dance show that they signed up for, and that I wasn't just another Hollywood kid who knew how to dance and choreograph. This was not even just about her learning how to ballroom dance. It was more than that. Somebody was holding her accountable, creating an environment where she could truly grow and learn and become the very best version of herself.

I understood what a vital part of the equation parents were, because I had encountered the situation again and again at Rising Stars. I was a product of an environment where my own parents had meant everything to my development as a dancer.

What the world saw that season, and ultimately what I'm most proud of, was how passionate I could be about working with young talent, how driven I was, and how focused I was. That opened doors to a whole different slew of fans, young fans, yes, but also older people to whom I showed a completely different emotional palette and a completely different style.

Being paired with a young partner helped me by taking the whole idea of romantic melodrama totally off the table. Instead of questions like "Are you guys an item?" we got queries such as "Wow, that was an incredible performance! How did that make you feel?"

"How it makes me feel is that I'm proud of her," I answered. "We're going to showcase her dance ability on a whole different level, showcase her star power on a new level, showcase her ability to learn something different outside of her comfort zone."

During the rehearsal period Zendaya introduced me to her tutor. Underage performers in Hollywood have somebody present who oversees their schooling every single day and who also counts how many hours they work. The woman pulled me aside.

"Hey, I really appreciate everything you're saying," she said. "You're telling her some really good stuff. Her parents aren't expecting this."

The vote of confidence from a tutor-slash-chaperone meant everything to me. By the end of rehearsals, her parents came to appreciate my tough-love style of teaching, too.

"I wanted to kill you, man," Kazembe told me later. "I'd never heard anybody speak to my daughter that way. Only I speak to my daughter that way. But I couldn't criticize or say anything to you, because you know what? That's exactly what I would have told her. You were saying the kind of things that I tell her."

We came in second that year, a close-but-no-cigar finish. The hardest thing for me wasn't losing, but the fact that I lost with a partner who was clearly a winner. My message to Zendaya had always been very simple. Work your ass off. Outwork the guy next to you and the rest of the business will take care of itself.

She had done all that, working as hard as she possibly could, giving me everything I asked for and more—but she didn't get the result that I felt she deserved, and it was my fault. At every point between our initial introduction and that second-place finish,

Zendaya had been excellent. In terms of content for the show and how much I was able to put across as a person, as a teacher, and as her partner, I probably had one of the best seasons I've ever had.

And it still wasn't enough. Zendaya and I would dance together again, going on to do many performances in different venues. We're still like family: she became my sibling, the sister I never had, not just for those three months on *Dancing with the Stars* but always. Once you invest your heart in a person during that difficult, inspiring, sometimes heart-breaking journey, the bond is forever.

MY TEENAGE
DREAMS COME TRUE

Life looped around, and it seemed as though I was always encountering faces and places from my past that came winging back into my present—some of them uninvited and unwelcome, but most of them a source of head-shaking, ain't-life-peculiar kind of moments.

I grew up watching the NBC sitcom *Saved by the Bell*, which was already into reruns by the time my family immigrated to the States, but which I could still catch at home even with basic cable.

As a newly arrived immigrant, I found that America was a place where you could say, "I was so poor growing up that I only had basic cable." In maybe nine-tenths of the world, American basic cable would be a dream come true. Among my friends, basic cable was a source of complaint that indicated a deprived childhood. When people started talking about the shows they watched as children, and they mention the Cartoon Network, my reaction is always "Oh, so you had money growing up, right?"

Maks and I had black-and-white pictures in our baby albums, not color ones. We were also poor in terms of the tube when we moved to Brooklyn, where we had access to a half-dozen channels—2, 4, 5,

7, 9, and 11—plus public television on channel 13, but who wanted to watch that? Come on, PBS? Come on, *Barney & Friends?* (No shade on PBS, since they broadcast the Ohio Star Ball dance competition, my second TV appearance after *Sally.*)

Don't let the word get out, but at the very beginning of my time in America I confess to watching a few episodes of *Barney.* Back then, "I love you, you love me, we're a happy family" was about my speed in the English language. The big purple dinosaur showed me a syrupy-sweet reality that even as a child I knew was too good to be true, though a part of me desperately wanted to believe in it. I quickly outgrew him after only a couple of weeks.

Saved by the Bell was *Barney* for adolescents. It depicted the quintessential high school experience that I dreamed about but never had. Looking back I'm glad I had the type of public school education experience that I did, because I came to understand that the world of *Saved by the Bell* didn't exist in real life. No one was having flash mob dance-offs in the school cafeteria. But for a quick minute when I was nine or ten, I thought Zack Morris, his sidekick Screech, his love interest Kelly Kapowski, and the righteous nerd girl Jessie Spano were typical American teenagers.

Along with shows such as *Family Matters, Blossom,* and *The Wonder Years, Saved by the Bell* entered the syllabus of my personal continuing education program, aimed at understanding "how stuff works in America." These sitcoms might have been a distorted lens through which to view my adopted country, but to my young eyes they were perfect. I was a sponge, absorbing the nuances of a culture that seemed impossibly cool, impossibly engaging.

I don't know if many people today remember the Hollywood catastrophe that went down next. The year after *Saved by the Bell* ended, Elizabeth Berkley, who had played Jessie, got swept up in a slow-motion car wreck of a movie, *Showgirls,* that became one of cinema's infamous bombs. Then a twenty-two-year-old, Elizabeth starred as Nomi Malone in what was essentially an exercise in R-rated soft-core porn. The release not only failed at the box office but it became a symbol of the movie industry's overblown budgets. What the filmmakers lacked in thought they tried to make up with money.

Later on in my childhood, my brother got his hands on a videotaped copy of *Showgirls*, and I watched it with him, stunned and fascinated to see the girl I knew as an innocent high school character let it all hang out as a Las Vegas stripper. I couldn't believe it. I personified what's today called "the male gaze," and *Save by the Bell*'s Jessie and *Showgirls*' Nomi collided in my mind, making for a heady, confusing mix.

This was around the time when I first got hard and noticed it, when I first put reasons behind getting aroused. Before that, I didn't even know what was going on down there below belt. As close as I was to my brother and dad, we never had the bird-and-bees conversation that was supposed to be everyone's birthright. We never spoke about sex, ever, ever, even when a Salt-N-Pepa song came on that put the raunch right up front. I was left to discover my sexuality for myself. Perhaps the old country's ways intruded into our New World household, making it unnatural for a father to sit his sons down for a discussion about sex. Whatever the reason, I never got one.

Showgirls was the first film that I remember arousing serious sexual emotion in me. I wasn't focused on the Nomi character necessarily. It was the whole vibe of the piece, how the movie put sexuality front and center, without apology. It was sinful, and I loved every minute of it. Even at age twelve, I recognized there were terrible choices being made by the production team. It stood as the ultimate 1990s movie, excessive and outlandish, though lately it's become a so-bad-it's-good cult favorite. Fans now prize the freshness of Elizabeth's performance.

But back then, when the entertainment establishment looked around for people to blame for the *Showgirls* debacle, it passed over the screenwriter, producers, and director—all men—and settled on the vulnerable young female star. The critics lashed out with a vengeance, and Elizabeth got thrown under the bus by Hollywood, demonstrating how vicious the town really could be.

The *Showgirls* controversy receded, but it left permanent scars, especially on the leading lady. She retreated from the Hollywood scene, bruised and emotionally battered. She still maintained her place in the erotic pantheon of my adolescence, but apart from a few indelible images that crossed my mind every once in a while, I forgot about the whole affair.

Skip ahead eighteen years to the fall of 2013, when Season 17 of *Dancing with the Stars* was gearing up. I was directed to an Equinox gym located in Century City, the high-rise development on the outskirts of Beverly Hills where a lot of show business types and entertainment lawyers had offices. The sound techs miked me up and I headed into the gym lobby for a first meeting with my new partner. They held me there while I waited for the mystery woman to show.

As soon as she did, Elizabeth let out a piercing scream, erupting in joy and happiness, and rushed over to hug me. A conflicted welter of thoughts rose in my mind. I knew who she was right away, but because of the cool, laid-back kind of guy I was, my first thought in reaction to her scream was a single slang word, "extra," meaning way over-the-top, way too extreme for the situation.

But I quickly realized that she wasn't faking it, that Elizabeth Berkley was genuinely excited to have me for a dance partner. My cynicism died and I couldn't help but feel flattered, humbled even. *Damn, that feels good*, I thought. Let's go! I considered how different this meeting was from my last season, when Zendaya displayed an effortless teenage cool, refusing to be impressed by anything.

Elizabeth was different, older, wiser, in her late thirties by then. I felt a crushing sense of responsibility. Here was a person who had gotten wounded very badly by Hollywood. But she had put together a great life, married to an incredible fashion designer, sharing a beautiful son together. She had created a popular online site called "Ask Elizabeth" to help young girls maintain their self-esteem and wrote a book on the same topic in 2011.

"Yes, I was a big star," she would tell her fans. "Then I did a movie that made me less of a star. Oh, wow, ouch, you know? But I still have a roof over my head, and that one bad thing didn't cost me my life. Thank God, I have a beautiful child. Life is beautiful."

In rehearsal Elizabeth was very good, loved to dance, and appreciated every second of the process. The elephant in the room was *Showgirls*, but it was a big friendly elephant, never dark, never aggressive. Elizabeth always embraced her inner Moni. If a fan asked her to sign a *Showgirls* poster, she hauled out her Sharpie without a hint of negativity.

I've said before that I was just as proud of my losses as I was of my gains, and she developed a similar philosophy. If you are going to own your victories, you have to own your defeats, too. No one could deny that in terms of a movie career, *Showgirls* was a loss, but a loss that shaped her life and helped make her into the happy, healthy person she was now.

I was just enough of an ass to inform Elizabeth that on *Saved by the Bell* the Jessie Spano character was never my crush.

"Jessie was cool, but Kelly was my girl."

Elizabeth gave me a wan smile and didn't seem to hold it against me. She refrained from pointing out the obvious: "Um, they were fictional characters, Val." In twenty years I hope I won't get offended if someone tells me they always liked Derek more than me. I hope my life will continue in the face of that withering piece of news. I won't be offended—actually, some small corner of me will probably get offended, but I'll get over it.

During rehearsals I couldn't help but notice Elizabeth Berkley had very arresting eyes. Actually one eye was blue and the other was green, which was a rare thing and rendered her gaze absolutely magnetic. She didn't look at a person, she looked *into* a person. At first, I found it almost overwhelming.

"Yo, wait, stop," I wanted to call out. Hold on a second, just hold up one second, please! I felt as though I had let somebody into the living room of my apartment, and immediately they start going through my closets. Yes, sure, okay, but one step at a time!

We bonded over love of family. She had a new son and a beautiful circle of friends and relatives. She told me that she grew tremendously on the show, that there were times, a couple of dances, where she was in heaven with the feeling of receiving the ecstatic gift of dance. At that moment in her life, outside of her son, her husband, and her family, *Dancing with the Stars* was the highlight.

ALL THE PROS ON *DANCING WITH THE STARS* CHOREOGRAPHED the routines that the judges then commented upon and scored. I've always felt choreography to be the hidden element of the show, with a lot of the truest artistry going on out of sight of the prime-time cameras. Choreography is the fuel, some of it high-octane rocket fuel, some of it regular unleaded. Everybody talks about sleek, beautiful race cars, but not many comment on the quality of gasoline that makes them go.

I have zero performance anxiety heading into a dance routine. Obviously there can be butterflies and all that, but I've been dancing for so long, and have competed so often, that I know I'm at my best when onstage. I believe in myself when I'm performing, with a confidence that arises not from cockiness as much as from exhaustive preparation.

But my insecurities come out in spades whenever I choreograph, and stage fright attacks me every time. I'm not quite sure why this happens. I've been directed all my life, primarily by Maks but also by other coaches, as well as by assorted other teachers and producers, so that serving as a director on my own can be intimidating. It is as if I were facing an army of ghosts from my past, all the people who have put me where I am today, standing silently by and judging my work.

It's important to know that for me, choreography is not just . . . steps. The gig goes way beyond simply blocking out a routine to include developing a story, a narrative, a vision, and then creatively directing the piece to bring it into fruition. A lot of "whats" need to be addressed before anyone steps out onto the floor, because I've always felt that if you didn't take care of the big-picture concerns beforehand, a routine could come off as shallow and uninteresting. What is the music saying? How should this dance make me feel? What is the essential dynamic here between the man and woman? What kind of conversation am I having with the audience, with the couple, and with those judgmental ghost armies of ballroom tradition?

Dance tells a story. Right there is the root of choreography for me, because even if the piece has very basic parameters, even if it is, say, comparable to an action movie with a shallow plot, it still has to have some sort of narrative. Not every routine is complex, just like not every novel is *War and Peace*. Although much depends on the song as well, the story forms a true basis of the action. The algorithm tends to be music, story, dance, in that order, or perhaps music + story = dance.

When I perform, my recognized strength has been spontaneity within the moment. The grace notes that I've added made the dance special, movements and rhythms that were unplanned and unchoreographed. Committed to paper, using an ordinary form of dance notation, the piece may have looked just okay. It's the way I perform within the moment that lifts a routine out of the ordinary, simply because I add different layers to it as I go.

Imagine a choreographer, such as Kenny Ortega of *Dirty Dancing*, writing down on paper a routine as mere dance steps, using those comical shoe outlines and dotted lines indicating direction. Scribbles on a piece of paper can't sum up what happens in the movie when Baby and Johnny Castle dance. Notation is a two-dimensional description of a three-dimensional reality, or maybe four dimensional, since the dancers are not just passing through space, up and down, forward and back, side to side, but moving in time also.

I'd like to take you through the whole process, then provide an example from my season with Elizabeth that shows how it all plays out.

"The name of the piece is . . ." I really do tend to start on that very basic level, and usually the routine simply takes on the name of the song, because the music inspires the dance. When I'm in conversation with the producers, their vision becomes obvious— let's say, in this case, they want a dance that is like a movie, a high-energy, buttered-popcorn, in-your-face dance extravaganza.

My initial conception might have been different. With the addition of the producers' input I would have to adjust my vision, no longer thinking in terms of a Woody Allen character piece, say, but now something like *Fast and the Furious 10* on the dance floor. I choreograph for different environments, different moods, and different strengths. Let's say the chosen music is an uplifting pop song then currently on the charts, featuring an EDM type of sound— meaning "electronic dance music," with lots of synthesizers and programmed drum beats.

Listening to the music, I would feel the pressure of the song's hype, the artificial inflation that takes place because everyone in the audience knows the tune. A popular song can quickly turn from novelty into habit, and habit can be deadening. But the music is still super sexy and super strong and there is a very solid male-female interaction running through the lyrics.

A cha-cha, I decide. A treatment begins to form in my mind, the story that I would write with this dance. At first I reference only fabric textures, different colors, the kind of dresses I envision for the girl.

"I want beaded fringe," I say, almost in a trance, like some poet making a connection with his muse. "Pearl gray, no frills."

Next a sense of dim, moody lighting comes to mind. "I want solo spots"—tightly focused spotlights on individual performers—"a very intimate feel in the beginning. I'll probably want a spot on her, and as she moves back, she reveals him. So he'll be in the foreground and is only revealed as the camera pulls back."

The difficult thing is transitioning between theatrical, competitive, and television routines. Choreographing for television is far different from choreographing for theater, which in turn is very different from choreographing for competition. In competition, we always have a standard, prerehearsed routine worked out in advance, but we never know what song the DJ is going to play. Every round, we are forced to customize our routine on the fly to match the music.

Because I studied the violin, I have a basic understanding of quarter beats, whole notes, bars, crescendos. Those formative years working out on the keyboard at Odessa Music Academy allowed me a general sense of how musicality operates within the context of a song. All that comes into play as I chart the ways the music can intersect with story and be transformed into dance.

As the pop song plays, I count out the beats in my head and watch the dance come together in my mind.

Cha-cha-cha, two three, cha-cha-cha, two three. Four-and-one, two three. Four-and-one . . .

I listen to the rhythm of the song. Where is the "four-and-one"? If there is no "four-and-one" beat, complemented by percussion instruments, the dance loses the essence of cha-cha. Each style of dance summons up different visions. Tango needs instrumentation that speaks of Argentinean dance halls, whispering of silvery passion and red fire. This cha-cha will be as sexy as a tango, I decide. A tango is . . . what? A man reaching out to a woman.

A plea.

A proposal.

A proposal of marriage—that is enough of a hook for me to hang my story on.

I settle on dim lighting throughout the routine, because nobody wants to have sex in Times Square. A dancer might kick and jive in the bright lights of Times Square, but for a man to propose to a woman requires a more intimate setting. Drama, mood, the environment, the genre—all of it comes together in my mind within the swirl of music.

After I choose the style, set the scene, imagine the costuming, come up with the narrative, consider camera angles, and decide on the lighting, then and only then do I go back and start putting steps to the piece. I try to freestyle it before I settle on the precise moves, so at least some spontaneous elements can crop up.

"That works," I say to myself. "Let's keep that."

When I choreograph, I paint with movement. I have a vision for what kind of dance I want, and the more I think the piece through, the more I start to see it in terms of actual pictures. The magic is seeing what's in my head coming to life on the dance floor.

Once I have the vision of the piece solidly in my mind, I bring in a rehearsal dancer, and of course she can be inspired in ways I might not have imagined. But I have painted the picture in my mind, and now I want to see what I was painting, so I have to direct her movement.

"No" is the strongest word I use when guiding my partner. More often it's "Yes, yes, I love that."

My preparation involves dancing the guy's part myself, choreographing it with the rehearsal partner, then moving on to the girl part so I can teach it to whoever would dance the part on the show. Learning the girl part is like stepping through the looking glass, where every day is Opposite Day. By the time I need to teach the piece, I already have it firmly in place.

Even though the word "choreography" means "written notation of dancing," I never write down specific dance steps. My notations run along grander, more general lines: "I want her to be fierce and contained, then rise like a phoenix, reborn out of the fire."

Next, we head into the studio and I just dance to the music. When I dance, I see the routine come together in my mind. I want the dance to satisfy the mood, satisfy the musicality, satisfy the story. Once I am happy with the way it feels, with the flow of it, and with how we marry the music with the movement, my normal thought is "I can't wait to perform it!" or "I can't wait to teach it!"

After painting the description and blocking out the moves, I have to hand the piece over to the producers to make the routine happen. I feel like a mom giving up her new baby to the hospital nurses. I will usually follow along the production process, attending the costume fittings to make sure everything is being done right, and check in with the other departments, too, the sound and lighting techs, the director, even the camera operators. When choreographing for television, I'd be an idiot not to be mindful about camera angles.

Television places your balls in a vise, compressing the creative process to an almost unimaginable degree. Whether it is on *Dancing with the Stars* or any of the other dance programs on TV, no one is given weeks to create a routine. I usually have two days, or five days at most. Process falls by the wayside. Trial and error became a matter of more error than trial, and results are judged on deadline.

In the heat of creativity, I can't very well ask the few dozen people on a production crew for more time. *Would you all please stand by and wait while I get ready for inspiration to strike?* No, I have to be ready.

I choreograph the piece, then teach it to my partner, or whoever is going to perform it on the show. At that point, the dance exits the realm of creation and enters the territory of collaboration.

Unless I am dancing a solo piece that I choreograph myself, dance is always a team effort, an act of cooperation and connection.

Originality is a difficult standard, because I am constantly influenced by other people's work, ideas, or just their general vibe. Originality in artists comes from their own integrity, their own strength of character. I respect the concept of sampling from its use in hip-hop, and I think it's important to be open to inspiration and influence.

But I also always feel compelled to add something of myself, even if the spark comes from the outside. It can be awesome to dress up who I am with other people's influences. But at some point, the dance has to be me. I have to make it my own.

Over the years, I've pitched a million ideas to the *Dancing with the Stars* producers, encouraging them to push the envelope. In one of my early seasons I wanted to try a spoken word piece that I wrote, professing my love to a woman. The camera would then pull out and reveal I was talking about my partner. Let me be charitable and say the idea didn't immediately grab the *Dancing with the Stars* producers.

The show had a million ways to say no to me, and rightfully so. But for the first time, in that season with Elizabeth, the producers approved one of my wild production ideas for a number. As a child of the 1990s, I was more interested in Elizabeth's *Saved by the Bell* past than her *Showgirls* past. I came up with the idea of a routine based on one of the sitcom's most memorable episodes.

Saved by the Bell was usually strictly middle of the road and light as a feather, but occasionally it would address weighty issues of the day. One plot thread indirectly dealt with drug abuse, showing Elizabeth's overachiever character, Jessie, taking "coffee pills" to stay awake in order to study.

One of the most famous scenes in *Saved by the Bell* had Jessie dozing off after a caffeine-fueled homework binge. Zack Morris popped through the window—it was a second-floor window, so who was he, Tarzan?—saying, "Hey, Jessie."

She woke up and freaked. "Oh my God—no, no, no!"

She grabbed the pills and started gobbling them down, behaving like a madwoman.

"Wait, wait, what are you doing?" Zack asked.

"I need the pills! I need some pills to stay awake for the dance."

He was there to tell her that she had already overslept and missed the dance.

"I'm so excited, I'm so excited," she repeated frantically.

Zack grabbed her and held her. "Jessie," he said.

"I'm so scared," Jessie whispered, and then started crying.

The coffee pills episode wasn't exactly a *60 Minutes* exposé on drug use, but it represented a big moment on *Saved by the Bell*. People talked about it—for a brief second it was a thing, a cutting edge TV moment.

Dancing with the Stars liked to do "Most Memorable Year" theme nights, and for Elizabeth they chose 1990, when her sitcom star was at its brightest. The producers re-created the whole *Saved by the Bell* set.

In the live performance, I played the Zack Morris character, jumping into the scene out of nowhere. Not little Potsie on *Happy Days* anymore!

"Hey, what are you doing? We've got to go jive!"

"Oh my God," Elizabeth said, in character as Jessie Spano. "I need my jive pills."

"Whoa, you don't need any jive pills!"

"I need my jive pills. I'm so excited, I'm so excited—I'm so scared."

I tossed her pills away and bam! The song "I'm So Excited" came on and we exploded into the jive number. This wasn't by any means the gorgeous Mandy Moore–choreographed opening sequence of *La La Land*, or Kenny Ortega's classic *Dirty Dancing* numbers. But it was a great moment for *Dancing with the Stars*, because the show brought back a famous, really special TV moment. And it was a great moment for me, too—reliving my nine-year-old self, sitting on a couch at home on West Street and Avenue Z in Brooklyn, watching *Saved by the Bell*, then years later being on live television re-creating a scene with a girl of my adolescent dreams.

THE SEASON AFTER I PARTNERED WITH ELIZABETH WAS, AS they say, déjà vu all over again. Someone had inadvertently pushed the repeat button. This time I went into the first meeting with my new partner to find yet another female icon from my youth. Danica McKellar had played Winnie Cooper on *The Wonder Years*, and was etched in my mind the same way Elizabeth had been, with a way-back sitcom laser.

But the journey we took on the show during Season 18 was entirely different. Danica hadn't wasted time sulking over the adult difficulties of a former child star, but instead had developed into a real brainiac, an author, an education advocate, and a champion of getting young girls involved in math and science.

I was having self-esteem problems of my own. Well, not really, I never have self-esteem problems, but I did have an internal struggle. I knew I was really putting in the effort on *Dancing with the Stars*, but I had never been able to grab a Mirrorball Trophy. What was going on? What was I doing wrong? Now matched with Danica, I was in my sixth season. With previous partners I had placed eleventh, tenth, third, and second, and in the previous season with Elizabeth had come in sixth.

I struggled to validate my presence on the show. All this effort was meaningless without at least one first-place finish, just one, just to say I was able to do it all the way to the end. I wanted a championship year, creating such an incredible platform for my partner that we stole the show and took the season. The choices that I made on her behalf would finally prove good enough for me to give my partner a *Dancing with the Stars* trophy. If I couldn't do that, what was I doing?

I began to ask myself a fundamental question. Was it better to have a partner who knew how to dance, or one who had never stood on a dance floor? Both options represented a challenge.

If my partner could dance, there existed the challenge of living up to her potential. She could dance, the audience knew she could dance, but she had to show me her growth. Being on *Dancing with the Stars* wasn't like creating a music video. It wasn't a single little performance. It was a three-month journey, for lack of a better word. In order to make it work, my partner had to not just show up, but also to learn the material and execute—show up, fall in love with the steps, become comfortable with me as her partner. Essentially, I had to make her fall in love, so that she knew to trust me. The process involved opening herself up, emerging out of herself into a new reality. Otherwise, she shouldn't take the plunge to begin with.

To me as a choreographer, the challenge with an accomplished dancer was to develop routines that would test her. With a dance veteran like Elizabeth Berkley, who was excited to be on the show, who had the eyes of countless people on her, how could I raise the bar high enough? My task was to make this the most incredible experience my partner would ever have.

Was that too ambitious? Perhaps, but it was always what I was going for. My approach encompassed the whole package: her as an athlete, her as a human being, and her as a dancer. I wanted to see her change physically and emotionally, her train of thought, inspiration, feeling, how she saw the world. I wanted her to end up with a whole new aura around her.

Becoming a better dancer was only number three in the formula, at least in terms of what inspired me when I walked into the studio. If my partner already had dance experience, yes, of course that made my life much easier. But dance was still only third in line among my priorities as a coach and mentor, behind athletic qualities and human character. So having dance experience helped, but it wasn't the main concern.

With a person such as Danica, who hadn't danced much before, the challenge was simpler. Everyone loves an underdog story. But just because I was teaching her dance at a more basic level didn't make the other elements in the formula go away. I still wanted to challenge her as an athlete and as a human being. That, for me, was what the *Dancing with the Stars* trophy measures. How much have I helped this individual develop in the last three months? How much has she grown?

I've learned a startling lesson on the show. Audience members have displayed an uncanny ability to recognize personal growth on the part of the contestants. I didn't believe it at first, but the results have proved it to be true season after season, year after year. It's a little odd, but the voters don't necessarily reward the best dancer. They have tended to support the person who has grown most significantly over the course of the season. That fact has reinforced my faith in my fellow human beings. It turned out that many people felt as I did, that what was important in life, finally, was not the glitz and glamour and the flashy step, but growth.

I've read surveys about what children enjoy most about participating in sports. Surprisingly, winning doesn't even make the top five. Number one? Getting better at the skills involved. In other words, growth. That is what makes people happiest, not only children but adults, too, the sense of achieving, improving, growing. That also happens to be the quality that most impresses the audience watching *Dancing with the Stars*.

These seasons with Elizabeth and Danica were where I built a whole new relationship with dance. From a very young age, the reality had been that I always looked at dance as a sport. I thought that if I wasn't winning, what was I doing there? The kids answering those surveys had it all over me, since they understood the truth of why we do what we do much better than I did back then.

I had an interview when I was fifteen, after winning the Junior Worlds. A journalist questioned me on dance and dancesport, how it was growing more and more popular, and how Russian immigrants were reshaping the international scene, competing and winning under the American flag.

The journalist asked a simple question: "What do you like most about dance?"

And in my Brooklyn accent I answered, "I like to dance because I like to win."

Now I can laugh at my young self, but at the time winning was the major motivator for me. Looking back I wonder if I would have kept dancing if I had been ranked 48th, or 90th, or 200th. If I wasn't in the finals, if I wasn't first at these competitions, would I have continued to pursue my life in dance?

I don't know. Perhaps I would have gone further in academia, or perhaps the violin would have won me over. There was no competition in violin, except for what section I sat in in the orchestra. It's significant that I finally abandoned my musical career when I went from concertmaster to last chair in the first violin section, before finally sitting in the second section. Then the violin stopped being my passion. So in my teenage years was my goal to be number one, or to pursue the art as a means of self-realization, to help myself grow, and help the world appreciate the music?

Being on *Dancing with the Stars* and experiencing growth through my work on the show, I built a whole new relationship with dance—not initially, but eventually. I started to appreciate the healing power of it, the creativity involved that went way beyond the competitive nature of the show.

My passion for winning a Mirrorball trophy, I realized, was still my old competitive nature creeping up through my DNA. I could never wholly resist the temptation to want to win. But the idea of victory began to take on a whole different color and shape.

For me, victory without actual growth wasn't worth it. That first win was still an important objective, simply to validate myself as among the greats who ever taught on *Dancing with the Stars*. But the seasons with Elizabeth and Danica were the beginning of my changing relationship with dance.

Common wisdom says that as soon as you stop wanting something you get it. I was about to test the truth of that concept.

RUMER HAS IT

A first-meeting moment I treasure came in 2015, on Season 20 of the show. But before I explain what happened then, I have to go back and first get into the previous season.

That installment of *Dancing with the Stars* established me as a contender on the show. My partner was actress Janel Parrish, who played bad girl Mona Vanderwaal on *Pretty Little Liars*. She proved to be talented, ambitious, and a super hard worker. But in terms of the competition on Season 19, no one ever gave us a fighting chance, since the fans all agreed it would be Alfonso Ribeiro's show all the way. He was going to own it. The actor and TV host had talked about wanting to do *Dancing with the Stars* for a long time, and he was perfect at it.

The producers paired Alfonso with a professional dancer named Witney Carson, who had appeared on *So You Think You Can Dance* when she was just eighteen years old, and had been a troupe dancer on Stars for multiple seasons. Witney was a bubbly, wholesome, girl-next-door beauty, so red-blooded American that when she came on the TV you could almost see an eagle fly by gripping the Stars and Stripes in its beak.

Alfonso and Witney. The viewers all thought the couple already had the Mirrorball all sewn up. The rest of us could just go home.

But I was telling myself, *Fuck that*. I looked forward to a great season with Janel. I swore that I would give the two of us the absolute finest, absolute toughest fighting chance that I possibly could.

"We're going for the upset," I said to Janel.

Looking back at that season I still believe I created the best choreography, best performances, and best content that I ever have produced for the show. I wasn't the only person who had a hand in creating what I did, of course. Family and friends supported me and helped the whole process immensely.

Janel and I made it to the finals and wound up taking third. Purely in terms of performance, the final product was outstanding. Season 19 had turned out well, but something happened in the aftermath that left a sour taste in my mouth.

Particularly in partnered dancing, what makes a performance so incredible was the same quality that makes the preparation hard to bear. Rehearsals can be exhausting, and the season with Janel was no different. Gradually all the interactions between us took on a highly personal flavor. We entered into a romance.

As happens all the time in ballroom, essentially Janel fell in love with her dance teacher. And her dance teacher (that would be me) was too weak, too stupid, and too trophy-hungry to take her aside and tell her, "Hey, I'm really not interested in this. I just want to dance."

If I had been a wiser man, that's what I should have said, would have said. But I was too blinded by the opportunity to play at romance in order to achieve the goal I wanted, which was holding up a Mirrorball trophy at the end of the season. I fell into the trap of letting relationship melodrama get in the way of me sticking to the script, which was to focus on dance. I let the line get blurred. I didn't separate the personal from the work.

The reason I came to look at Season 19 as disappointing wasn't a result of the content or not winning, but that what appeared to matter was the romance, not the performances. I wound up feeling empty about the effort I had put in, creating the experience and crafting an environment to help the two of us to succeed.

I have always enjoyed a great performance, and obviously I can't have a performance without my partner. Janel reciprocated every effort that I made. But at the end of the season she seemed to be more concerned about our personal relationship than excited about the great dances we had created, the flashes of artistic lightning that we had managed to catch in a bottle. For me, the heart of the show was always the dance.

Ballroom is intimate enough, so I don't need to have sex with my partner to dance the way I do. When I dance, I'm in the moment, and in that moment, I'm in love. The person I'm dancing with is the most important person in my life.

For the moment.

Because of that, because I pack into every routine as much passion, nuance, and commitment as I possibly can, the audience inevitably feels the intimacy. For a man to approach a woman in the way I do when I perform, it's almost inevitable that people conclude we're fucking in real life, since the only time two people come together with such high volume of passion and comfort and turmoil is if they are in a physical relationship.

A good dancer can display a wide variety of emotions. I don't have to be intimate with a person to create a passionate performance. In fact, being intimate, actually being sexually involved off the dance floor, can wind up being counterproductive. When you long for intimacy, yearn for it, but never consummate, dance becomes an exercise in catharsis.

Complicating matters is the fact that there are usually other people involved. My significant other needs to understand the process, and I need to work extra hard to make sure that she knows that she's still number one. I have to communicate the truth to her, assure her every day of the week. *No, I'm not interested in her like that. No, really, I'm not—I'm only interested in you that way. I'm only loving on you.* Dance is emotionally so powerful, with such weight beyond even its essential physicality, that there is no way to prevent conflicted feelings.

That holds true for me, too. For example, I'm now in a relationship with an incredible dancer, an incredible talent, just an incredible young woman. I'm so lucky to have her. But she's like me in a female body, and that scares the fuck out of me. Every time she performs, a small voice inside me wonders, Am I going to lose her?

Finding myself in this situation has made me a better, more conscious person. What attracts me to her—her name is Jenna Johnson, by the way—is also what makes me insecure and jealous. I'm an artist, and I do the same thing she does all the time, and to her credit she sticks by me without fail. Lately I've felt occasional twinges of jealousy, not because I don't trust her, or because I fear that she's not coming home to me, but because she might share a very special moment with somebody else, and I want all her special moments to be with me. I want to be the only special moment she has, especially on such a high level of emotional tension, and especially when it comes to intimacy.

The Capezio is now on the other foot. Seeing her dance with a male partner, I have to consider what happens when I perform and Jenna watches. The only solution that I can come up with is to employ reason. Think it through. Understand that what happens on the dance floor stays on the dance floor. Reason has to play a bigger role in my emotional makeup, because life is not as simple as it used to be, and love is not either.

My girl can get very jealous, but she's a lot better about it than I am. Jenna loves me more than she's jealous, way more. So maybe reason isn't the driving force, maybe it's simply pure, unconditional love. She challenges me to rise to that same level.

Watching her dance with another man, I have to be willing to say, This is Jenna's moment, and I need to celebrate that because I love her. That's how I'll know I've found the person I want to be with, when we can celebrate those moments together. At those times, I can almost feel our connection growing stronger. When it comes to love, you've got to dance in the big picture as well as the small. Sometimes it's your moment, and you've got to love that, and sometimes it's her moment, and you've got to love that, too.

It's the nature of alphas, especially creative alphas, to generate overwhelming degrees of passion when creating or performing. Passion is part of creativity, more addictive than any drug in the world. It's a hard job. You have to dig deep down. It's like coal mining for the soul. The history of artists and their significant others is often not a pretty one. Check out Picasso's biography, for example, or the life story of almost any one of the greats.

I'm in love with love. I'm in love with being in love. And I'm also in love with being an artist. Every day is a tightrope act to make sure those two loves don't send me tumbling off into space.

Hollywood loves romance, and in Season 19 the romantic melodrama overshadowed all the good performances Janel and I were racking up. Our efforts on the dance floor were getting blown away by the soap opera swirl that seemed to be all the viewers wanted to talk about.

I told myself enough was enough. Never again would I be weak-minded, never again would I allow a romance that wasn't entirely there to inflame the imaginations of millions of viewers, never again would I neglect to stand up for my craft. From that point forward, I would strictly separate the personal and the professional.

I've always liked a line from the Irish poet William Butler Yeats: "How can we know the dancer from the dance?" Dancer and dance—they're all wrapped up in each other, right? You can't separate them. But going forward after Season 19, I swore that everything would be about the dance, and that I'd let the dancer take care of herself.

ON A BRIGHT SOUTHERN CALIFORNIA DAY IN SPRING 2015, I WAS about to roll into a first-meeting shoot for Season 20 at Rockwell Theater. I had been to the venue before, to attend a tribute program called "For the Record" about the film director Baz Luhrmann. The piece was a musical that featured songs from his movies. Of his work, the film that hit closest to home for me was Luhrmann's first, *Strictly Ballroom*, a broad comic portrait of the competitive dance scene in the director's native Australia. But I loved his *Moulin Rouge*, too.

For Season 20's meet-your-partner segment, the *Dancing with the Stars* producers wanted me to drive up to the theater. To capture the moment, they put a field producer with a camera in the car with me.

"Do you have any idea where we're going?" the producer asked.

"No."

"Are you sure?"

"Absolutely not," I said.

When we pulled up to the Rockwell, another segment producer met me at the door.

"Do you want to maybe come in with flowers?" he asked, offering me a dozen red roses.

"No, I don't want to come in with flowers," I said, annoyed at the offer.

I learned the hard way that giving flowers casually was a kind of behavior that did not translate well on *Dancing with the Stars* or on American television in general, much less in day-to-day life. You have to understand that in Ukraine presenting flowers to people was a very common practice. On a first date, or meeting the teacher at school, or going on a vacation—any occasion called for a big bouquet. Men in Eastern Europe gave flowers to women all the time, a gesture of respect first, romance second. In the West it was much more about romantic flirtation.

The fans of *Dancing with the Stars* always liked to mix in a little bit of *The Bachelor* into the show, playing up the relationship dramas between the dancers. Were the dance partners an item? Had love bloomed on the set? Since I'd been caught in that web before, I swore to myself that the new season would be different.

In the past I had been a willing participant in the whole playboy business. I did the media appearances and had the sex symbol conversation. Repeatedly. To some degree I gave in to it, but it was depressing to me that my aesthetic might somehow be linked to a kind of pretty-boy reputation that would overshadow everything else that I was. Besides, the credit for my physical self is all due to my parents, who gave me my genes. Being a sex symbol isn't even close to what I really hold dear—my thought processes, my ability to speak, reason, learn, create, dance, work, practice.

Listen, I enjoy feeling good and looking good. I like the energy that it gives a person. But I've learned that if you feel sexy and confident and strong, the way you look doesn't really matter. Your energy is what makes you interesting. The rest is just window dressing.

I hear the comments. "Look at this stud, I mean, he is *on point!*" Do you think I wake up on point? No, I wake up with the same eye garbage and the same morning breath that stinks like shit. I wish my six-pack had magically developed during the night, but just like everybody else, I have to do the stomach crunches to make it happen.

You think I work this hard just to be another pretty face? No. First and foremost I need to be in shape, physically strong, to continue to create on a high level. Looking good is completely secondary to the primary focus, which is health, and the ability to be an artist as long as I can. The paintbrush is my body, and I have to take care of it.

That's why I chose not to present my new partner with flowers, because I just didn't want to head down that road. Previously, my status as some sort of hottie had been pushed front and center, and my personal relationship with partners somehow became more important than the work. I entered into the new season on the lookout for anything that would veer toward romantic melodrama and distract from the immediate business at hand.

Outside the Rockwell that day, I tried to get my opinion across to the segment producer. "Don't you think the soap opera is kind of shallow and getting old? I've had all that up to here last year. I've learned my lesson. It's not happening again."

Needless to say, he reacted with surprise. The kind of reaction I was giving him wasn't even on his radar. How could I not be interested in playing the game?

I headed into the theater's green room. The production crew hadn't seen me in a few months, and they erupted in "Hi!" and "How are you?" There was a lot of embracing, a lot of Hollywood style "air hugging," the kind that left plenty of open space in between the huggers. By contrast, we Russians went in for the whole-body clinch.

The producer guided me over to a young woman with long brown hair and large brown eyes who stood shyly off to the side. I recognized Rumer Willis, and could not help reacting with astonishment that she was present as a Season 20 contestant.

"Really?" I blurted out.

It didn't seem to fit. *Dancing with the Stars* was great, and being involved in the show changed my life. But I have to admit that the program was always associated somewhat with a certain kind of audience, with stronger viewership numbers in the rural areas and the suburbs, rather than the "cool" urban neighborhoods.

Like a lot of stereotypes, that reputation didn't always hold true.

I know some legendary rappers who love the show. Bun B, whom I met through the popular radio show *Sway in the Morning*, and A$AP Rocky both told me they watched it all the time. "That's a big show, bro," Rocky said, a comment that gave me the same flash of pride I had getting applause as Potsie in grade school.

But in general *Dancing with the Stars* was supposed to represent the opposite end of the spectrum from cool. Meanwhile, here was Rumer Willis, Bruce and Demi's daughter, one of the coolest girls I knew in all the world, putting herself forward to participate. I had met Rumer at the Rockwell the previous year, when she and Janel performed onstage in the Luhrmann tribute.

I tried to imagine her life, growing up fast amid the swirl of movie-star celebrity. She was not only born at one of her father's film-set locations, but her mom had arranged to videotape her birth, so she had come into the world already onstage, on camera.

We didn't exactly hang out together, but at the Luhrmann tribute and later, when she visited the *Dancing with the Stars* set, I got to know Rumer some. I remember thinking that children of stars must have a difficult path to walk. They didn't ask to be thrust into a world where paparazzi flashes were always going off like firecrackers every time they stepped out of their front doors. Life in the limelight couldn't help but put someone off balance, and the track record of celebrity offspring demonstrated that.

Rumer had also appeared on a few teen TV dramas, but I knew and respected her as a performer when she sang in small underground music clubs around Hollywood, the Sayers Club in particular. The place reminded me of New York, and I used to go there all the time to listen to live music. It really made me feel at home. I saw Prince at the Sayers with a live band, doing an hour and a half set. And it was there I saw Rumer, live and in her element, doing her thing. I thought of her as a real artist, seeking real fulfillment.

Her background was quite opposite from mine in a lot of ways. We might have been similar in sensibility, but we came from completely different worlds. She seemed to be miles beyond me, moving in circles of the coolest kids in Hollywood.

Catching a glimpse of her standing there at the Rockwell, I was struck once again how she could appear alone even in a crowded room. She reminded me of the song "Nature Boy" that was sung by David Bowie in Baz Luhrmann's *Moulin Rouge*, about a "very strange enchanted boy." "Enchanted"—that was how I saw Rumer. I wondered if I was supposed to wake her up or allow her dream to continue.

"Hi, I'm Rumer," she said, slightly shy, a little awkward. "We've met before, I think, remember?"

"Sure, of course I remember—right here in this theater. Isn't that crazy?"

"Yeah!"

"You two know each other?" someone asked. I could see the romantic melodrama already developing, and I hated it.

"We got acquainted through a mutual friend," I said curtly, trying to keep it professional. Folks were looking at us, so I took Rumer by the arm and moved her away from the buzz of gossip.

"What are you doing here?" I tried to lower my voice so the sound techs wouldn't pick up my tone of disbelief.

"I don't know," she answered. "I thought it'd be fun to do it."

"Really?" I said again, still unable to hide my surprise.

"Yeah, dude! Honestly, I came to the show in the audience a couple of times, and I really enjoyed it. I'm so excited. I want to learn how to dance."

"All right," I said. "Awesome. I'll teach you how to dance."

I was silent for a beat, looking into those big brown eyes. Then I snapped out of it. "Okay! Then let's get started! You know what? I'm going to make this one of the coolest things you're ever going to do. And you're going to tell all your cool friends how cool their grandma's favorite show is."

During that first-meeting session with Rumer, I managed pretty much to keep my own excitement in check. When I got into the car for the drive home with Maks and Peta, we stayed silent as we eased out into L.A. traffic. Then I let my feelings bubble over.

"Yo! Yoooo! That's Bruce Willis's daughter!" I exclaimed, kind of out of nowhere.

"Yes, she is, Valya," Maks said. He still calls me by my Russian nickname "Valya" once in a while, just as he did when we were growing up in Odessa.

"Demi Moore's daughter, son!"

"Correct you are again, my friend," Maks said, laughing.

I've never really been starstruck about anybody. "They're just people" was a philosophy that I tried to hold onto. Bruce and Demi were real Hollywood royalty, not as much for me as for my parents. My mother and father didn't know much about celebrities, but they knew who Bruce and Demi were. Meeting them, my dad had stars in his eyes, which was funny because he and Bruce Willis look somewhat alike.

Rumer proved to be pumped for the opportunity to accomplish something for herself, to come out from the shadow of her famous parents. Performing on *Dancing with the Stars* meant she would be venturing beyond the family profession of acting, and she'd be doing something completely different courtesy of none other than me. Even though Rumer had plenty of curiosity, experience, and ambition, underneath it all I saw a person who was really very vulnerable, who didn't have a lot of confidence.

During our first rehearsal, I assured her this was going to be the greatest experience of her life. She smiled as though she believed me. That statement was tying me down to a very big responsibility, but one that I would embrace wholeheartedly, with undivided focus and unlimited passion.

"Where do you want to be after the season is over?" I asked. "I know you can sing. But I'm going to teach you how to dance. We're also going to create performances that you can be proud of, a repertoire you'll be able to present professionally, not just value personally."

"I love Chicago," she said quietly.

"The city or the musical?" I joked sarcastically.

"It would be amazing if I could do *Chicago*, Val," Rumer said, using the same soft tone.

"Let's make it happen then," I answered.

For the next three months, that simply expressed, heartfelt wish of Rumer's gave me an immediate purpose. Over the weeks we worked together, I discovered what made her special. It was the element of surprise, the fact that while on the surface she was always this child of privilege, in truth she had given up the chance to enjoy the most beautiful things in life, which are the little things. She was no victim by any stretch of the imagination, but she did experience her own share of disappointments and challenges. She could not perform the smallest gesture in public without triggering cascades of media criticism. She had to keep the most innocent actions private, so that they didn't wind up in the pages of a tabloid.

Rumer did not possess even a hint of arrogance, something that I really appreciated about her. But I knew that, oddly enough, a certain brand of arrogance sometimes protects you when you're performing. It is a quality that as a dancer you should be able to access at will. Playing a role served as an escape for her, where she could be anything she wanted with little or no outside judgment.

Whatever the case may be, arrogance was not in Rumer's vocabulary. She was a beautiful person with an impulse to veil her inner light. I wanted the world to see how beautiful and special she was, just on her own, without any affiliations to anyone else in the world. It was as if I was trying to surprise her with herself.

Before the first show of the season, Rumer understandably had jitters. During the pause before the storm in the green room—or, on *Dancing with the Stars*, the Red Room—I spoke a few sentences of encouragement.

"You know what?" I said. "We're not going to care about the judges. We're not going to care about this audience. The only thing we're going to prioritize over the next minute and a half is ourselves and our loved ones. Let's perform with gratitude, let's perform with love."

She and I went out, danced, and stole the night. It was very clear that the audience felt our intensity. Bruce Willis, Demi Moore, and two of Rumer's sisters, Tallulah and Scout, were seated near the front rows. Amid all the applause when we finished our routine, I saw brave, bad, *Die Hard* Bruce Willis with a tear rolling down his cheek. Dad was crying out of pride. Seeing her family celebrating Rumer's accomplishment was one of the most beautiful moments I've had on the show. It was as if the family was coming together, and coming together because of her.

That was a secret about what I did, how I motivated myself, and how I approached life in general. During a performance, I never worried about the judges, audience, or viewers. I tried to keep my focus firmly on the foreground, never on the larger picture— because my partner and those closest to her represented the biggest picture of all.

Challenge after challenge, dance-off after dance-off, as the season went on Rumer and I survived, killing it, getting high scores from the judges. The clever producers had her dance to "Rumor Has It" by Adele. She did a *Swan Lake*–based routine that absolutely killed it, and also exposed me in an all-white tutu costume that judge Bruno Tonioli had personally requested. He even signed my jockstrap, which I never wore again.

Success feeds confidence which feeds success, and I remember thinking that we were being lifted by a tide of good feeling. Rumer had a great capacity to work harder, the closer we got to our goal.

In the finale, we took home the Mirrorball Trophy as the best dancers of Season 20. It was a jewel encrusted, all gold, tenth anniversary edition of the Mirrorball. It was the most expensive trophy to date, but for me, the value of it wasn't in the material, but because it was my first, and I got to win it with Rumer Willis.

Rumer's performance brought Bruce and Demi together with their children, celebrating as a family. It was difficult to reach people who have seen it all and felt it all, to create a lifetime memory for a family that already enjoyed ten lifetimes of memories. That single tear from an action movie star meant more to me than any Mirrorball Trophy.

Later that year, after our time on *Dancing with the Stars* ended, Rumer called me to announce excitedly that she would be making her Broadway debut in her dream role, Roxie Hart in the hit musical *Chicago*. Oh, how beautiful life can be sometimes.

PART 4

A JOURNEY IN
LIFE

RISING STARS

Just like the Bronze Age or the Iron Age, in our family we had what we called the Pickles and Milk Era of the mid-90s—where if I swung open the refrigerator door all I saw inside were pickles and milk. I guess it could've been worse—I could've been lactose intolerant.

A few months after arriving in the States, we had moved into low-income housing in Brooklyn, and the struggle for money was a daily grind. At the time we weren't the only ones in the neighborhood having a hard time making ends meet. Being poor and hustling was an immigrant's rite of passage—at least, that's how I looked at it, even at a young age. We did what we had to in order to survive, to assimilate, and, one day, to thrive. The mood was stressed-out and intense.

I'm not sure all my current peers can relate to waking up in the morning and hearing endless talk about money, money, always money. My parents never argued about anything else. They clearly loved each other. We all loved each other. But there was a huge elephant in the room at all times, and that was lack of money.

There was love everywhere in our household, mostly unconditional—except, of course, when it came to my report card. Then love came with one condition: I had to get straight As. But no matter how well I did in school, or how rich we were in "love currency," in reality there was still no money. And yes, money isn't everything, but when you don't have any, it becomes paramount.

This awareness we had as kids, my brother and I, gave rise to a heavy sense of accountability. We knew that our parents were going through tough times and we couldn't bear it. We couldn't stand seeing them struggle, sacrificing their own happiness, their own needs, and sometimes even their own sanity for my brother and me to have whatever we needed. In those circumstances, you tend to grow up quickly, accepting a responsibility that not all kids that age have to embrace.

My brother and I would speak at night in whispers, top bunk to bottom bunk.

"*Blyat*, it sucks that they have to work so hard," Maks would say, speaking about our parents. "You know how to dance. You and I, Valya, we need to start working. Why not?"

No one needed to tell me twice. I was twelve going on twenty-five, overflowing with energy and curiosity, always seeking adventure. I was ready to contribute. I was ready to get my hands dirty, or in my case, get my dancing shoes dirty. I knew my brother was *podrabatyval* (Russian for "hustling" or "moonlighting") in Brighton Beach restaurants on the weekends, dancing with his partner for $25 a night. I wanted to be part of it. I, too, wanted to perform and get paid, using my skills to take some of the pressure off my parents and help us all make a living.

I mean, shit, I could do it by dancing! How much fun was that? It wasn't like I had to wash dishes or lift bricks. I got to do what I love and get paid for it. I completely disregarded the fact that a twelve-year-old had no business spending late nights in crowded, smoky, mob-owned joints that reeked of vodka and herring. Good thing the owners of these Russian nightclubs chose not to believe that child labor laws applied to them.

In their defense, half the time I don't think they realized I was twelve, perhaps assuming I was just a young-looking adult. How were the club owners supposed to know how old I was, anyway? I was giving off so much swag at such a young age—it was unbelievable, LOL! I tried my best to look older than I was. I slicked my hair back, wore a leather jacket (with no shirt underneath, obviously), and donned a pair of sleek black dance pants.

My patent-leather dance shoes had been donated to me by a fellow student in my dance class. They might have been secondhand, broken down, and worn out, but I cleaned and polished them with elbow grease, restaurant napkins, and spit, perching on the edge of my bunk bed and working away like some tiny shoemaker's apprentice. By the time I finished with those damned kicks, they shined brighter than the mirrorballs that hung over the nightclub dance floors. I loved this shit.

When I joined Maks in Brighton Beach, I could have billed myself as "Lil' Tony Manero," except this wasn't a *Saturday Night Fever* gig, but rather more like *Strictly Ballroom* meets *Eastern Promises*. Most of our jobs were forty-five-minute, two-couple shows at Russian restaurants that called themselves Paradise, or Odessa, or National.

Yes, Paradise. The irony could not have been more perfectly executed. A live band executed to perfection Russian songs along with incredible versions of Italian pop songs (Russians love Italian music). The decor was downright tacky, and if you ever blundered into the place in daylight the shabbiness showed around the edges.

Despite all this, or maybe because of it, Paradise truly was a paradise to me. I realized only looking back that I was experiencing what true happiness really is. They say happiness is when you love what you do. And I agree, but it goes further—happiness is doing what you love with people you love the most. And at a young age

I was in paradise, making $25 a night, working alongside my best friend, my brother. Those were some of the greatest times of my life, even though they had no business being so.

Even though a nightclub might not have been a Broadway showcase, I was still racking up priceless experience. I learned how to perform in any circumstance, how to dodge, weave, and politic my way through an intimidating environment, and how to deal with a rude audience or even a pair of split pants. Talk about wardrobe malfunctions! I had plenty of those.

Nights at Paradise and the other clubs also taught me something truly important: the vital lesson of *earning*. Those hard-won dollars—grimy bills smeared with sea salt and tobacco—went straight into the communal Chmerkovskiy family pot. This was more valuable to me than any thousand-buck payday I'd pull down later in life. What a miracle! I could hardly believe it. I was able to take my place among the earners of the world. The Paradise is long closed now, but brief as it was, my experience there paid off in residuals that I would always carry with me.

Knocking down $25 a night and $75 for a three-gig weekend, I found that I could buy my first Nintendo Game Boy with my own money. That meant I finally got to "flex"—show off a bit—in school and start to fit in.

To be honest, I was already growing out of my obsession with Nintendo, but I did what I had to do to attract the attention of Vanessa. Who's Vanessa, you ask? Just the most beautiful girl in the world who happened to sit next to me in fifth grade. Expertise at the game console was the key to popularity at P.S. 216. I could not get over Vanessa's eyes, which in my young lovesick mind appeared to glisten brighter than a million stars on the darkest night. Girls were definitely becoming a main motivator in my life, mixed up in a swirl of chivalry and romance. I couldn't resist trying to win Vanessa over.

Seventy-five bucks might have been a nice enough payday for

a twelve-year-old trying to impress a fifth-grade crush, but it certainly wasn't enough for my seventeen-year-old brother.

On the brink of adulthood, Maks was feeling overwhelmed and underappreciated. He worked hard and hustled constantly, but wound up confused and uncertain. What kind of man did my brother want to be? What could he bring to the family table, figuratively and literally? Was his destiny limited to hustling at Paradise and doing low-paying teaching gigs assisting at the local dance school?

By this time my father had finally landed a well-paying job, making $80,000 a year as a computer programmer, which was all the more impressive given that he had never set hands on a computer before he came to America. I figured we had our family situation all set. More than that, I thought we were "holy shit rich."

There would finally be bread in the house along with the pickles and milk, perhaps even a treasured delicacy that was more precious than gold—Nutella. The chocolate-hazelnut spread had become a marker of wealth to me. My friends all seemed to be drowning in it, but Nutella-on-demand would elude our household for many more years.

But even without Nutella, our family's prospects were looking sweeter than ever. I could focus on my grand plan for life, which was to do well in school, play the violin, dance, then get better and better at basketball until I could enter the NBA as the only fiddle-playing point guard in the league. I wish I could tell you this was solely a childish dream of mine, but in truth I held on to the ambition until only a few years ago. You will see me at a celebrity all-star game soon.

Regardless, I was happy, everybody in the family seemed happy apart from Maks, and the constant, worried chatter about money did slowly subside.

One Saturday my brother sat sullen-faced in our kitchen, eating borscht and complaining. He was upset about being underpaid and undervalued at a dance studio in the neighborhood, where he was "assisting" the studio owner in teaching students.

"'Assisting,'" Maks groused in Russian. "That means I do most of the work and get compensated the least."

This being the weekend, my father was in the kitchen washing dishes, a chore he found therapeutic and meditative. As the saying goes, "No woman ever shot a man doing dishes," and my mom certainly didn't mind her husband receiving some Palmolive therapy every now and then. She worked elsewhere in the apartment, cleaning, while I pretended to be studying, sitting on the couch not too far from the kitchen.

"*Maksush,* you okay?" my dad asked, using the nickname, an adoring way of saying his son's name. Russian is the greatest language in the world for nicknames. There are variations and variations on the variations. "Dima" for Dmitri, "Masha" for Maria, "Vova" for Vladimir, and "Sasha," my own father's nickname, for Alexander. I was often "Valya" and Maksim was often "Maksusha."

As tough and strict as my father was, he would always use such endearing nicknames when speaking with us—at least when he was washing dishes. I guess taking grease off plates was the secret to taming the Beast from the East.

"*Da vse normal'no,*" my brother muttered. Yes, everything's fine.

"Look, if you're unhappy assisting this shmuck," my father said in Russian, "why don't we open our own dance studio? Then you won't have to assist anybody."

The proposal seemed to come out of thin air. Pops could have said, "Why don't we fly off to outer space?" and it would not have surprised me more. He had never danced a step in his life. He not only had two left feet, he had two left hands, two left ears, two left everything. My brother, on the other hand—on the other foot—had danced his entire life, but was only seventeen years old at the time. This was the dynamic duo that would open their own business? It seemed unlikely to me.

"All right, Papa, I'm in," my brother responded simply, not fully grasping the magnitude of what he was agreeing to.

"What about your computer job?" I called out from the other room.

"I like being with people more," my father responded. "I don't want to be sitting in front of a screen all day, locked up in a cubicle like an animal."

And that was that. In a simple two-minute conversation, my dad and brother displayed the kind of pride that defined our family. Pursue what you love, and be willing to be miserable. My dad, who was getting well paid in his corporate job, said fuck it, I'll starve again. Maks was too young even to think on that level, but he agreed instinctively to give up the best years of his life to pursue a dream. If you want to understand my pops or my brother, all you need to do is examine this scenario that played out at the kitchen table over borscht.

The decision was made that would alter our lives and eventually send ripples out into the lives of many other people. Thank God my mother couldn't hear the exchange over the sound of the vacuum she was using in the next room. I'm sure she would've chimed in and perhaps derailed the whole train of thought before it even left the station. She always was the reasonable one in the family, with her feet firmly planted on the ground. It was the fellas who lived in the clouds, imagining that their ludicrous ambitions might give them wings and actually let them soar.

Back then, I didn't really understand my father. I have more insight now. At that point in time he chose to return the family to financial instability rather than be stuck in a dead-end office position, seeing his dreams turn to dust as he wrote code in a cubicle the size of a jail cell. For my father an office job was a ticket to the gulag, maybe even worse than prison. He is and always was a man fueled by pride, not money. No compensation in the world was worth selling his soul.

Sitting there listening, I thought of our family crashing back to the earth financially. I saw the sweet dream of a Nutella-spread sandwich as it was whisked away from me by my brother, a bitter teenager digesting his lunchtime borscht. I cursed my luck.

That fuckin' borscht, damn it!

My brother wanted appreciation and my father wanted to be his own boss. I guess they both wished for a sense of fulfillment. Pops had been hustling all his life. Hustle was built into the hard-scrabble world of Odessa. A nondancer opening a dance studio was a slightly nutty, fairly risky proposition, but risk-taking was the essence of the hustle. He would only be doing what he had done all his life.

Not in Brooklyn, though. We would not open a studio in Brooklyn because the whole borough was saturated with dance academies. Many of them were operated by friends and acquaintances in the tight-knit Russian immigrant community. My dad didn't want to step on anyone's toes—no pun intended. He didn't want to create competition and animosity. In hindsight he was foolish to believe he could ever hide from those two inevitable companions. Competition and animosity would follow us everywhere we went, for years, until we built up an immunity to both.

"Let's go as far away as we can," he said. "That way we'll maintain good relationships with people at home."

"Where, Papa?" I asked. "Where do we go?"

"New Jersey," he said.

Those two words sounded like a death sentence to me. If you are twelve, uprooting yourself is a major tragedy, especially when you have been trying hard to assimilate yourself into the Brooklyn school system. In the three years since I had shown up in Brooklyn, I had worked hard to make friends, first through basketball, before I had any English, and then through school. I felt as though I was just getting a toehold in our new home country.

"New Jersey? Yer crazy!" responded one of my New York friends, when I told him we were moving.

Don't think that this was a discussion in the sense of the whole family weighing in on the options and voting. The Chmerkovskiy family was not a democracy. The sense of responsibility instilled in us by our parents' sacrifice made us want to sacrifice, too. If my father said "New Jersey," then fuck it, Jersey here we come.

My parents, who had so little money, somehow managed to scrape up the funds to open a new business, offering a single product. Ballroom dancing was the draw, yes, but really what they were selling was Maks Chmerkovskiy as a teacher.

Maks was great, Maks was handsome and impressive, all right, but I could barely imagine the pressure being put on him to deliver. He was seventeen years old and not even out of high school, but my father would be offering him up as a professional dance instructor—my father, who didn't know a cha-cha from a choo-choo train. To him, Maks was like the champion thoroughbred in the stable, the one that was going to win races and bring home the prize money. For his part, Maks simply could not conceive of refusing.

Saddle Brook, New Jersey, was a half-hour drive from the George Washington Bridge and Manhattan. Very few Russians lived there in 1998, and those who did preferred their kids to participate in good old all-American football, not ballroom dancing. That was an old-world activity, a blast from the past. It wasn't something to push on your children if you wanted them to be modern and assimilated. We had no friends in the area and no support. So the Chmerkovskiy family was entering into uncharted territory.

We found a location, and the first time I saw it, my heart sank. The building on North Midland Avenue lay between a cemetery, a set of busy New Jersey Transit railroad tracks, and a small makeshift farm. In the farm's stable stood a forlorn thoroughbred named Rocky, an elderly former race horse living out his retirement years not in Kentucky bluegrass country but in gray, rainy Saddle Brook, New Jersey.

Saddle Brook and the nearby towns of Garfield, Elmwood Park, and Paterson weren't rich suburbs, but rather blue collar. This was strange and alien territory for me, not because they were blue collar but because they were suburbs. It was actually quiet at night, and that really freaked me out. I needed the ambulance sirens, I needed the subway, I needed my city.

We planned an open house for our school, which we named Rising Stars Dance Academy. Maks and I beat the streets of local communities with our father, making the rounds to barbershops, nail salons, delis, and restaurants, handing out flyers.

Rising Stars focused entirely on teaching kids, following the pattern of dance schools that my dad had seen in Brooklyn and back in Odessa. "Give me a child by the time he is seven and I will mold him for life" is a motto of the Catholic Jesuits, and that was our idea, too. In order to build up a healthy ballroom dance culture in the United States, we had to start them young.

I watched my dad passing out our ads, interacting with the suburbanites of Ho-Ho-Kus, Saddle Brook, and Fair Lawn. "Hey, guys," he would announce in his broken English, "we opened a dance school, Rising Stars Academy. Take lessons, ballroom dance." He finished off his little presentation with a charming smile. Maks and I inherited our charisma from our father, so we smiled, too.

In return, we got a lot of looks like we were crazy. The shop-keepers we approached usually were polite enough, but it was clear to my preteen mind that nobody really understood what we were trying to do.

Maks was front and center, put forward by my father as a brilliant young teacher of dance. I was the silent one, watching the whole process, on the inside, but seeing it from the outside. I was young, I was small, but I was conscious. I witnessed the burden being placed on the whole family, but especially on Maks. He was our workhorse. Everything depended on him.

The dynamics between my father, mother, and brother appeared

My parents romantically walking through the streets of Odessa. *sarcasm*

And on this day Larissa Eremenko officially became a Chmerkovskiy, Pops looks mischievously excited. He was nineteen and she was twenty at the time.

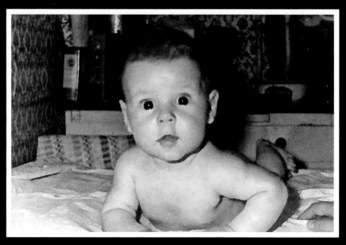

Here I am in our apartment just keeping it casual, butt-naked on the kitchen table that doubled as my changing table when I was a baby.

Ah, my young parents taking me for a stroll around town. Smiling was illegal in the Soviet Union.

But not for us. Here I am with Maks, teeth and no teeth, loving life. You could tell he loved having a little bro.

I must've just learned how to walk and you can see Maks keeping me balanced, making sure I wasn't going to fall. It's so dear. This picture truly captures our relationship for the next twenty years.

Taking in the sun at the famed Odessa beach on the Black Sea. Folks still not allowed to smile, something's got me over-analyzing life already, and Maks is totally owning that speedo.

Taking a bath. In a metal tub. In the kitchen. Life was so simple back then.

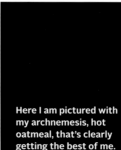

Here I am pictured with my archnemesis, hot oatmeal, that's clearly getting the best of me.

Maks taking this whole "she loves me, she loves me not" thing way too seriously.

I think Pops was trying to dance with me. I look petrified and confused all at the same time.

Okay okay, now I'm getting the hang of it. That bathrobe though!

Here we are on a family trip to our local circus. I hated being placed on my Mom's lap, Maks is just awkward, and Pops is being Pops.

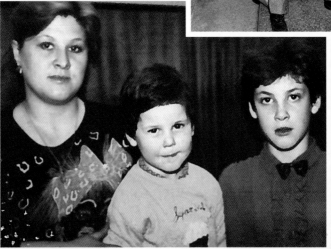

I love this picture of my beautiful mother. You can see the nurture in her eyes, yet incredible strength at the same time.

End of first grade class picture in front of the world-famous Odessa Opera house.

My very first dance recital at the age of six with my very first partner, Tanyachka, and we're doing the polka. For real, the polka.

In Maks' hand-me-down onesie looking like a gentleman.

At my uncle's wedding, entertaining the keys.

At my very first competition in America with my new partner Anna. The balloons say it all, still

Riding along our Brooklyn neighborhood in those infamous rollerblades. My brother was nowhere in sight.

In our kitchen, at our South Brooklyn apartment with my Easter eggs and Pops' translations on the wall. He was learning English; we all were.

Celebrating my ninth birthday in our living room, with me entertaining of course.

I was obsessed with Steve Urkel from *Family Matters*, and my family was obsessed with me pretending to act like him at family functions.

My eleventh birthday, I think. I honestly just counted the candles.

The Jordan cut-out my brother got me for my birthday. He forged "To Val, from AIR." with a sharpie thinking I'd fall for the fact that Mike's signature wasn't stock and personalized. I love my brother for that.

Pops teaching me the game of life, on our bunk beds.

Outside our apartment building on West Street and Avenue Z.

Violin recital, sneaking a peek at the sheet music.

Victory pose with my partner Diana, and yes that's an American flag dress. Tacky? Maybe. Patriotic? OH YEAH!

This "standout violinist" trophy taking a picture with its recipient. It's huge.

This is the moment I truly felt American, waving the American flag at the Junior Worlds, becoming the first American to ever win the championship, just a month after September 11—easily the most meaningful moment of my dance career.

Here I am mid-dance with my partner Valeria, and I had recently discovered sheer. This was a beautiful disaster.

Hitting a figure called the "New Yorker" with my partner Sandy. I have now rhinestoned my sheer. (Hand on face.) © Jonathan S. Marion

With Elisabetta at my very first Judges' feedback ever on *Dancing with the Stars*. That smile was short-lived . . . *Photo by Dave Levisohn*

Sherry being Sherry. *Photo by Dave Levisohn*

Sometimes emotional difficulties can be conquered through a beautiful dance—this was one of them. *Photo by Dave Levisohn*

Redefining the term blood, sweat, and tears. All three are real in this picture at dress rehearsal with Zendaya, it was a great season. *Photo by Dave Levisohn*

One of the more important times on *Dancing with the Stars*, not a time that I won but a time that I lost. *Photo by Dave Levisohn*

Me doing my best version of Zack Morris alongside the real-life Jessie Spano (Elizabeth Berkeley). *Photo by Dave Levisohn*

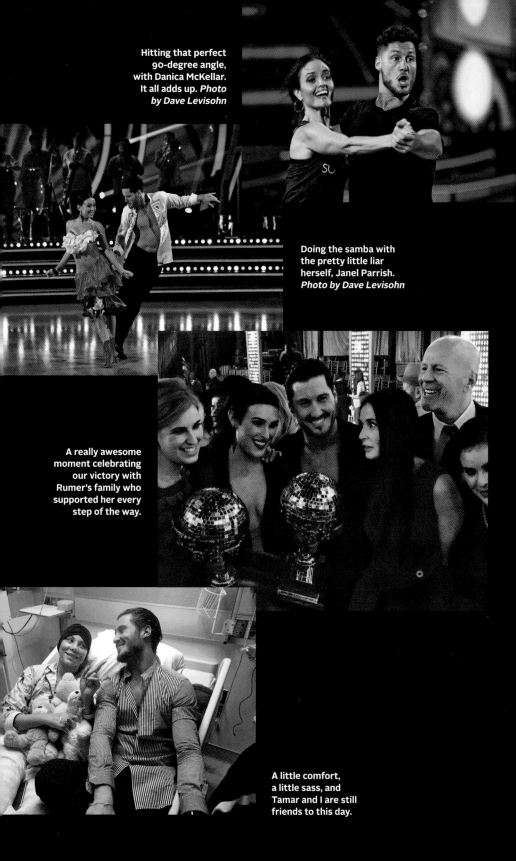

Hitting that perfect 90-degree angle, with Danica McKellar. It all adds up. *Photo by Dave Levisohn*

Doing the samba with the pretty little liar herself, Janel Parrish. *Photo by Dave Levisohn*

A really awesome moment celebrating our victory with Rumer's family who supported her every step of the way.

A little comfort, a little sass, and Tamar and I are still friends to this day.

Ginger assuming mommy duties straight after her performance. Moms really are the best.

Laure bringing out the kid in me.

Guiding Normani through her breakthrough performance. *Photo by Dave Levisohn*

Proving to the world with Victoria that you don't have to be able to walk to be able to dance. *Photo by Dave Levisohn*

Still a kid at heart, paying it forward at the Kipps Scholars School.

Inside the Hammerstein Ballroom with Jenna Johnson (left) and Maks (right)—we sold out the place.

Who did it better? Just being bros on the set of *DWTS. Photo by Dave Levisohn*

This was a number to *Fiddler on the Roof* in our tour, Our Way. The dance symbolized us moving to America.

Thankfully, smiling is legal in the U.S. This was taken at my thirtieth birthday, surrounded by my parents, Maks, Peta, and my grandmother.

My father. My hero. He can finally smile.

supercharged. I would think to myself, *Fuck, look how stressed out they all are!* My parents planned to open a new business only three years after arriving in a new country. They had no experience and had never even danced before. This was not just an entrepreneurial move, it was pure insanity.

After two weeks of door-to-door promotion, the time for the open house at the studio rolled around. We threw our doors open at ten o'clock on a rainy Garden State Saturday morning. A superstition in Russian culture—one of the only nonpessimistic folk beliefs that actually works in favor of an enterprise—was that everything good and successful starts with rain.

Despite the mystical blessing of rain, no one exactly lined up outside our doors. At ten fifteen there was still no one there. Crickets. It was agony. Everyone in the family had the same thoughts swirling around in their heads. *Bills are going to have to be paid. Pops doesn't have a job. We're going down in flames!*

At ten thirty a mother brought in her seven-year-old girl, bright smile, half her baby teeth missing. Then another kid showed up. In all seven students presented themselves at the open house that day, and it was definitely a "be careful what you wish for" scenario, since now that we had potential customers we somehow had to take the next step and actually provide a service.

"Shit," Maks muttered to me. "I've got to figure this out."

He turned to me. "Val, front and center—okay, let's go!"

Suddenly I understood my place within the scheme of things. I would serve as the guinea pig, the example of what Rising Stars Dance Academy could do for a child. It was like a three-headed attack. My dad was making sure that the parents were signing up, taking care of the managerial element. Maks was out on the floor, mostly faking it but stepping up to the occasion. And I was the undercover one, the example they were led by.

Meanwhile, Maks seemed to have only the loosest grasp on what he was doing. "More, more, more!" he yelled at me. More?

More what? I squeezed out every ounce of my talent to be able to deliver Maks's "more." In hindsight he was doing his absolute best, using his limited experience of simply being an older brother to me.

From that small, unsteady beginning a business was born, but more than that, a community developed. I saw it happen. The family element was the main attraction. We began spending all our time at the studio. Because we were the only game in town, the only Eastern European–style children's dance program in Northern New Jersey, people slowly gravitated to us. I became a product of that school. The experience helped shape me into the dancer I've become today.

Our students weren't all Russian. The melting pot was still bubbling away in America, and we drew Italian kids, Cuban kids, all kinds of kids. I knew we had turned a corner when other dance studio owners started to bring their own children to our school to get an education. They understood that we were creating camaraderie and a communal spirit, that everything at Rising Stars was about being part of a family. All for one and one for all.

Community was the key, community was everything. Some of the students may have lived in mansions, but they wanted to visit our apartment on the second floor of a two-family house. Because of the warmth that our family had, it was fun for others to hang out with us and be part of whatever was going on, to enjoy my mom's cooking, listen to my dad's gruff lectures, be a member of the dance crew that was slowly developing.

When I turned fourteen I was thrown into the mix, too, promoted from student to instructor, teaching five-, six-, and seven-year-olds. I felt crazily out of my depth. How do you communicate with a five-year-old? How the hell did I know? Even though I wasn't that far removed from being that age myself, the students appeared like little aliens to me, strange beings from another planet who just happened to stumble into our school.

"Come on, man, you can do it!" That was the teaching style of my fourteen-year-old self. I could never quite master my brother's drill-sergeant approach, so effective when instructing kids. I imagined myself more of a wise, mystic sensei straight out of the movie *The Karate Kid*. The problem was that I wasn't wise, and any sense of mysticism I possessed came out of early illicit experiments with marijuana. Just like my brother, I always tried my best, even though my best as a teacher wasn't always good enough.

The school started to enter competitions. A fierce loyalty developed among the students, who called the place by its intials, RSDA. When we went to Nationals one year in Minnesota, we traveled in a raucous two-bus convoy, a twenty-hour ride that was somehow made not only bearable but enjoyable because of the sense of togetherness it fostered. The parents got involved and the whole experience turned from being a duty into an attraction.

We'd do things that were a little out of the ordinary in the tradition-bound dance community. Our studio became notorious for having real cheering sections. A mechanic father of one student brought along an air horn to the competitions. We crossed boundaries. Our energy shook up the world of ballroom dance. If the judging seemed unfair, we would boycott, making protests that were not strictly ballroom, as though we were the outlaw renegades of the dance world.

Old friends from other dance academies back in Brooklyn also began joining our community. This was another breakthrough development, because while private lessons are one thing, what is most important for kids are group classes. The students feed off each other's energy and commitment, and the lessons become a series of friendly, informal competitions. That is how you breed excellence, by having excellence standing next to you.

We built a business around family. Did that make Rising Stars a family business? Maybe. Family businesses have this kind of small-town essence to them. What that really means, I guess, is heart. We were turning into a big company, too, but one that was built on the morals and atmosphere of a tight-knit family business. That's what helped make us approachable.

Three years after we started, the school that had begun with seven kids at a studio open house was able to foster a national champion in the Junior 1 age category, a Junior 2 champion, and multiple finalists and semi-finalists as well. Somehow the crazy, makeshift organization of the school was able to work magic. With Maks as the artistic focus, my dad as administrator, my mother as the power behind the throne, and me as a model student, the package turned out to be a winning formula.

Five years after we started, Rising Stars Dance Academy had developed into one of the premier dance education programs in the country. Everybody in the Chmerkovskiy family concentrated on the school, and it represented a huge chapter in our lives. Maks and I met most of our best friends there. No one could ever understand me or my family without having a sense of what Rising Stars meant to all of us.

We were swimming in success, but not in money. The realization came only gradually, but there was a fundamental flaw in the business plan. It took a major change in direction before we could remedy the situation, a vital next step that would lead to astonishing transformations in all our lives.

CHOICES

As the older son, Maks willingly accepted the responsibilities our family handed him, but doing so had a huge impact on the adult he would become. The most extreme example of my brother's sacrifice came while he was in his early twenties, when his role in life was still strictly limited to teaching at Rising Stars.

It has always been hard for me to separate Maks my brother from Maks my teacher. As long as I've known him, which is as long as I've been alive, he's taught me, first informally as an older sibling and then formally as a dance teacher. Actually, he became more and more a dance coach, rather than just a teacher, which is a crucial distinction. A teacher can show you the steps. A coach focuses on the larger picture. A coach can put you on the winner's platform.

Maks's style of teaching has always been strict. He could be *brutal*, demanding, disdainful—and that was if he was in a good mood. He wasn't an iron hand in a velvet glove, because with him, the glove came off and got tossed away, or had never been put on in the first place. It was tough love all the way, and although sometimes the emphasis was on the "tough" and not the "love" part of the equation, I thrived under it.

Maybe because he was teaching constantly, Maks was forever stressed out. He was totally invested in the students, but naturally he wanted success for himself, in his own individual career in ballroom dance competitions. The tension between his teaching duties and his own ambitions weighed heavily on him.

Even while working sixty-hour weeks at Rising Stars, Maks tried out with partners who were high in the competitive dance world hierarchy, which was much more developed in Europe than in the States. Europe offered a viable career path, a big-league opportunity that could give my brother freedom for the rest of his life, both financial freedom and freedom as a person.

But a terrible conflict lay at the heart of my brother's dreams, because Rising Stars Dance Academy simply could not survive without him. My father had his entire life invested in the school, and our family's financial security depended upon it. Since Pops had no idea how to dance, he never tried to teach—he believed that would have been an insult to the craft. He would never dream of hustling anybody in that particular way. He was only going to do what he was great at, and it wasn't dancing.

In hindsight, those years as a teacher at Rising Stars were the best thing that ever happened to my brother, including the friendships he developed and every sacrifice he made there. He gave up ninety percent of his school friends in favor of the young students at the dance academy, but because all those kids grew up adoring him, they remained an essential core of people who helped make his life great.

Smack in the middle of his time at Rising Stars, a golden opportunity landed at Maks's feet. A Belgian dancer named Joanna Leunis, who would go on to be a professional world champion multiple times, and who at that time was world champion at the Amateur age level, lost her partner, a Ukrainian dancer with the consonant-crunching name of Slavik Kryklyvyy.

Joanna searched the world for a new partner and eventually

reached out to my brother. He was floored and overjoyed by the call, since she represented a gateway to the high-level world of European ballroom dance. Joanna Leunis was at the top of her game, and Maks had not even competed all that much. For her to recruit him from a family-run dance school in the backwater of Saddle Brook, New Jersey, was an amazing stroke of good fortune.

She was in Amsterdam working with her coach, Ruud Vermeij, who had been one of the greats as a dancer before going on to become a superb mentor, teacher, and self-proclaimed "first doctor" of ballroom. Maks flew to Holland. Vermeij watched the two of them dance and judged their energy as a couple to be superb. Joanna told Maks she felt comfortable with him and liked the chemistry they had.

"We'd love to go forward with this," she said. "But you would have to live over here. I'd like you to move to Belgium or Amsterdam, somewhere that would make it easy for us to work together."

Maks called my dad. Here was a twenty-one-year-old kid looking at a chance to become a champion, with an opportunity to study ballroom in Europe, dancing with the best, competing among the best, and ultimately becoming the best.

If Maks signed on with Joanna he would be living in Europe, not in Saddle Brook, motherfucking New Jersey. No offense to Saddle Brook or Jersey or the upstairs apartment that our family rented from the people downstairs. Whatever the attractions were back home, they didn't include recreational marijuana, a red light district, the Anne Frank House, Rembrandt, Amsterdam. In other words, civilization.

Taking the call at our home base in New Jersey, my father could hear the pride in his son's voice. He was silent, listening to the spill of words about Joanna, Ruud Vermeij, Europe, and the excitement of ballroom competition. Maks finally stuttered to an end, waiting for a reaction.

"But, Maks," my father asked quietly, "who's going to teach at Rising Stars?"

Just that single, plaintive, heartfelt question. My father didn't have to say anything else to my brother. The simple summons to hold fast to family responsibilities was enough. *Keep your neck in the yoke and your nose to the grindstone* was the unspoken message.

To his credit Maks never wavered when it came to family. He told Joanna that their partnership wasn't going to work out and flew back to the States.

I tried to imagine what it must have felt like for him to return to Rising Stars, to stand in that makeshift ballroom studio, where his pops had laid the parquet floor despite having never laid parquet before in his life, and where we had installed a graffiti wall because all the students were little fucking hoodlums. The studio would have still smelled of sweat from the night before, and if Maks turned to look outside, what would he see? The cemetery next door.

Meanwhile, his younger bro comes up to him, empty-headed, happy, and carefree, with precious little awareness of how his older brother's hopes and ambitions had just gotten crushed.

"Hey, Maks, how you doing?"

He was carrying all the weight in the world, that's how he was doing. That was my brother.

Later on in life, whenever he thought about this period, Dad would sigh with genuine heartbreak. He could barely forgive himself for placing so much responsibility on his son at such a young age, even though Maks wanted it and willingly took it on. Our father should have known better.

Maks's interior voice back then might have sounded like a broken record of "I coulda been a contender." In a few years my brother's life would take a couple of spectacular turns. A wise man once said that we don't know enough about the future to be pessimists. Dark as my brother's life seemed at that point, a light would soon break.

COMPETITION (1)

What was I doing while Maks was chained to his post at Rising Stars, facing the most agonizing choices of his young life? I was busy becoming the superstar of the family, the *wunderkind*, the world-beater, absolutely killing it in ballroom dance competitions on the national level and, finally, on the international stage.

I've spent most of my life involved in competition. Charles Darwin taught us that struggle is the truth of the world. The peak moments I cherish the most came in the middle of competitive environments, either in a dance contest or on the basketball court or at a concert recital—the venue didn't matter as much as the spirit of the struggle.

I hate losing more than I like winning, and that's a fact. Winners focus on winning. Losers tend to dwell on winners, looking on from outside the winner's circle, perhaps a little envious and self-pitying, refusing to grasp the fact that they themselves had a hand in what has happened to them.

To create a culture of winning you have to put together the whole package, an attitude, a lifestyle, an energy.

It's not about the word "win" or the word "lose."

It's about effort, honest, unconditional effort.

When you give your all, there's no way you don't win. You either bring home a title or a trophy, or you take away a hard-earned lesson. Either way, you win. You will always be in a better situation if you've worked hard. If you put in one hundred percent of your effort, then automatically you've entered into a win-win situation.

On the other hand, if you put in, say, only ninety-nine percent of your effort, then the situation can turn into a nasty lose-lose proposition. Because at ninety-nine percent effort, even if you win you might somehow feel you don't deserve it, since you didn't give everything you had. In that case, how sweet can winning be? And if you lose, you're left with a sour taste in your mouth. *If only I had put in that last one percent of effort.*

Hard work. I don't believe in anything else.

The peak experience of winning is like the tip of the iceberg, where the huge mass of effort is submerged out of sight, so that all anyone else sees is the win and not the work supporting it.

Effort created the most monumental winning moment of my life. I witnessed my father, almost insane with joy, shouting "U.S.A.! U.S.A.!" and rushing to my side to gather me into a huge bear hug of love. I heard a crowded arena in Italy rock with the chant "U.S.A.! U.S.A.!"

That incredible event happened in November 2001. Nothing else in my life has come close to that singular experience, a crowning achievement in my young competitive life. To demonstrate why it meant so much, I have to go back to the heartbreak that came before it.

A year and a half earlier, in the spring of 2000, when I was fourteen, I traveled with my partner, Diana "Deena" Olonetskaia, to Sarajevo, Bosnia for the Junior World Latin Dance Championship. It was our first time going to a world championship together.

The country of Bosnia and Herzegovina still showed the wounds from the civil war that had torn the whole region apart in the early 1990s. Flying in, we could see the devastation in Sarajevo, bombed-out neighborhoods reduced to rubble, old scars across the landscape. Beyond all that I could still appreciate the beauty of the city, its red roofs nestled among the green surrounding hills.

On our way into town we passed an elegant modern building that looked as though it had been blown in half. "What's that?" I asked the bus driver.

"Oh, that's our Parliament," he answered.

The trip went wrong from the start. At the airport we had discovered that the airline had lost our luggage, which was bad enough in the normal scheme of things, but which now meant we were without our show costumes. Costumes are such an intimate, fundamental element of ballroom dance that they are like another character in the drama. I never take what I'm wearing for granted, and now there I was at the Junior Worlds, and it looked as though I would have to go out and dance buck-ass naked.

My partner's mother, Yelena, served as a chaperone on the trip. Yelena's specialty was freaking out. She made a huge scene at the airport, complaining loudly and at length in frantic, broken English that the lost luggage would rob her child of the chance for a glorious future.

Not an auspicious beginning. I worked frantically to cobble together some sort of outfit from odds and ends given to me by sympathetic fellow dancers. Like a beggar, I went around pleading for clothes. A Lithuanian kid lent me shoes he had used to practice for a previous competition. I would dance in the cast-off pants of a teenage dancer from Italy. I went to a mall and bought a shirt, purchasing a woman's blouse because it was a little more flamboyant than anything else available.

You have to understand that at the turn of the millennium, America still had pretty much a zero profile in international dance competitions. No one from the States had ever won a world championship at any age level, Junior, Youth, or Amateur. Here we were, Deena and I, venturing into the gladiator's arena wearing cast-off clothes and hand-me-down shoes. On our way to the venue we could see bullet holes everywhere, left behind on buildings and walls. Blue-helmeted United Nations soldiers from several different countries patrolled the streets.

We arrived to find a typical Eastern European arena, where basketball games were played and political rallies took place. Not the most glamorous spot in town, but the huge space helped render the occasion grand. Because I was accustomed to competing in American hotel ballrooms, the arena offered a whole different energy. European dance took place in a ruthless, more competitive atmosphere than in the States. But I was coming off a lot of good showings at national competitions back home, and I was focused and hungry.

Occasionally, I was literally hungry, as in famished, since the American organizers of our appearance in Sarajevo did not exactly have their business together. Everything was done on a shoestring budget. Unlike other, more experienced contestants, we didn't have a coach by our side, since the U.S. dance organization couldn't provide accommodations for coaching personnel.

My partner and I were so sad-looking and so obviously intimidated that we appeared like refugees who just wandered into the arena. We were nervous as it was, because we had never been to a world championship. There was no cheering section out there for the American interlopers. It was just me, my partner, and her mother, the three of us against the universe.

The day before the event, the organizers held a rehearsal for the parade of flags planned for opening night, an Olympic-style procession that would feature all the countries involved. This rehearsal session also allowed the dance couples a chance to get a feel for the floor. At the rehearsal, the announcers went through the list of countries in competition, calling them out in Bosnian.

The language was confusing and somehow Deena and I missed our call. Yelena concluded that the organizers had skipped over us and had one of her patented stage-mother meltdowns.

"What about the United States of America?" she called out, jumping to her feet and bringing the whole procession to a screeching halt. Deena and I felt as though we wanted to crawl into a hole. The obnoxious American—or really, the obnoxious Russian-American—had struck again.

When competition commenced the next day, I first encountered Nino Langella, a kid who would go on to become my rival, a beloved rival, a respected rival, but a rival all the same. At that time, my favored dance was the jive and Nino's was the samba. He was super rhythmical and light, with a balletic speed and the ability to put a subtle, exquisite bounce to his moves. On the floor he gave off a sense of beautiful finesse.

I was jealous of Nino, but I loved his style and was inspired by it. I was a fan. My jealousy was not the kind filled with hate. He was an Italian kid from Naples, a little kid from the street, just like I was a Russian kid from Brooklyn. That's why we related so well to each other, because we came from similar worlds and had similar stories, which we translated into our performances. Nino's dances were unique because he was unique, because he came from a unique place.

The Junior World Latin Dance Championship, where we met that year, was all Latin, all the time. Everyone competed in all five of the Latin dances: cha-cha, samba, rumba, paso doble, and jive. Nino was good at all of them. He was the more beautiful dancer, with better lines, but I had more power. We both displayed adolescent charisma, but which one of us you preferred depended on whether you liked finesse or sheer passion and power.

In *Rush*, the based-on-fact Formula One racing movie that's one of my favorite films, there are a couple of lines that I always remember. An injured Niki Lauda says to his rival, James Hunt, "Watching you win those races while I was fighting for my life, you were responsible for getting me back in the car." Later on, Lauda formulates the sentiment into a rule of thumb: "A wise man can learn more from his enemies than a fool from his friends."

That's how I felt about Nino, and that's how I felt about competitors in general. I needed my rivals. I possessed an athletic or a sports mentality as much as an artistic one. I had to have Nino or someone like him to challenge me. I didn't want to win without facing the best in the world, and to me, Nino Langella was the best in the world.

At the 2000 Junior Worlds, Nino fucking killed it and took home the championship trophy. That year, appearing at our first international competition, Deena and I came in thirteenth place, which wasn't good, but wasn't that bad, either. Thirteenth was close enough for me to be able to smell first place, but far enough away for me not to get cocky.

A loss is a loss. I'm not here to make excuses. Excuses are a waste of my time, a waste of people's hearing, and, honestly, a huge case of disrespect to all my mentors. For me to make excuses undermines the whole spirit of competition. So I keep them to a minimum. I am too proud for excuses.

For me being too proud of victories veers into a boasting mentality, and that's not part of competition for me. I am proud of accomplishment, of course. I am proud of Deena and me giving it our all, and proud of making it to Junior Worlds so that I could finally see what winning could look like, and what losing felt like. But I am proud of what my defeats gave me, too. I'll defend my defeats all day long, because what I take away from losing is the stuff I'll spin into pure gold later on.

I RETURNED HOME FROM SARAJEVO IN THE SPRING OF 2000, not as the conquering hero, but as just another kid with homework and chores and friends to come back to. That fall I entered my freshman year of high school. In our household, extracurricular activities such as dance or violin did not let me and my brother off the hook for our other duties, particularly academic responsibilities.

Along with everything else I had going on, I had to have good grades. Growing up, whenever I got a B, it came with an ass whooping. When I received an A-minus, I got a dirty look and a question about it. If I scored a 97 out of 100 on a test, my mom might be even more upset than if I had gotten an 82.

"Those extra two minutes that you wanted to go and spend on that America Online Instant Messenger"—this was back in the AIM days—"you could have just as well been studying!"

Later on, when I got my first tattoo, my mom was devastated, heartbroken. "I've failed as a mother! I raised a child that lowered himself down to the level of getting a tattoo!"

No matter that by then I had completed three years of study at Pace University while holding a 3.7 GPA, had won two world dance titles, had never been arrested—not that my mother knew of, at least—and was a loving, studious, violin-playing paragon of a son. But because of a tattoo, she had failed as a mother. And what did I choose for my first ink? A script on my left bicep that reads "Family Over Everything."

Such was the household where I grew up. "Accountability" was the byword. Everyone had to work. Nobody was dwelling on the fact that there was a *wunderkind* in the household. My brother was definitely not bowing down before my achievements. He was more interested in kicking my ass.

My parents had no money, but they managed to hire violin teachers and send me to Europe for dance competitions. None of those activities put food on the table or paid for themselves. I felt the need to pitch in, too. I carried a burden of responsibility through the world, not as heavy-duty as my brother's burden, but there all the same.

I had to achieve. I had to do it for Maks, had to do it for Moms and Pops, had to do it for my friends, too.

During those high school years, my mom drove me everywhere. Moms are crazy, moms are amazing. She wasn't out there boasting about me, and wasn't often on the sidelines. Instead, she was in the car waiting for her son to finish this or that lesson. For the past year, I had been attending the Hudson School in Hoboken, New Jersey, which I traveled to via the commuter train that ran through Saddle Brook. My mom was the person who picked me up in Hoboken after school to drive me to a youth orchestra on the Upper West Side of Manhattan. Then we'd sit in traffic, heading back through the city in order for me to rehearse ballroom dance from nine to eleven at night, because my dance partners all lived way out in Brooklyn.

During all this shuttling back and forth she would always have sandwiches. Yulia, my mom, everyone was always making me sandwiches. On the way back home I would eat and we would talk. I'd play hip-hop music and my mom hated it, saying, "This is garbage!" but still letting me play it. I'd be blasting "Juicy" by Notorious B.I.G. as my personal anthem while Moms winced behind the wheel.

We drove nearly every day from Jersey to Manhattan to Brooklyn to Jersey, and meanwhile I'd be worrying to myself, "Holy fuck! How am I going to do my homework for tomorrow?" Then, answering myself, "Oh, okay, I'll do it on the train in the morning."

That was it, that was our routine. For years. There was so much time, so much love, and so much sandwich-making invested in me.

That first Junior Worlds championship, where Diana and I came in thirteenth place, was held in April 2000. The following year's Juniors were scheduled for Turin, Italy, in October 2001. So it was a year and a half between those two competitions, and after that year and a half I was a completely different dancer. I had turned fifteen by then, and the difference between a young fourteen and an older fifteen was a difference of cigarettes, girls, and a little bit more teenage swagger.

Two crucial competitions led up to the 2001 Junior Worlds in November: the German Open and U.S. Open. That August, I entered the German Open with Deena. It was a competition that had always been good to me. My first appearance on the international stage had been there, with another partner, three years before.

This time around, I was third. Because of age limitations, Nino Langella did not compete at the German Open that year, which robbed the event of some magic. Alex Zampriello came in ahead of me, an amazing dancer, but a by-the-book systems guy. He danced with his sister as his partner. Where's the chemistry in that? What can that arrangement be but synchronized movement? When you're dancing with your sister, how much fire can that rumba have?

A week after the German Open, still at the end of summer 2001, I met Alex again at the U.S. Open in Miami. As I mentioned, in Latin dancing the order of the five dances is cha-cha, samba, rumba, paso doble, and jive. I had a rule of thumb for winning: it wasn't how you start out in the cha-cha, it was how you finish in the jive.

Jive was my shit. I owned it. One of the reasons I excelled was that I played basketball my whole life, almost every day since I had come to America. In Brooklyn, round-ball represented a way to make friends when I didn't speak the language. The basketball moves carried over to dance. Jumping, twisting, using my legs, it all filtered into the jive, where my athleticism combined with my love for rhythm and movement.

In jive, only the strong survived. The dance wasn't only a certain style of energy—the jive had nuance, not just the rock 'n' roll aspect but the jazz rhythms that were deeply embedded within it. The jive energy came into the world over the last hundred years, and it burst into competitive dance only in the past few decades. As a ballroom dance form, jive was influenced by East Coast swing, West Coast swing, the Lindy, the twist, rock 'n' roll—it was an all-American creation. I made my name with that dance.

At the U.S. Open that year, I again came in third. I couldn't believe it. By the end of August 2001, leading up to October's Junior Worlds championships, I was hungry, starving for a win.

For the first time in my life, I consciously gave myself an ultimatum: *I gotta get this.* I had been dancing since I was a kid, and I was willing to do whatever it took. My dad and I always spoke about the opportunity for me to be the first American dancer ever to win four World titles, a champion in each age category: Junior, Youth, Amateur, and Pro—sort of the grand slam of ballroom dancing.

But if I didn't win the Juniors in 2001, I wouldn't get another chance at a grand slam, because by the next year I would age out of the Junior category and be bumped up to the Youth class. Beyond the grand slam, I just wanted to be the first American to win the Juniors, period. That would put me in the record books, and I wanted to live forever. I wanted to come back to my home country and be like, "Yo, I just won Worlds! I'm the best in the world! I'm a champion!"

But a dark element in our lives belittles every single effort that we make toward what we love. In a minor-key counterpoint to crowing over successes, don't we all hear the chorus of discouragement from our interior nag? I know I did. *What are you doing? Man, you're not even that good!*

That negative voice has met me at every single stage of my life, and thank God for the fact that every time I've encountered it, I've been able to dismiss it. As I've said before, pride worked to save me.

Pride killed the cat—or, no, really, curiosity killed the cat, but pride was there as a coconspirator. Pride can be a force for delusional behavior. Being too proud to fail can suddenly turn into being too proud to try at all.

But that wasn't the case with me. Not only did pride fail to kill off my ambitions, it *made* my ambitions. It *made* my work ethic, made me want to work hard enough to win, harder than I'd ever worked for anything before. And it was that same pride pushing me forward as a recently arrived immigrant who wanted to be the first American to ever win a title at Junior Worlds—Valentin Aleksandrovich Chmerkovskiy from Brooklyn, motherfucking New York.

COMPETITION (2)

What happened next, just a month before the 2001 Junior Worlds, was obviously not about dance at all. At that time my brother was twenty-one, and Brooklyn College had just started a dance program. He was way overqualified, but he represented a huge "get" for the school, so they gave him a free ride as long as he would participate in dance classes.

I was still going to the Hudson School, and Maks and I usually took the train together in the morning. I would hit the streets in Hoboken, and he would continue to Manhattan on a PATH train, switching to the subway at the World Trade Center station to carry on to Brooklyn College. There was a Century 21 store across the street from the World Trade, and on that Tuesday, September 11, 2001, my brother, always the garment enthusiast, had a momentary thought that he might go over and check out some fashion.

Maks decided against it, got on the subway, and headed over to Brooklyn. As soon as the train emerged from the tunnel beneath the East River, every cell phone in the car started going off.

Behind him in Lower Manhattan, the World Trade Center was on fire, and the world as we knew it had ended.

My school was located across the Hudson River from Downtown Manhattan, and we witnessed the tragedy in real time, as it was happening. The Twin Towers were *right there*, only a couple of miles away. Of course the situation was pure mayhem, and the school administrators sent all the students home. My parents were frantic, but thankfully Maks was okay, I was okay, everyone in the core four was safe.

In the aftermath, the whole New York City area was paralyzed with grief and uncertainty. What do we do? Do we go to school and work the next day? Everything normal had crashed to the ground with those towers, the attack on the Pentagon, and the nosedive of Flight 93 into a field in Pennsylvania.

A lot of Russian immigrant families were in computer programming, and many of them worked in the World Trade Center. My father's first computer programming job had been in the towers. The Twin Towers represented New York City for me, and as far as I was concerned they made up the skyline of the world.

Like a lot of people, after 9/11 happened I went a little numb. I concentrated on putting one foot in front of the other. Ballroom dancing had been placed in a harsh perspective, fading into insignificance, yet on the other hand it was all that I had to hold on to. On September 12 Rising Stars reopened, basically because we didn't know what else to do.

I called my partner, Deena. "Are we practicing today?" The Junior Worlds were a month away, coming up in October. We would be returning to the competition where we had placed thirteenth the year before. As I said, I had changed since then, and definitely the world had changed utterly when the towers fell.

It's an odd reality, but as trivial as dancing appeared to be in the wake of an enormous tragedy, somehow I became all the more intense in my devotion to it. Dance seemed to me to be some sort of fortress that I could erect against all the evil, all the violence, all the hatred in the world.

I began to train with a vengeance, channeling my anger, fear, and hurt into making my muscles scream for relief. A combination of factors figured in, not only the events of 9/11, but my responsibilities to my parents and brother, my third-place finishes in recent competitions, and my unyielding determination as an immigrant to do my country proud.

Most mornings before school, my father would take me to a track at a nearby Boys & Girls Club. I'd put on my headphones and listen to Nas's *It Was Written*, running laps until I dropped. I would swim twice a week, too, run the other days, and I came to love the burn.

No one else in ballroom dance was doing anything like that. Especially in the United States, dancers weren't generally into body conditioning. They treated ballroom as a hobby, while I had begun treating it as an athletic enterprise, as well as a lifeline in times of despair. Working out saved me.

There was no accepted exercise regimen for ballroom dancing back then, and I had no one to look to for a blueprint. The more it hurt the more I loved it, because the more I knew I was growing.

"If you cheat on your road work in the dark of the morning," said the boxer Joe Louis, "you will be found out in the big fight under the bright lights."

I had tunnel vision, focusing on the belief that hard work would always pay off.

In the middle of October 2001, we headed off to Italy for the Junior Worlds once again: my father, my partner, Diana, and her mom, Yelena, and dad, Valodya.

This time around we didn't lose our luggage. This time we weren't rookie outsiders. This time we were ready.

ON THE DAY OF THE COMPETITON, I STOOD WITH DEENA ON THE sidelines, preparing ourselves mentally for what was to come, listening as the opening announcement came over the loudspeaker. "The Junior World Championship is a celebration of international community through ballroom dancing," said the announcer. "This year we even have representation from the United States of America."

The night before the contest started, my dad and I had taken a walk around Turin together. It was late, but Italy keeps a late schedule, and there were still people in the restaurants. The tradition before competition was usually very strict. You go to bed early in order to wake up early. There's a whole schedule that I would normally adhere to. But my father was clearly in a thoughtful mood, so we strolled in the darkness along the river Po.

We didn't speak much, just quietly enjoyed each other's company. I've always raved about what a great father he is, how supportive and motivating he'd been to me, but in truth he was still awkward as fuck around his sons. We never had the sex conversation, for example, we never had a heart-to-heart about weakness, say, or nerves, or courage. My dad always kept it simple.

"You physically ready? You good? You need anything?"

Our walk that night was not about talking so much as taking in the environment. The weather was warm and perfect, and in Italy the air always smelled like history to me. We both realized the magnitude of the occasion, how close we were to our dreams. There were no fancy speeches. For my father, action always meant more than words. But I'll take to my grave that near-silent walk along a river in Italy. It was a moment suspended in time.

"Go to bed now," my father said to me as we returned to the hotel. "You need to get some sleep."

I woke up ready the next morning. As a pregame ritual, my father always helped affix the competition number to the back of my costume. The numbered placard was made out of paper and when you sweat it could become a little ragged. You attached it to your costume with four safety pins, but not all competitions provided the pins, so Dad always brought his own. He also had clear Scotch tape that he would wrap around the number to make it solid, so no amount of flop sweat would matter.

My dad was a man of consistency and a certain devotion to regimen and patterns. We never compromised. If we had pinned the number on and wrapped it in tape before, we would do that again for every competition. It wasn't about superstition, really, so much as being in the moment and remembering the details each time I stepped out onto the floor. As a father-and-son duo we weren't perfect, but the bond between us was unbreakable, because an immense sense of gratitude lay behind all these small, seemingly insignificant actions. The pinning on of the competition number was a pure gesture of fatherly love.

That morning I danced in competition with a little American flag sewn onto my shirt. It really wasn't something that you do in ballroom dancing, not at all. There was a high risk of offending the traditions and conventions of the dance world. I also had a track-suit with an American flag on the front and "USA" emblazoned on the back in large letters.

You could say it was too much, that it was jingoistic, but you have to bring yourself back to the period I'm talking about. Many Americans were driving around with the Stars and Stripes on their car antennas. As a display of patriotism, it wasn't much, but as a country we were desperate for solidarity.

This wasn't to say I walked around after 9/11 pounding on my chest, shouting, "America! America!" Yes, there was a huge sense of pride in my country, but that pride was there before the World Trade Center was attacked and will be there forever afterward, too.

The tracksuit also helped me feel like an athlete psyching my-self up for a big game. When I walked onto the competition floor and warmed up, wearing the flag provided an extra sense of drive. Deena and I already stood out, because at the Juniors that year we were the only U.S. couple in competition. In that sea of tracksuits we were two American flags, floating free.

"We have a really incredible opportunity here," I told her. "Let's take advantage of it. We have a chance to do something great. Let's do it, okay?"

In hindsight I have to second-guess myself a bit. "You little fifteen-year-old shit! Who do you think you are, Russell Crowe in *Gladiator*?" Actually, that's exactly who I thought I was.

We went into the competition and started killing it. The dance felt good, and the good vibes only increased as Deena and I survived cut after cut. By the time we got to quarterfinals—the top twenty-four couples—the event had gone into an evening session that started after the same formal parade from the previous year's competition.

I'm not going to lie, my dad and my partner's dad might have had a drink or two that evening. As Deena and I walked in the parade, the production values were a little higher, the spotlights were a little brighter, and the audience was a little louder. I was feeling it. But I was also feeling the flag I was wearing.

"Yo," my cocky fifteen-year-old Brooklyn self said to my partner. "We have fifteen more dances. Let's do this!"

I could not wait for the music to start. Deena and I killed in the quarterfinals and went through into the semis. Now we had five dances in a row. Ordinarily contestants get to take a break, catch their breath, or talk some strategy. A coach or parent might come over to say, "Hey, you really aced the cha-cha." My father would never do that, but I would look over at him and he would always throw me a thumbs-up. When I got that thumbs-up I became bulletproof. I turned into a superhero.

The semifinals came down to the top twelve couples, and we were all out on the floor at once, so there was a direct comparison of dancers right next to each other. We started out the semis with the cha-cha and we were both on a roll. We were cruising. *We have a chance to do something great.* It was just a tiny bit of grandiosity from a young kid, but it had the effect of putting Deena and me on the same page.

Ballroom dance judging was always subjective and open to political influence, and contestants didn't make the step from the semis to the finals for a lot of different reasons. Shit happened. I didn't know what kind of political game existed among the judges, but I did know there were two Italian couples who were definitely in the top rank, as well as two Russian couples. I felt as though Deena and I should definitely be up there, too, but I really didn't know how it would fall out.

But we did end up making the finals, so I was riding on an enormous wave of energy. By this time both our fathers were feeling extra loose and courageous, and in an arena full of Italians these two drunk Russian-American fathers made more noise than anyone, waving an American flag in pride and intoxication, hand in hand with this symbol of freedom.

The MC introduced the remaining six couples. I experienced mad fears. I had these two inebriated dudes, shouting "U-S-A! U-S-A!" and I was afraid we might get disqualified simply because of the antics of our supporters. We performed our bows and right afterward they made an announcement in Italian.

"One last time, please give it up for your finalists and their last dance, the jive!"

Poet that I was, I heard the announcement's rhythmic energy build and could anticipate the music starting. I began doing the moonwalk in silence right in front of the judges, arriving perfectly in time at the perfect spot. It was fly and it felt good. Even so, I was terrified, thinking my American showboating might offend the international judges.

No one in the audience could help themselves. Every eye in the place turned to us. On the floor stood Alex and his partner, and they had claimed their space, but I passed right in front of them. It was as if they weren't there. Once I managed to claim the crowd, no other couple in the arena had an audience. The air sort of went out of everything that everyone else was doing, which was a pretty disheartening development for them. It wasn't just the judges who noticed the shift in attention, but everyone in the hall.

I performed my little moonwalk introduction, and right as Little Richard slammed into the title words to the song "Tutti Frutti," I jumped into a half split like James Brown, bounced back upright, and started the routine.

It was incredible. The moonwalk and the James Brown split have nothing much to do with ballroom dancing. They are both just subliminal influences for me, because I wasn't even that much of a Michael Jackson fan as a kid. But that little move, that small, riffy variation, that divergence from the norm, with a melting pot of pop music elements poured into the dance—that was the American in me, and that's what made the routine unique and special.

We finished the finals. It felt incredible, all right, but who knew what the outcome would be? Judges were fickle. "Adjudicators," they are called within the dance world, and they had the power to adjudicate me right out of my socks. Dances had felt incredible to me before, and the results never seemed to match my enthusiasm.

We did our final bows, and one of the traditions was to link arms with all the finalists and run across the floor together. It was a tradition that the pros started, and I had seen them, exhausted after the finals, linking arms and doing their run together. My whole life, I had wanted to make that run, but you could only do it if you were in the finals at a major competition. As we joined together and dashed across the floor, I flashed back to all those mornings running laps at the Boys & Girls Club in Jersey. The moment was awesome, it was cool, but then we had to await the results.

The announcers called out the sixth place couple, fifth place, fourth place, third place . . . and Deena and I had wound up in the top two. We were either going to win or be the runners-up.

I stood back. As I've said, I'm not much of a religious person at all. I was raised with plenty of tradition and culture, with Eastern European and Jewish influences, but I didn't have that intimate a link with organized religion.

I had my relationship with God through dance. I have such a great appreciation for the spirit of the universe, a connection that flows directly from my heart. I felt it strongly at that moment. Fingers crossed, I was praying for a win.

Then a spill of Italian words echoed in the hall, and the announcers named Deena and me winners of the 2001 Junior World Latin Dance Championship.

What happened next was pure chaos. The word "celebration" took on a whole new definition. My dad ran over, grabbed the American flag, and raced up and down the floor, leading the chant of "U-S-A! U-S-A!" As shocked as everyone was initially, soon afterward the entire arena in this little town in Italy began chanting the three-letter abbreviation of my home country.

They played the victory chords as Deena and I took a bow. Then I bent down and I kissed the floor. My fifteen-year-old self was way extra on everything. I had watched too much Michael Jordan, too many athletes winning it all, and seeing what they did, I sought to emulate them.

When we received our medals and stood on the podium, it turned out that they couldn't raise the American flag, because my dad still had it. He had to walk across the floor, and I had to step forward to take the flag from him. It felt like some sort of ritualized, formal handover. All I needed at that moment was a bald eagle on my shoulder.

Then they played the anthem. I didn't see a dry eye in the house, but I couldn't be sure because my own eyes were full of tears.

At that time I probably couldn't have put the feeling into words, but in my heart I was thoroughly and completely convinced that hard work and sacrifice always paid off. You will never be able to tell me otherwise.

Happiness is relative. Moments aren't bought, they're earned. They're felt in the present but are created by the past. Ultimately, at the heart of every moment is the effort you've put in to make it real. Your effort determines how much the moment matters to you and to the people around you, the ones you love who share the experience with you.

I looked to my left and there was a couple that Deena and I had never beaten until now. I was in a country where I'd never taken first place before, in a competition that no American had ever won before, and I stood with a flag that I felt had never been raised so high before. To me, this was the beautiful realization of the American dream.

DANCE WITH ME

In the opening years of the new millennium, if you cast your eye across the dance landscape in America, a few realities would become immediately apparent. While dance in general was hugely popular, ballroom dancing was far from the most fashionable form, rarely appearing in the curriculum of schools, colleges, and academies. Instead, classes in jazz, ballet, and tap were much more common, lately joined by hip-hop. These were the dance styles that were ingrained in the culture, especially among kids in this country.

Ballroom dancing was something our grandparents did, old and outmoded, an outlier in the field. Nobody under thirty knew who Lawrence Welk was, even though he had hosted a ballroom dance show that was among the longest running programs in television history.

Even when considering this smaller slice of the larger dance demographic, what Rising Stars did—teaching ballroom dancing to children—was a negligible, almost nonexistent sector of the market. The ballroom dance scene at the time was dominated by something called social dance, which was where maybe ninety percent of the ballroom action went down in America. Social dance lessons taught ballroom dancing to adults, and were a whole different animal compared to what we offered at Rising Stars.

Two social dance franchise chains, operating under the names of famous dancers Fred Astaire and Arthur Murray, had studios all over the United States. They were the giants within the still-limited field of ballroom dance. The atmosphere in these kinds of studios was very social, very laid-back, very much a case of go-at-your-own-pace.

Only a small amount of instruction focused on preparing clients for dance contests, because in the eyes of the schools they were just that, only clients. It was almost always older adults who were doing the competing. Whenever they did bother to concern themselves with competition, the big social dance studios concentrated on events that were labeled "pro-am," for "professional-amateur," because both teachers and students would enter.

If studios in the Fred Astaire or Arthur Murray chains offered instruction to kids, the classes were usually tossed in as an afterthought, typically scheduled at eight o'clock on Saturday morning, which for most working parents might as well have been before the crack of dawn.

At Rising Stars, we might have appreciated the big chain studios teaching social dance as huge businesses that dwarfed ours, but we knew we rode in an entirely different lane and had an entirely different approach. We were hard-core ballroom dancers with a laser-like focus on helping kids to succeed in the cutthroat world of competition. There weren't many other people who were doing what we did, and within that small sector of the market, Rising Stars had soared to the top of the heap.

As every schoolteacher understood all too well, there were problems and challenges associated with teaching kids. While social dance studios catered to the adult ego and petted and pampered their clientele, kids needed more structure and authority. Rising

Stars should have posted a sign at the entrance reading Check Your Ego at the Door." Instead, we had my dad, who served as the authority up front who kept everybody's egos in check. Trust me, that was not easy to do, especially with the parents of the students.

One of my father's favorite phrases summed up the situation: "Ninety-nine percent of success for kids is due to the parents. And ninety-nine percent of failure is also due to the parents."

A woman from Long Island named Jhanna Volynets had enrolled her two children, Nicole and Teddy, in a Brooklyn ballroom dance school. Jhanna was a powerhouse. Emigrating from Ukraine in that first wave of refugees during the 1970s, she had risen in the ranks of Wall Street as a stock broker, making her first fortune within a decade after arriving in America. Then she switched over to real estate investment and made a second fortune doing that. She was smart as a whip, beautiful, and confident, and she wanted to give her children a taste of the ballroom world that she had experienced growing up in Ukraine.

After a year and a half taking lessons in Brooklyn, Nicole Volynets accompanied Jhanna to a competition held at the New York Marriott Marquis in Times Square, the Empire Dance Championship. There, something beautiful happened that changed this energetic mother's mind about the approach she was taking in teaching her kids ballroom dancing.

She happened to catch a dance performance by Maks Chmerkovskiy.

With his partner Elena, Maks competed in the Latin event. I remember the evening well. After he performed a paso doble, my brother walked off the floor. I was barely sixteen years old, and thought I had to function like a cornerman in boxing. I rushed up to give Maks water, quick-like so he could take a sip and replenish himself midcompetition. The moment really did resemble a pause in a boxing match, lacking only the ring girls parading around with placards announcing the round.

I threw some water on the floor for Maks to wet the bottom of his shoes, a typical ballroom hack that helped give friction to the soles so they didn't slip and slide.

"Go out and kill the jive," I whispered, knowing that the final dance in the series was most important. (To repeat my rule of thumb: "It wasn't how you start out in the cha-cha, it was how you finish in the jive.") Then I wished him luck, told him how great he was doing, kissed his cheek, and sent him off.

And Maks did kill the jive that night, mesmerizing the judges, the audience, and the other dancers. He also floored one onlooker in particular, Jhanna, who watched transfixed and totally charmed as my brother danced.

Jhanna was too stunned to approach her new ballroom crush right there and then, but she made sure to check the program and try to figure out how she could get in touch with him.

"Where's this kid's studio?" she asked everyone around her. "Because I am going." She found that Maks worked out of Rising Stars Dance Academy, and in the days following the championships she called to sign her daughter Nicole up for a private lesson.

Driving her children to Jersey from Long Island, Jhanna arrived at the smelly, nothing-fancy studio, its walls cluttered with graffiti, competition numbers, and ballroom dance trophies won by our school's students and instructors. The story is family lore, and I still have a mental image of that day. Jhanna wore a mink coat and perhaps $200,000 worth of jewelry on her person, and looked as out of place as a royal duchess in a boxing gym. She came off as possibly the most bougie woman in the world, definitely the most bougie person who ever walked through the door at Rising Stars.

What resulted was the creation of the oddest of odd couples— not Jhanna and Maks, but Jhanna and another, just-as-unique member of the Chmerkovskiy family.

ON THAT FIRST VISIT, JHANNA WAS IMMEDIATELY MET BY THE manager and all-around boss of the academy, my dad. Ms. Wall Street, meet the Beast from the East.

You have to understand that my father did not exactly exhibit the most inviting energy. Even when in a good mood he looked as if he were pissed at something—charmingly pissed, beautifully pissed, but nonetheless still fairly intimidating. He had the syndrome commonly identified nowadays as "resting bitch face," and he carried it off pretty well and quite consistently.

Underneath it all, my pops was a real teddy bear. He was just results oriented, not comfort oriented. Sure, he received newcomers politely, but he lacked the fawning nature of a restaurant maître d'. At Rising Stars, we were *not* at your service. This was an academy that had trained some of the best athletes in the world. If you chose to be a part of it, you were very welcome. Come in, sign the paperwork, hit the floor, and start working.

Jhanna told me later that the vibe was *this is an intense place.* Tacked to the wall behind my dad's front counter was a handmade poster with his motto spelled out in large letters: "Fail to prepare, prepare to fail."

There was minimal nonsense and very little lip service paid to conventional niceties. Nobody was there to small talk you into liking us. We were going to show you results and that was why you were going to love us—not pretend to like us, but really and truly appreciate what Rising Stars had going on. We didn't exist to raise the esteem of parents, but to realize the potential of their kids.

"I have—my daughter, Nicole, she has a private lesson with Maksim Chmerkovskiy," Jhanna said when she met my dad, stuttering a little but pronouncing the last name flawlessly.

"So, a lesson with Maks?" he said. "You will just wait in the seating area and he'll be right with you."

"Okay," Jhanna said, looking around a little helplessly. "Um, where can I put my coat?"

My dad shrugged. "Put it in the same closet with everybody else's jacket," he said simply, and wandered away. *Honey, hold on to the mink if it's so precious to you* was the not-quite-subliminal message.

Instead of being put off, Jhanna was actually impressed. Okay, she thought, this is refereshing. I think our studio might have reminded her of the old-world dance academies that she hadn't seen in twenty-plus years.

It didn't matter where you were from or how much money you had. At Rising Stars there were no separations based on class, race, or social status. We could not give a fuck about where you came from or who you were. We based our judgments on how you acted and how you treated others. We were not going to be flexible with the individual, but rather the individual had to be flexible within the Rising Stars system, which was all about family, camaraderie, and equality.

As usual, I was working out on the parquet myself, and I sort of idly surveilled Jhanna as she sat in the waiting area with her mink coat wrapped around her. *"Rich bitch"* was the two-word rhyme that passed through my mind. She watched Nicole have a first lesson with Maks—Maks the charmer, Maks the charismatic, Maks the larger-than-life personality that they both had first encountered the previous weekend, winning the Empire Championship. But here was a very different Maks—Maks the drill sergeant.

No coddling went on out on the floor. No empty compliments either, not, "Very good, very good, oh, very good," but instead "Not enough, that's not enough, that's not enough!" If you wanted compliments you earned them at the competitions, where they were called medals. So the lesson ended with "Now go home and fuckin' practice this, you little shit."

Well, not those precise words, of course, but that was the sentiment that came through loud and clear from my darling, cut-the-crap brother.

I thought that might be it for Jhanna, that she would head out the door and never return after witnessing Maks at work. Once again, though, Jhanna was less offended than startled and impressed. The studio still struck her as pretty stinky, but somehow the stench now indicated hard work and perseverance, like discipline was in the air. She fell in love with the whole package.

After the hour-and-a-half lesson, she collected her daughter and approached my father in the front office. "That was great!" she said. "How much do I owe you?"

"Eighty dollars," he said.

"Well, here's eighty," she said, counting out the bills. "And here's a hundred for the kid."

I stood there as a silent witness. *Uh-oh*, I thought. Here comes a stern correction from my dad.

He stared at the woman, then glanced down at the bill in her hand.

"What? What's that for?"

"Oh, you know, for the kid," Jhanna repeated, referring to my brother. She wanted to tip my brother. As though it were radio-active, my dad carefully took the hundred, smoothed it out, and gave it back.

"We don't tip here," he told her, more gently than I had expected. "This isn't one of those places."

I saw a moment pass between them, two very different but like-minded people crossing each other's paths at completely different times in their lives. "Um, okay," Jhanna said, tucking the bill back into her Givenchy.

My dad wasn't being rude and neither was Jhanna. This was a woman who had an old-world upbringing, who had raised her kids in a new-world atmosphere, but who was now linking back up with an old-school environment at Rising Stars. The style of the place was familiar to her, but unfamiliar to her children, and she loved Maks's tough-love attitude. Being denied the acceptance of that tip made her understand that our school was not driven by money, but by passion and people.

That first visit thoroughly seduced Jhanna Volynets. She enrolled both Nicole and Teddy at Rising Stars and began driving from her home on Long Island three, four, and finally five or six times a week. She would occasionally rent a room at a nearby hotel on Friday night, so she and her kids wouldn't have to commute back to Jersey for a Saturday morning lesson. During this time, it wasn't just Maks teaching—I was there, too. I witnessed the lessons unfold and watched as Nicole and Teddy grew better each week.

Now it was our turn to be impressed. Wow. Here was a lady putting in two hours each way, in traffic, for her kids to be able to take lessons with us. We examined that fact and thought to ourselves that it didn't really matter who she was. Whether she had five dollars or five thousand dollars in her pocket, she was going to get our very best. Nicole and Teddy would receive our undivided attention, focus, and effort, because Jhanna reminded me and Maks of what our mom used to do for us.

Here was a model parent, I thought, the kind who was willing to go the extra mile—in New York traffic—for her kids. In my dad's formula of attributing ninety-nine percent of success or failure to the parents, Jhanna was the kind who helped ensure her children's success. Both Nicole and Teddy thrived at Rising Stars.

We started building a relationship, a friendship between our family and hers. Soon Jhanna no longer had to book a room at the local Marriott, because she stayed with us in our crummy second-floor apartment. She loved my mother and the warm style of the household. Slowly, as others had done before, she fell in love with our world, with its twin draws of my mom's cooking and my dad's lectures.

Her interest expanded to embrace not just her kids, but to

our business itself, because she was an expert businesswoman who sensed an opportunity.

"I've seen it all, you know?" she told us. "I've traveled the world. I've done it all. I've put Nicole and Ted into a million activities, from karate, sports, gymnastics to art, to *everything*. And only Rising Stars stuck. And why did this stick? What is it that you have here that's so magical? And how can you expand it?"

We had never before really looked at our business from a business standpoint. We considered Rising Stars more of an institution, a place that probably should have received government arts funding, if only we could figure out how to apply for some.

As my parents built a friendship with Jhanna, my father began to open up to her, a little more after each family dinner we shared, a little closer after each round of vodka. It was as if she were peeling away at my dad's thick, gruff layers in the course of a series of dinner conversations. At first, he dismissed out of hand the ideas that she would throw his way, but then he slowly began warming to them.

Soon enough, I noticed the pronouns had shifted in Jhanna's conversation, switching from "you" to "we." As I said, my family was a "we" kind of environment.

Together, my parents and Jhanna developed Dance With Me, a social dance studio aimed at adults. With Maks as lead instructor and me with my national and international competition trophies, Dance With Me was an immediate success. We opened more branches, still trying to retain the warm, community feeling that was featured at Rising Stars.

In all our enterprises, we insisted on keeping that family environment. The heart was going to always be there, we told ourselves, and we were never going to sell out. The emphasis would always be on people, never on how beautiful our decor was, or how fancy our chandeliers were, or how clean-cut, suited-up, and fresh our staff was going to be—even though all those would be true in our case. My father's pride, Jhanna's ability to create a high-end product with superior execution and beautiful attention to details, and their shared work ethic and the camaraderie between them formed the foundation of what Dance With Me ultimately became.

Jhanna didn't stop there.

"Why don't we start a nonprofit organization to support dance instruction?" she asked. "We could call it 'DanceTeam USA.'"

She suggested ways such a move could benefit the world of ballroom.

"I have some rich friends, basically," Jhanna told us. "What a nonprofit organization can do is receive donations that the donors can then write off. In return, you'd have a way to provide scholarships and sponsor competitions. Dance lessons are expensive. There are a lot of kids out there who can't afford what Nicole and Ted's family can."

Like a one-woman rocketship fueled by enthusiastic energy and the spirit of philanthropy, Jhanna swept everything along in her wake. Rising Stars Dance Academy was already the leading school in the nation for instructing children in the art of ballroom dancing. Now, with DanceTeam USA and the Dance With Me studios, the Chmerkovskiy family began to widen its sphere of influence, becoming players in the dance world as a whole.

In the sometimes incestuous, claustrophobic world of ballroom, quite a bit of animosity arose over the alliance between my father and Jhanna, because outsiders rarely grasped that we were connecting on a level that had nothing to do with money or status, but instead had everything to do with passion and purpose.

Together, Jhanna and my dad embarked on different projects. He loved that we were expanding and enjoyed working with a savvy business partner. The mood was not always babies and butterflies, because as with any enterprise involving strong personalities there was some tension. These were two very passionate, stubborn people, and they bumped heads a lot of the time, but out of that friction came magic. My father believed that there was nothing wrong with confrontation, or with a couple of fiery people going at it hammer and tongs. As long as there was a common goal, he felt, there would be a great end result.

Operating as DanceTeam USA, we founded new competitions at the Junior and Youth age levels, the Grand Dance Sport Cup. We discovered a gorgeous, classic venue, the Grand Prospect Hall on Prospect Avenue in Park Slope, in Brooklyn, which reminded all of us, Jhanna included, of an Eastern European ballroom auditorium. I loved the large Victorian-era building, which featured an exterior in the French Renaissance style, a soaring entrance lobby with an ornate gilded ceiling, twin marble staircases, and plenty of room inside for a dance competition.

It was perfect. The event could be an escape for young kids to play dress up and be little kings and queens for the day. Why not put them in a place where they could really feel like royalty?

We had the space and we had the event, and finally we could link together a circuit for Junior-level competition that would help reshape the dance landscape in the whole country. Young ballroom students now had a series of events and a point system similar to professional level competition.

They say as one door closes another opens, but the opposite is also true. By opening the multiple doors of DanceTeam USA, Dance With Me, and the Grand Dance Sport World Cup, Jhanna and my father helped broaden a world formerly limited to Rising Stars Dance Academy.

But just down the line another door would slam shut from two thousand miles away, robbing us of our very own rising star, the hardest working stallion in the family stable, a figure that everyone else in the core gang of four revolved around. Out of that development, in turn, came success on a whole other level, breaking our world open as though it were a piñata, showering us all with candy.

In Hollywood during that same period, without any of us knowing anything about it, a reality TV show was taking shape, with an odd format that paired celebrities with professional ballroom dancers.

LUST

Before I started competing on *Dancing with the Stars*, I'd had just seven partners over my entire competitive dance career—deep, serious, long-lasting relationships that for me formed the most important bonds outside those with my family. The decision to leave a partner was always an agonizing one, and likewise, the decision to take on a new partner was huge. By comparison, *Dancing with the Stars* has created a totally different, somewhat unreal and artificial situation whereby I have had to take a different partner every season.

But whether stretching over years in reality or compressed into a short three months on reality TV, competing as a ballroom dance couple represented a total immersion in another person's being. I got to know everything about my partner, her laughter and her tears, what motivated her, what left her cold. Over the course of the rehearsal period, I would discover how she looked, felt, sounded, smelled—all the senses except taste, I guess, but some of these women could have activated the taste buds pretty well, too.

It has seemed to me that the obvious comparison was marriage, and some of the same dynamics applied. If my partner and I were growing as a dance couple, then the relationship was healthy, but if we were stale creatively, I'd know we were in trouble. Since I have never been married, the comparison could be false in any number of ways and I wouldn't know it. But I understand that the intense, heightened feeling of dance is similar to lovemaking, involving supercharged episodes of sensual communication between a man and woman.

Or, for me in my younger days, between a boy and a girl. I took dance lessons and entered competitions long before I ever had sex. It was an odd situation, because in one way or another ballroom is all about sex, or, to put it a more academic way, ballroom is a highly stylized performance activity based on the exchanges and postures involved in human sexuality. So when I started taking lessons at age four I lacked a fundamental understanding of what I was doing. It was like learning to drive a car on a closed racecourse without knowing anything about steering a vehicle in traffic.

I felt like a very lucky man when I reached adulthood, because ballroom helped me learn how to approach a woman, how to relate with sensitivity to another human being, how to embrace the lessons of chivalry and empathy. From a very young age I was in close physical proximity with the opposite sex. We had to touch, hold hands, embrace, and do it all without losing our shit. The social awkwardness that other kids went through totally disappeared under constant, almost daily contact. Relating to a girl on a one-to-one basis simply became a natural part of my young life.

In contrast, during youth sports, say, players weren't normally exposed to the opposite sex at all. Being on an all-boys team tended to reinforce preconceptions about girls, rather than work to dismantle childish prejudices.

Because I started learning ballroom at such a young age, sex was in my life for a long time before I even knew what it was, an 800-pound gorilla I lived with even though we had never been formally introduced. Later on, when I showed up in Brooklyn, I was plunged into a culture that was very different from my Eastern European background, and it took me a while to get my bearings. In America, the reality of the street was hot and wild and loose in ways it could never be in Odessa. I witnessed violence in the hood, yes, but I also encountered a sexually charged atmosphere that was intoxicating, mystifying, and frightening all at the same time.

Even with all that, I didn't get into self-pleasuring until I was eleven or twelve, and I didn't have my first real girlfriend until a couple years later, when puberty hit me like a truck. I was fourteen, but with braces I looked like a solid thirteen. She was sixteen, and hung out with eighteen- or nineteen-year-old dudes who smoked cigarettes and drove.

Of course she was a dancer. I have always loved dancers, not only because they share the social circle that I move in, but because dancers are just naturally tuned to the world of sensuality and romance. She danced in an older, under-twenty-one category, so at first I encountered her only from afar, as a spectator.

I don't think I'd ever really looked at girls like that before in my life. But when I gazed at her dancing with a partner, displaying all the elaborate moves of ballroom, I felt a sick urgency to be near her, to spend time with her, to hear her speak. Watching her dance was a revelation. It was as if after all those years I suddenly understood what ballroom was all about.

Lilya, beautiful Lilya. She was a Brooklyn girl, which meant you could add ten years to her chronological age in order to understand her level of sophistication and cool. She came out of the Russian immigrant community, and that helped us to connect over our common background. But because I was living in Jersey with my parents and had no access to a car, we were impossibly separated geographically.

What was love? I had no idea back then, but even as a kid I'd always had an appetite for more, a questing, restless, hungry attitude toward the world, lusting for more experience, more sensations, more *more*. Whether it was turning ambition into art, or approaching competition either on the dance floor or on the basketball court, that same instinct sustained me. Right from the start, the hunger followed me into my love life and my interest in women.

What did I want from Lilya? More.

Grown-up, fully developed sexual attraction was something I was feeling in my body for the first time. This wasn't the puppy love I'd felt for Vanessa back in grade school. I had never before experienced a type of desire so overwhelming.

At the same time, I was definitely punching above my weight class, and there was no way in hell that I had a chance with this girl. Though I had started to man up a little bit, I still had braces, like I said, and how was I going to kiss with a mouth full of prickly metal?

Lilya didn't dance at our studio, but was at a Brooklyn dance academy where my best friend took lessons. But within our little world of ballroom, I was the alpha kid in my age group, so of course she saw me, she knew me.

We went to some of the same competitions, and at one, the Ohio Star Ball, I sat behind her with my two best friends, Igor and Alex. I thought she probably saw us as a trio of gnats buzzing around her head, but an amazing thing occurred.

I said something funny and Lilya laughed.

Oh my God, I could now die happy.

"I think I have a shot with her," I whispered to my buds. They howled, dismissing the whole idea. Later, when Lilya left her seat and walked away, I turned to them.

"I'll make you a bet," I said. "I'm going to win her over."

They thought I was out of my mind. The prospect was so far beyond the realm of possibility that they only laughed at me. But it wasn't the first time I heard naysayers mock my ambitions.

Later that night, after the competition, Lilya and I ended up in a room together, among friends, and we all started playing a game of Truth or Dare. Somebody dared her to make out with me. To this day I owe that kid a solid. It was the greatest thing in the world. From that point on, and for the next half year, Lilya and I were constantly in touch through AIM.

For the first time in my life, I almost flunked one of my classes. My grades dipped dramatically in ninth grade, because I was chasing this girl. Every night I would wait for everybody to go to sleep, log in on the computer, and instant message with her. I always worried that the electronic squeal of a dial-up internet connection—something not many people remember nowadays— might wake my parents.

We would "talk," and I suddenly became Shakespeare. That's really where all my writing comes from, the source from which everything else flowed: writing poetry to Lilya trying to win her heart.

At that time, what was I except a kid with nothing? I had no car, and I still slept on a bunk bed in a second-floor apartment in Garfield, New Jersey. Garfield. Even the name of the town made me sound like a loser. I couldn't pull up stakes and move to a more prestigious address, couldn't suddenly materialize a driver's license and a car. I had to work with what I had. I took up smoking Marlboros, figuring that looking cool was worth the risk to my health.

Making a catalog of all my pluses and minuses, I came up with a precious few of the first and a lot more of the latter. I realized that on the plus side I didn't possess much more than ambition and intellect. But even back then I grasped a simple fact of life, that there was nothing more sexy to a woman than a man with talent and ambition. If you also had a brain attached to that combination— and with me the jury was still out in that respect—you were golden.

I was still determined to move my relationship with Lilya from the digital to the physical, from AIM to something real. We never danced. Or rather, Lilya and I never partnered, never entered competitions as a couple. She danced competitively with a kid who was eighteen. At that point I was dancing up an age level, competing with fifteen- or sixteen-year-olds. Not only were Lilya and her partner older, they were better dancers than me and my partner. I continually felt defeated and deflated. All my poetry, all our online messaging amounted to nothing. Whatever we had together— whatever it was—was still secret, intimidating, and impossible.

"Lilya is totally out of your reach," whispered a small interior voice, the voice of failure.

We had started talking in November 2000—and it wasn't talking, really, just online communicating—and a month later we ended up at the same New Year's Eve party. I had heard through the grapevine that Lilya would be there, and though the obstacles against me seemed insurmountable, I vowed that I would somehow make it to that party. But I was stuck at a New Year's celebration with my parents, which was a tradition in our family. I had to beg my brother for help.

"You've got to get me out of this party and into that party in Brooklyn," I told Maks. "Please! Tell the parental units some shit, anything—vouch for me, bro! Tell them it'll be all right for me to do this."

Not for the first time and not for the last, Maks came through for me. He finagled permission from our mom and dad, then drove me to Brooklyn and dropped me off at the party.

I was ecstatic. That first taste of adulthood was the sweetest thing ever. First, I was drinking and, second, I was smoking cigarettes. For the *wunderkind* from Garfield, New Jersey who always did what he was told, it was heaven. I knew everybody there, but they were older, so underneath my surface bravado I knew I was bluffing.

Nothing happened between Lilya and me. Being together at that party represented only the most limited kind of interaction, because Lilya seemed to be caught inside this cloud of insane sexual energy. Other dudes constantly buzzed around her. She was the sun, and I was like the moon, with no light of my own except what little reflected off her, constantly eclipsed by the shadows of all her male friends.

That night left me heartbroken. What had I expected—some sort of reverse Cinderella tale where I was magically transformed into a prince? Instead, I was like, *Damn, is that all there was?*

But then the next day she reached out again. As far as I could understand through the medium of instant messenger, she was in love with me just as much as I was in love with her.

I sent flowers to her on Valentine's Day. In late February, I cut school and we met at Battery Park in Lower Manhattan. It was so wintry that the whole city seemed frozen solid. The wind knifed in off the harbor as we took a walk in the chilling-ass cold.

Purely as a matter of survival, I thought our only option was to get as close as two humans could possibly get. Oh, it was one of those slow-motion young-love moments, where we beat around the bush for a second and then just jumped into each other's hearts, with the greatest taste of joy, I think, that I had ever felt up until that point.

We made out and that was it, that was when we swore our love, right then and there among the shrieking seagulls.

From that point forward we might have been technically and officially dating, but I still lived in Garfield and still was too busy studying ballroom and violin. I didn't talk to anyone about this most monumental development in my life—except, of course, for telling my boys that they had lost the bet and to pay up. Lilya and I developed a kind of long-distance, interstate, greater New York metropolitan area, Brooklyn-to-Jersey relationship.

Two months later, I ended up losing my virginity to her.

Forgetting that Lilya herself was also very young, just sixteen, I had this whole mistaken notion that she was somehow very experienced in the ways of love. I was just a kid, while she had grown men looking at her. But she was in love with me and didn't want anybody but me, because, as I said, there was nothing sexier than talent and ambition with a little bit of intellect thrown in.

Ahh, fuck yeah.

That spring I turned fifteen and she turned seventeen. I wanted to be older for her, more mature, more experienced. I asked myself, *Where are the notches on my belt?* I thought I had to have a bunch of notches, a bunch of sexual conquests, so Lilya would see me as fully grown up.

I played around and lost her. It was my first lust, my first love, and I was devastated when it ended. My GPA took a further nosedive, I didn't get enough sleep, and I no longer gave a fuck about dance, the violin, or anything but her. I wrote agonized poems on the subject of lost love. I was Yevgeny Onegin, the title character in Pushkin's novel who writes a poem to the love of his life before going out and dying in a duel.

For sure it changed me, being introduced to that type of heavy emotional involvement. I returned to high school as a sadder but wiser man of the world. Saving the money I was making teaching dance and performing with Maks at Brighton Beach nightclubs, I took a train into Manhattan and bought Lilya a ring. Not an engagement ring or anything like that, but I just wanted to give her jewelry, being maybe a little unclear on the concept that you should give a ring to mark the start of a relationship, rather than its end.

Lilya stood at the beginning of my life as a romantic adult, and sex and lust have woven themselves through my days forever afterward. I want to recount the story of another time when sexual attraction changed the course of my life, but it might take some telling before the lust element finally enters, coming in from offstage at an entirely unexpected time.

IN 2003, JUST BEFORE MAKS WAS FIRST RECRUITED FOR *DANCing with the Stars*, I hit a period where I wanted to dance but I didn't want to compete. With my girlfriend and new dance partner, Sandra Udis, and I had just won the Youth World Latin Dance Championship, one age level up from the Junior Worlds I had won in 2001 with Deena.

I was ready for a break from the rigors of training. So we developed a two-couple tour: me with Sandy and my brother matched with Elena, a brilliant Moscow-born dancer who had been his partner since the previous year.

Sandra, a blond-haired, blue-eyed stunner, looked like a Barbie doll next to me as Ken. I was really passionate about us as a couple and felt that we had complementary forms of energy, a well-put-together woman and a man with an overtly masculine look. Sandy was the all-American girl and I was the exotic import.

At one of our shows, after we finished our fourth dance and before starting our last one, I had to perform a quick costume change, so my brother took the mic to say a few words. People who know my brother know that in his hands a microphone can suddenly transform into a grenade. He had the ability—some might say disability—to pronounce the most ordinary, most politically correct words in ways that never seemed to come out as he intended.

I don't know how to explain it, but in the ballroom world the way girls spoke about competition was very different from how boys talked. Whenever people got into a conversation about results, girls used identifying markers that were always from the costumes. "Who came in fourth?" "Oh, it was the girl in the yellow dress." "Who was third?" "You know, the girl with the pink-vested dress?"

I saw it all the time, and that's just how the chatter went. But among guys, the way to list results was merely to mention the first name of the male of the couple. "Maks was second, Joe was third, Mike was fourth, Tommy and Jackie were fifth, and you know Anthony from Ohio? Yeah, he was in sixth."

It was assumed that the guys were talking about both members of the couple, and they weren't trying to disrespect anybody, just keeping the conversation moving. That was just the insolence of the game and how competition results were described. But Maks made the mistake of using that inside-ballroom language in public.

"It's a very special moment for our family," he announced to the audience as I was backstage switching costumes. "Since we're here, and all of our friends and family are here, I wanted to share something very special that happened last week. Val won Worlds!"

The room blew up with applause, so even if Maks wanted to go on, he wouldn't have been heard. He could have continued and said, "Obviously my brother couldn't do it without Sandra Udis, and the whole Udis family was incredible," but for a long moment he couldn't say anything, because he had to wait for all the applause to finish.

In that interval, Sandy's mother had just enough time to get infuriated. She was a woman of status in Brooklyn, a person of large personality and larger ambitions. If there is ever such a thing as *Real Housewives of Brighton Beach* (not a bad idea), she could be the star of the show. Her husband was also a powerful man locally. The whole family, Sandy included, was for better or worse very much a product of the Brighton Beach social hierarchy.

To add insult to injury, Sandy's mother had a good friend by her side that night, and this friend leaned over to rub a little salt in the wound.

"So? This Val person, he won the contest all by himself?"

Because of that acid-tongued friend, what would have been a simple gaffe by my brother turned personal. Even though none of this should have been about a stage parent in the first place, Sandy's mother seemed embarrassed, because the friend she'd brought along had now witnessed the incident.

What could I say? We—not just I—had indeed just won the Worlds. A year and a half prior to that, Sandy had been ranked sixth in the United States. After our championship at the Youth level, she rose to be ranked first in the world, due to her talent, of course, but also due to my brother's coaching and what we were able to accomplish together, the three of us.

My father's old ninety-nine-percent-was-due-to-parents rule came into play again. Right away I realized that Maks had fucked up. So while Sandy was still backstage, I rushed out and finished changing on the floor, managing smoothly to snatch the mic away from my brother.

"You know, hey, guys, yes, Sandy and I won," I said. "I just want to give a special thanks to our parents." I gestured vaguely in the direction of my partner's mom, who still had steam coming out of her ears. "Sandy and I would have never been able to accomplish what we did without our incredible parents. Please give it up for Sandy's parents and my parents!"

I tried to remedy the situation as much as I could, but the damage had been done, and there was no going back.

I turned to Sandy. "Are you cool?"

"Are you kidding me?" she responded. "I don't give a fuck." She knew that this was a simple slip of the tongue, which was very common for my brother, and he obviously didn't mean anything by it.

Sandy's mom really lit into my father, who kept his tone very polite, apologizing again and again. But after saying "I'm very sorry" a few times, an edge crept into his voice.

"We just took your daughter and we made her into a world champion," he said, quoting the facts from his perspective. "We did that for your daughter and with your daughter. All you had to do was write the check and show up at the airport. And now you're giving us a hard time?"

The woman would not leave it alone. She called the next day to harangue my father some more.

"What do you want me to do?" my dad asked, becoming exasperated. "Do you want me to apologize a hundred times? Maks made a fucking mistake. He apologized for it. Let's move on, you know?"

She didn't want to move on, and finally my father had had enough.

"Is this about Sandy being offended, or is it about you being humiliated because your stupid friend was talking shit?"

Sandy's mom reported the incident to a friend, who apparently told someone else, who then called and threatened my father. This guy—I don't know how else I can put it without getting in trouble with the libel lawyers—but he was the type like maybe you didn't want to ask too many questions about his business.

Now we were getting death threats for a silly mistake behind the microphone?

My brother overheard the menacing conversation, and while he and my father would normally never share something like that with me, when we hit our bunk beds that night, the truth came out.

"Somebody called Pops and was threatening him," he said.

"What? Over this Sandy thing?"

I couldn't believe it. I leaped out of bed and paced the floor. "Okay," I muttered, more to myself than to Maks. "Okay, we're done."

"What do you mean?" Maks asked. "Who's done?"

"Sandy and I," I said. "We're finished."

In a split second, my reality shifted. This wasn't a girl that I just danced with. Sandy and I were dating, too. But with zero hesitation I decided on the spot that she and I were over.

As far as I was concerned, Sandy's mom preoccupied herself with stroking her own ego, instead of supporting and celebrating her daughter. In my view, as a parent she didn't deserve to have the trophy in her household, didn't deserve the accolades, and most of all didn't deserve our effort.

The next day I headed out to Brooklyn. My parents counseled

against any rash moves. "Are you sure? Don't worry about us. We're fine. You don't have to split with Sandy just for us."

"Dad, are you kidding me?" I said, getting up on my teenage high horse. "I am doing it for you. I'm not going to coexist with somebody who is willing to put your life in danger!"

Keep it moving, I told myself. Always and forever.

I met up with Sandy, and telling her we were breaking up was one of the hardest things I've ever had to do. I remember we were in Brighton Beach outside of her luxury apartment building. I had come out with two of my friends, Eugene and Andrei. They waited across the street, just kind of looking out, because there were really scary people in the Russian immigrant community of Brighton Beach. I felt as though I had to have some backup.

"Listen, Sandy, I love you," I said, one eye on my boys and the other on the front door of her house, in case her father charged out. "I would never want to make you feel bad, and I know you still have to listen to your parents, but the truth is I just can't deal with your mom anymore. It's not right, and it may not be fair . . ."

Then I shrugged my shoulders and pronounced a phrase just then coming into vogue. "But it is what it is."

Though Sandy told me she understood, I might have broken her heart right there. She was kind, sweet, and vulnerable, but strong in her own way. And she actually might have saved a life afterward, because a little birdie informed me that even though emotions still ran high in Brighton Beach against the upstart Chmerkovskiy family, Sandy insisted to her parents that nothing bad should happen to me.

"I'll run away and never talk to you guys ever again," she warned them. At least to her, the situation seemed just that serious, just that intense.

After things settled down somewhat, Sandy's mom called me to plead for her daughter's reinstatement as my partner.

"Come on," she said. "You know I was just joking and that nothing was ever going to happen."

"I'm sorry," I said, a little man who was trying to man up. "It's over."

LIKE A LOT OF PEOPLE WHO PUT THEIR FOOT DOWN, I DIDN'T think about what was going to happen afterward. Having just won the Youth Worlds with Sandy, I was at the peak of my competitive career, except now I no longer had a partner. Blackpool was coming up, and skipping it wasn't an option. I had to find another person to dance with, and I had to do it quickly.

Julianne Hough, one of the best dancers in the world at my age level, might have been a candidate if she hadn't quit competing a year before to concentrate on a potential music career. Even though Julianne was currently (and famously) saying no to ballroom, I still felt there might be a little wiggle room, and maybe I could reach out and convince her to partner with me.

Julianne and her longtime partner Mark Ballas were awesome and incredible, and she had quit kind of suddenly. I had a hunch that you don't break it off at age seventeen with someone like Mark and then never dance again. That's just not the way things happened. Ballroom was like the mob: the only way out was in a casket.

So Julianne was on my radar as someone to fill the void left by Sandy.

A whole day had already passed, and I didn't really have a moment to waste. I turned to my most trusted ally.

"Hey, Maks," I said. "What do you think? I want to dance with Julianne."

"Yeah, great," he said. "Only maybe you forgot, but Julianne's not dancing."

"Maybe she will for me. Let's reach out and see what happens."

It didn't take long for me to find her number. In the meantime I had all these local girls, great dancers who were ranked second in America, or third, fifth, or whatever, and they were hitting me up for a chance to be my partner. I didn't pay anybody apart from Julianne any mind. Why beat around the bush when I knew exactly what I wanted?

In situations like these, one thing that was popular in the ballroom world was holding tryouts. The candidates and I would perform some basic steps, do some choreography together, and then maybe have a coach come in to judge if we were aesthetically a compatible fit, if we harmonized, if we looked good together. I found the whole business loathsome and humiliating for the girl. I didn't like it, and maybe I was wrong, maybe I was overanalyzing, which I always did and always do.

Every time I split up with a partner the situation already had reached the level of the catastrophic, so that it was a very painful process, literally like a divorce. After splitting with Sandy, I was feeling cored out and emotionally exhausted. How was I going to go through yet another heartbreak? And who the fuck did I think I was, to have one girl after another come in and try out, only to have them hear, "No, sorry—next!" These were people's lives I was dealing with. Who was I, the fucking Bachelor?

As far as ballroom couples went, I believed in arranged marriages. Find the person that you want, get in the room together, and say, "Hey, are you into doing this?" To me, "love" was always a verb. Love just didn't magically happen—I had to make it happen. No angel would descend from heaven and present herself as my perfect partner. My job was making the perfect couple, to find a way to love that person, cherish her, and help her shine.

With Sandy, that had been the case, too. She wasn't on my level when we started, but she inspired me, and that was enough. Our mutual effort took care of the rest, and we worked and worked until she was the number one dancer in her age group.

"I'm not going out there, you know, trying out girls like I'm shopping for shoes," I told Maks, tearing into a rant. "I know what I want. I want to dance with Julianne. No offense to anybody, but I don't want to fucking hear from anyone else. I don't want to waste my time, I don't want to waste their time, and I don't want to get their hopes up and then shut them down."

"Well, maybe you should talk to—" he began.

"No one! I don't care. I want to dance with her. I don't care that she quit. I don't care about anything. We're reaching out and we're dancing with Julianne. Boom! That's it!"

"Okay, okay," Maks said, accustomed to seeing me go off in that manner.

I finally called Julianne. "Hey, it's Val."

Everyone knew everyone in the small world of competitive ballroom, so I didn't have to give more than my first name. "Oh, hi! Wow! My God, how are you?"

"You know, I have no idea what you're doing right now," I said. "I don't know where you are with dance and everything, but I'd love to compete with you. I'd love to dance with you."

"You know, Val, I haven't competed in some time, and to be honest I'm pursuing my music right now. I'm in L.A. and actually finishing up an album."

We went back and forth a few times, but Julianne wouldn't budge. She was out of the world of ballroom competition. I was disappointed but tried to put the best face on it. "All right, cool," I mumbled halfheartedly. "Well, you know, it was worth a try. Good luck out there. Keep on killing it. And thanks for taking the call."

I added one more "cool" for flavor and hung up. That was on a Thursday. On Friday, I got a call back from Julianne.

"I've reconsidered and you know, for these last eight months, I've been thinking about ballroom a lot. I definitely miss dancing, and miss competing, and to be honest, all those times I was thinking about it, the only person I could ever see myself coming back to competition with was you."

I was overjoyed. "Whoa! Holy shit! That's awesome!"

"The only thing is, I might need a couple of days before I could fly out," Julianne said. "I could probably be in New Jersey by Monday."

It was coming up on the weekend, so I told her Monday would be fine. Suddenly the recent events in my life made sense. Thanks, Maks. Thanks for taking that microphone and almost getting our father killed and busting up my partnership with Sandy, because now I was going to dance with the one woman in the world who represented everything I wanted in a partner.

Or so I thought.

THROUGHOUT THIS PERIOD MY FATHER AND BROTHER WERE getting bombarded with calls from John Kimmins, president of the World Federation of Ballroom Dancers, the umbrella organization for ballroom dance in America.

"Val absolutely has to do a tryout with Lera," John said. He meant Valeriya Kozharinova, whom everyone called Lera. Here we are, back in the world of Russian nicknames.

I knew Lera. I had actually considered taking her on as a partner before I went with Sandy. I'd had a little crush on Sandy at the time, and though I knew this girl Valeriya was awesome, I'd heard little hints that she could also be very, shall we say, *dramatic*.

Back then I had a friend who danced with her. When we hung out I would see him getting constant texts from Lera: "Where are you? Who're you with?" Calling, texting, reaching out.

"Man, she seems like a little a lot," I remember commenting at the time.

So I went with Sandy and never regretted it. Now I tried politely to put off Mr. Kimmins, sending the message that I had already settled on a partner. There was another side of the triangle: Julianne's brother, Derek, had recently split with his partner, too, and was seriously seeking to dance with Lera.

Kimmins would not take no for an answer. "You've got to have Val take a trial with Valeriya," he told both my parents and my brother, during multiple calls over the course of the weekend.

"Listen, he doesn't want to have tryouts," Maks told Kimmins. "He's not interested in tryouts, doesn't like them, doesn't want them. We have our mind set on somebody and it isn't Lera."

But Maks was working on the other side of the fence, too, trying to convince me. "Look," he said. "This guy just keeps calling. You don't want to piss off the president of the Dance Federation, do you?"

I had recently lost a competition at Blackpool, England, taking second by one mark. Among the thirteen adjudicators that day had been John Kimmins, and he had cast a tie-breaking ballot in the finals.

Going in, I had been ecstatic because it was the first time I had seen an American judge at Blackpool; in the past the judging panel was comprised solely of old British farts who made Len Goodman look like Brad Pitt in his prime. I thought I would have politics working in my favor for once. But Kimmins consistently marked me as second, and his mark was the deciding factor. If he would have given one first place—not five, just one, in a single one of the dances—I would have taken first at Blackpool.

I never placed the blame on him, because I should never have let it get that close. But you expect support from the people who represent the same flag as you. Maybe to him I was just some Russian kid from Brooklyn. Half a year later, I wasn't exactly holding a grudge, because everything happens for a reason, right? But I shut down Kimmins when I talked to Maks.

"I'm not going to listen to that dude," I said to my brother. "I don't give a fuck about who's president of anything. It's not like these guys do me any favors anyway. We've always been free agents, we've been doing our own thing, and it's worked out fine. We're Monaco and he's France. You know what I'm saying?"

Maks did know what I was saying, all right, but he insisted I see Lera. So that Saturday, fresh off committing to a partnership with Julianne Hough the day before, I found myself in the Rising Stars studio, waiting for a woman I knew for certain I was going to turn down. I remember I had all my boys there, because they were all teaching or practicing, but also because once again I felt as though I needed backup.

In came Valeriya. This chick was a fucking character. First of all, her presence. She was sexy and dark haired, with huge eyes and long legs. She looked like a Bond girl, maybe in *From Russia with Love*, only this was more like *From Russia with Lust*. She was the polar opposite of Julianne.

I felt it instantly. Julianne was the girl next door, a Disney heroine, or maybe Jennifer Aniston, while here was Angelina Jolie, straight up. Lera had *presence*, an exotic kind of crazy energy. She was unconventional and clearly over the top, but in the most striking, most incredible, most Greek goddess way possible. She might have acted a little insane, but was insanely beautiful because of it.

As soon as I saw her, my inner voice started mumbling *shit, shit, shit*, knowing that she was going to upend the apple cart. But I played it cool.

"Hi! How are you?"

"*Harasho, vse, normalnya,*" using Russian to answer, which was to me so extra, since she had lived in the States for years by this time. But like I said before, she was a character.

She vaulted off to the changing room, and I looked over at my guys. Their eyes followed her out like she was the sexiest thing they had ever seen. She came back flustered and all over the place, and I was reminded again why I didn't like tryouts, because of the stress they placed on the other person, and on myself.

As she headed onto the dance floor, her shoe strap broke. I immediately took it for an omen. "Okay, God, thank you for the sign. Got you. Good." The decision was going to be easy, then.

But Lera had brought along another pair of shoes.

She was wearing a dress designed by Espen Salberg, who was an ex-dancer, now a legendary coach and teacher. If there was a Mount Rushmore of ballroom dance, Salberg would be right up there. Like any ambitious, restless artist, he was eager to branch out. He got into dance fashion and then started making dresses. His style was totally, aggressively off the hook.

Lera wore that black Salberg dress as though she had been born into it, and she didn't bother with a bra, either. Everything about her was on a higher level of maturity than I was currently enjoying. I was just coming off a competition that was open to everyone under eighteen, and I was a fucking child compared to this woman.

The male brain tends to become a little oxygen-starved at such moments, since all the blood is rushing to another part of the body. "Holy shit" was about the only kind of thought I could entertain. "She is so hot."

My brother stood by the music machine. I had my crew lined up and sitting against the wall, Kiki, Cole, Serge, Eugene, and Teddy, all of them. Lera, her nipples hard and poking through the dress, warmed up her long-ass legs by doing her rumba walks, exhibiting a physical confidence that filled the room. Thank God the boys were all sitting down, because otherwise it would have been a little embarrassing for everybody.

Lera and I started dancing together, and we literally did two basic steps before I was seduced. I was seduced not only by her physical self, but by her energy. She had a different air about her, a subtle quality of movement that wasn't so much athletic as artistic. Again, the way she moved rose to a whole other level of maturity.

She was a woman, not just a talented girl. For the first time in my life, I felt as though I was dancing with an adult.

I understood that in any partnership with Lera there would be a huge potential for me to grow, because I would have to step up and become a man in order to complement this woman, just to be able to stand next to her.

That was it. She won me over. The challenge of it enticed me. I decided I wanted to dance with Lera, starting right at that moment and continuing into the foreseeable future.

We did five steps and an overturn. The thin fabric of her dress moved with her. There was a minor wardrobe malfunction and we stopped abruptly.

"Hey, let me go change," she said.

"Yeah, you should probably do that," I said, practically choking on the words. She left the room, and I turned around and all my boys were sitting there with their mouths open and their thumbs up. I looked over at my brother.

"Maks, what do you think?"

"Bro, I've never seen you be able to create this kind of image before. This is the shit that you're a fan of. When we watch and we like who we watch, *this* is what we like."

I was sold. Lera and I finished the tryout and said our goodbyes.

"Okay, well, see you later?" she said, letting the question trail off.

"Yeah, we'll give you a call," I said, feeling foolish.

"Okay, *ladna harasho*," she said—"okay, cool"—giving me a slight kiss on the cheek as she left.

My brother and I drove home, and I had one word to say to him: "*Blyaaaat.*"

That was a curse word in Russian, one of the most common expressions from Moscow to Odessa and beyond. The literal definition was "whore," but it was a tofu word, taking on the flavor of the context around it, so it could just as well mean "shit," "fuck," or "wow," depending on the speaker's intention.

"What are we gonna do?" I wailed to Maks. *"Blyat, blyat, blyat!* We had this whole plan. It's Saturday, and we've got Julianne flying in on Monday. What the fuck are we gonna do?"

"Bro," Maks said, all sober-like since it wasn't *his* problem, "it is what it is. What do you want to do? Do you want to dance with Lera, or do you want to just go ahead and dance with Julianne?"

I owed Julianne. She had just dropped everything, put off a recording session in Los Angeles to fly to New Jersey and dance with me. I felt like a complete asshole. I had *promised* Julianne. Was I going to let a simple little nip-slip turn my head? That would be a dick move, and I knew it.

Unaware of the drama going down on my end, Julianne's father called my father.

"Hey, this is Bruce Hough," he began crisply. "This partnership idea with your young son and my Julianne? I just want you to understand that I'm totally against it. I don't even know where Saddle Brook, New Jersey, is. If she does end up coming out there, which I'm totally against, she has to stay with a Mormon family somewhere in the area, good people who could introduce her at their temple."

My dad was at a loss. "What? What? First of all, I don't even know whether Mormons exist here in New Jersey. I thought they all were confined to Utah."

At that point in time—at pretty much *any* point in time—my dad had a hundred thousand things to worry about, beyond trying to track down a Mormon family in his immediate vicinity.

"Blyaaaat," he said to himself and hung up the phone.

What was good about Bruce's phone call, I realized when Pops told me about it, was that at least it gave us some sort of excuse for why a partnership with Julianne might not work out. Otherwise we had none, nothing, *nada*. Julianne had just changed all her plans for this thing, and I felt terrible. We felt terrible, the Chmerkovskiy "we"—Maks, Dad, Mom, and myself. We all felt ourselves in the wrong, and that just didn't feel right.

I felt terrible, but I was that type of person—I had tunnel vision and I could not help it. That's my normal MO: I obsess. I don't admire, I don't love, I obsess. When I wanted to dance with Julianne, she totally entered into my head. Then Lera came along and swept all those thoughts clean. All I could think about was the look and feelings that I had when I was dancing with her. That was it. I didn't care about anything else. I never want to second-guess myself. I see what I see. I feel what I feel, and I go for what I want. I don't question it.

We went home, where my dad said, "Listen, you've got to make the call to Julianne."

My brother said, "Just man up. It's not the end of the fucking world. Just talk to her."

My mother chimed in: "Call her, Valya."

In the meantime, Valeriya was also under the gun herself. I heard a rumor that Shirley Ballas, the mother of Julianne's former partner, Mark, was pressuring Lera to come to England and try out with Derek, who was Shirley's student and like a son to her.

Along with her husband Corky, Shirley was a major power in the ballroom world, the self-styled "Queen of Latin." She and Corky had not only raised Mark and their whole family of other champions, but also mentored the Houghs, both Derek and Julianne.

Shirley wanted Lera for Derek, and what Shirley wanted in ballroom she usually got. Lera texted me, her words seeming to come out breathless from a lack of commas. "What is the prospect here because I need to figure out what I'm doing because I don't want to go to England I want to dance with you but I need to know this—*pazhallusta* [please]!"

"Well, first you didn't want to piss John Kimmins off," Maks said, laughing off my predicament. "Now you're going to piss Shirley Ballas off. Good luck with your results next year, buddy."

I felt like I was James Dean in *Rebel Without a Cause*. "You're tearing me apart!"

I was stuck. It was now Saturday night. I had just finished a semester at school, so we had plans to celebrate. My brother and I were in the car, heading out for the night, and he would not let up.

"This is dumb. You'll have plenty of Saturday nights in your life. Meantime, Julianne's flying in Monday morning. You've got to get on the phone and tell her you're calling it off."

"I can't," I said pathetically. "I just had a conversation with her about flying out here and how, like, we were going to put her up and take care of everything. I can't call her now and tell her, 'Hey, by the way, all that shit I promised you? None of that is happening because we're not dancing with you.'"

I turned to Maks with a big-eyed kid brother look that had worked with him when I was young. "Will you call her?"

He exploded. "No! I can't fucking call her. It's your mess, you clean it up."

"Please, bro, will you? I really can't do it."

"Shut up. Just make the call. You're seriously pissing me off."

I sank back in the car seat. "Okay, okay, I'll call. But listen, let's pick up our boys first, okay?"

As always, I needed backup to inject a little steel in my spine. We were on our way to collect Eugene and Andre at work, and when we got there, I left Maks in the car while I went in to fetch the boys. I found them hanging out in a stairwell, the smell of weed strong and potent.

"Want some?" Eugene asked, offering the joint to me.

"Are you kidding?" I was stressed out and needed a break from reality.

When we got back to Maks, waiting in the car, he knew instantly we were all high as apple pie.

"Bro, what the fuck?" he asked, clearly disgusted.

"Listen," I babbled. "I'm in no position to call. You have to."

I admit, I was a coward about it. My brother was the one who ended up getting on the phone and breaking a girl's heart.

"Hey, listen, Julianne," Maks said smoothly, "we decided to go in a different direction and we're sorry and *blah blah blah*." I tuned his actual words out, unable to listen.

Julianne was indeed upset, but what was there to be said? "Okay, cool," she sighed, practical and gracious as ever. Then, to be fair, I did end up speaking with her the next day, when my brain got unscrambled and I was able to apologize like a human being.

Choosing Lera as a partner wound up being the biggest favor I could ever do for Julianne. Yes, she might have been heartbroken because of all my foolishness. She never did return to ballroom competition, with me or with anyone else. But a short year later a certain reality TV show about ballroom dancing came along, and with that a young star was born named Julianne Hough. She ended up doing the show, released her amazing country albums, and became a huge Hollywood star.

If it hadn't been for a single little innocent nip-slip, who knows? Julianne and I might be married right now, or dancing and competing as partners. It's crazy how the world works. Sometimes the things that don't happen have the biggest impact on your life—not the things that do happen.

I look back and marvel about Maks and me and Julianne and Mark and Derek, the multiplying connections we all have, originally arising from the limited world of ballroom, but now magnified by the wide world of television. Our relationships stem from a series of small, mostly unknown episodes, but, man, do we go back.

"It's a small world," said the comedian Steven Wright, "but I wouldn't want to paint it."

At the time, the whole business with Julianne and Lera was fairly unbearable, though in hindsight it makes me laugh. I just hope all my future problems turn out so well for everyone.

THE UKRAINIAN BACHELOR

I didn't go with them, but my brother and dad returned to Odessa in 2007, visiting the old hometown. It might have been a mistake. The city looked terrible, they reported, its shit gone gray and dreary. My father and Maks found the old estate house with the courtyard, and I think my dad might have shed a tear about how rundown the place was, how there was little upkeep, how the building appeared to be somehow sinking back into the earth.

As much as his heart still felt connected to Ukraine, my father saw the visit as a sad confirmation that he had done the right thing for his kids. Maybe we were all delusional about what our surroundings looked like when Maks and I were little. Or maybe the old homestead struck my brother and father as shabby because of how we now lived in America, which had such a different environment and different style of energy.

The separation between Ukraine and the States showed itself not merely in the physical things, but also in a mentality among the residents, a vibe in the air. This is not to say that our Ukrainian life was hard and our American life has been easy. Our lives in the States have never been easy, but as poor as we were at first, at least moving to the States had turned out to be worth the discomfort.

The lack of ease was justified. You've got to pay your dues to live in this amazing beauty of a country. Hard work is worthwhile because it pays off. In Ukraine, nothing paid off. Hard work was just . . . hard work.

In America you could have goals and make progress. Everything seems possible. But back home (I still catch myself saying "home" for Ukraine, when really I know in my heart that America is my home) there was this depressing, defeated attitude. What exactly am I paying my dues for? Oh, I remember now! I've got to pay my dues to get the hell out of this country!

I've returned to Ukraine only a few times in my adult life, but have never yet gone back to Odessa. If only because my grandfather was buried there, I know that at some point in the future I'll make the pilgrimage. It's as if I'm saving up the experience for when my days and ways quiet down a bit, when I possess the emotional balance to make the trip meaningful.

I had a near miss with my old hometown in 2009, when I spent some time in Kiev, the capital of Ukraine, three hundred miles to the north of Odessa. Typical for that period of my life, I was at a ballroom dance competition when the opportunity arose to go to Kiev, and since the competition was being held in Moscow, I was at least in the same time zone.

I got a call from my brother. "Hey, yo, can you do me a favor?" Maks asked.

The producers of the Ukrainian version of the hit reality show *The Bachelor* had contacted him, he said. Maks's first impulse was to turn them down flat.

"It's a crazy idea," he told me. "I don't think I want to do it."

The producers heard that I was in Moscow, and suggested I might act as my brother's scout in Kiev.

"Yo, they'll fly you down there," Maks said. "Just meet with them, give me the overall scope of things, and tell me what you think."

I was there for two days, during which the producers wined and dined me to within an inch of my life. If you've ever experienced Ukrainian hospitality, and can recall the fog of toasts and banqueting, you know what I mean. My hosts were execs from the STB network, which operated Ukraine's most popular commercial channel. They had licensed the rights to *The Bachelor* concept from Warner Bros., creating what they called *Holostyak*, Russian for "bachelor."

As soon as I arrived, I understood immediately what a big deal the show would be. For the time and place, the budget was huge, more than had been spent on any series previously. I could see that the entire network was behind the show, which had the potential of being a game changer in the limited world of Ukrainian television. I took meetings with execs, who were all really jazzed about the project. They had brought in consultants from all over the world. They would devote the resources, they assured me, to make the program look sleek and professional.

Then I visited the TV studio where the show would be shot. I remember my conversation with Maks from that day.

"Hey, bro," I started out, giving him our traditional greeting. "You know when kids pretend to be an astronaut, and they use a cardboard box for a spaceship?"

"Yeah?" he asked, wondering what I was getting at.

"Well, the soundstage where *Dancing with the Stars* is shot, that's like fucking NASA. This place in Kiev, the TV studio here is like the cardboard box."

The infrastructure wasn't even worthy of being in the same conversation, it was so poor. But I noticed something else, too, on that visit. All the executive producers at the network were young, in their midtwenties, but when they opened their mouths they sounded as if they were eighty years old. I met a few of the girls they were considering casting on the show, and they came off as mature beyond their years, too. A young woman would speak to me in Russian, and even if I didn't follow everything that she was saying, I could see depth in her eyes and detect a wisdom in her words. It felt crazy to me, because obviously they were young, but it helped me to understand that people grew up fast in Eastern Europe.

This was before civil war kicked the stuffing out of much of the country, but in some ways, even back then Ukraine felt as though it had slipped down from second world status to border-line third world. I noticed that the billboards featured not celebrities but rather large pictures of ugly politicians. On the other hand, big American stars like George Clooney were featured all the time, doing product endorsements on TV commercials translated into Russian. Seeing George do it gave me an idea, providing the logic for encouraging Maks to participate in the Ukrainian *Bachelor.*

"Listen, you'll be a superstar here," I told my brother. "Unlike Clooney you can speak Russian, and they won't even have to translate you. We're talking about a financial opportunity *and* an opportunity to increase your visibility in a whole different market. [Yes, we really do talk like that to each other occasionally.] It's far enough from America that no one back there will give a fuck if it's a fail. And even if it turns out not to be the best look for you, you're still appearing on far and away the biggest TV show in the country."

Maks didn't even have to say anything for me to summon up the cynical expression that was probably crossing his face at that moment. I shifted my argument into overdrive.

"You're handsome as fuck! You *are* the bachelor, dude! What better storyline could there be? Here comes a son of the great Ukrainian nation, who went to America and found fortune and fame but couldn't find love. Now the only love that he wants, the someone he dreams and yearns for, is a Ukrainian princess. He wants to make her his international queen."

Talk about a fairy tale. How could anyone say no to that? In the end, I convinced him. He did the show and blew up as big as it was humanly possible to blow big in Ukraine, a humongous star, Prince Charming, a local boy made good. The show did smashingly well, too, at one point managing the feat of beating out a broadcast of a EuroCup game, Ukraine versus France, the first time any Ukrainian show had received higher ratings than soccer.

A couple of times, I flew out to see Maks on the set of Ukraine *Bachelor*. My first impression was that he spoke Russian much better than me. My mind was blown seeing him with the lineup of twenty-five Eastern European women. They appeared to me to be hard women ready to eat my poor brother alive. I didn't think I would have liked to meet any one of them in a dark alley, much less the whole platoon. All I could do was mentally wish him the best of luck.

The *Holostyak* producers seemed to be willing to spend money, and the show filmed all over the world, in the Canary Islands, in Paris, and in Italy. There were scenes with Maks arriving to pick up a girl for a date in a vintage 1956 Rolls-Royce Silver Cloud.

My brother had plenty of insecurities about women, but he also possessed a simplicity and honesty on the direct opposite end of the romantic spectrum from the fake figure presented by *The Bachelor*, which practically shouts "douchebag." *Hey! I want to find love on television as millions of people watch!* Let me go on TV and pick the love of my life from a group of twenty-five women! And let's all pretend that this whole business is the most natural thing in the world!

Plus Maks was selling the concept to a totally flat-footed society. America loves *The Bachelor* because most people get the joke. The U.S. audience watches to get away from everyday woes and laugh and smile and not take things too seriously. Eastern Europeans know how to take things just one way, and that's extremely seriously. They're the people at the party who don't get the joke.

Maks won over maybe eighty percent of the audience, with the other twenty percent hating him out of pure spite. The show painted my brother as a super-successful entrepreneur and celebrity superstar from America, rolling up to luxury venues in luxury cars. You think Hollywood is the land of make-believe, but this was a whole different kind of fairy tale. Maks looked good in the role of the young prince, which not everybody in the world can pull off. Flying in a private jet, stepping out onto the tarmac—you try that sometime, and see if you can manage not to look like an ass.

At the same time Maks put across his essentially humble nature, emphasizing total respect for the women involved. Success matched with humility was a killer combination, wholly novel in Ukraine, where financial security was unfortunately synonymous with a certain attitude of entitlement. *Fuck everybody! You know who I am? Outta my way—I've got money!* In the United States there can be a similar attitude, but it's never as flagrant as in Eastern Europe.

Maks was something new under the Ukrainian sun, a rich kid (at least on TV) who was also approachable, respectful, and not a total asshole. The combination made him a star among men and women both.

Until the finale. Then Maks's choice came down to two girls. One was like a version of Miss Ukraine, super beautiful, charming, and gushingly in love, to the point of being borderline embarrassing when expressing her emotions. The second finalist was a much chillier bitch, a little thinner, a little hotter, a little more put together.

The options were laid out clearly, the Western-style City Chick versus the All-Ukrainian girl. It wasn't a reality TV show anymore. *Holostyak* had become a test of the national character.

Maks went with Sasha, the City Chick, and the country immediately exploded.

You cannot imagine the extremity of the reaction. Maks gave me the numbers, which I don't know if I can believe: Out of a population of forty-five million, twenty-three million watched the show, with the remaining twenty-two million not connected to electricity. On Google's trending topics in Ukraine, *Holostyak* ranked number one. It *mattered* to folks.

This was in the aftermath of the 2004–2005 Orange Revolution in the country, when confrontation loomed between Ukraine and Mother Russia. But forget about that boring political stuff, let's talk about Maks and Sasha!

People were hugely invested in the results and reacted to the outcome with rage in their minds and spittle on their lips. *What a fucking piece of shit that Maksim Chmerkovskiy is! What an idiot! Sasha is gonna play him, doesn't he see that?*

According to the concept of *The Bachelor*, Sasha was the supposed love of Maks's life. She lasted with my brother for all of two days.

He called me with his report. "We landed at LAX and she wasn't interested in her surroundings at all, never asked me to help her get a job or figure out how she was going to make her way in Los Angeles. She was like, 'Hey, I want to get a pair of shoes I really like. Can I get your credit card?' Of course like a softie I gave her my credit card and pointed her to Rodeo Drive. But I didn't think that should have been the first thing coming out of her mouth, you know?"

So the relationship came to an abrupt end. In the aftermath, Maks revealed his strategy to me, which was actually pretty smart. "Look, I knew that any relationship that began on *The Bachelor* probably wouldn't last. I figured it would be a lot easier for the public over there to buy the fact that me and this girl Sasha didn't work out. They would expect that. But the public would go berserk if me and Miss Ukraine didn't get married and live happily ever after."

The logic made sense to me—for once my brother had an actual logical point. Take the loss now to position himself to win later.

Season 12 of *Dancing with the Stars* aired live in the States just as *Holostyak* was being broadcast on STB in Ukraine. Maks killed it on *Dancing with the Stars* that season, pairing with actress Kirstie Alley and finishing as runner-up, his best showing up until that point. The show peaked, too, with one episode watched by over thirty million people, a record.

As a kind of anticlimax, my superstar brother was required by contract to return to Kiev and make an appearance on a last, follow-up episode of *Holostyak*.

"You want to come with me?" he asked. It was characteristic of the Chmerkovskiy brothers to enlist backup when entering dicey situations. Plus I still owed him for having my back during the Julianne disaster.

We flew into Kiev to be met with the biggest media cluster-fuck I've ever encountered. I couldn't believe it. We collected our baggage, stepped out the airport door, and ran into a solid wall of cameras. Later on I would enjoy my fair share of celebrity, and experienced emerging from a theater, say, to find tons of scream-ing fans greeting me. This was on a whole different level, this was David Beckham meets Barack Obama meets the resurrection of the living Elvis.

The Bachelor returns . . . to be greeted by utter pandemonium!

When it came to fashion, swagger, and demeanor, Maks and I were the real American deal. Ukraine had seen modern Ameri-can style before, of course, but mostly secondhand, on television. And the country had also seen its share of Russian style, which was sort of a bootleg American vibe crossed with vodka-infused tackiness.

What Ukraine hadn't seen was us. In Maks the country saw the epitome of cool, someone they could idolize. Without too much patting ourselves on the back, I have to say we came off as from Brooklyn, successfully assimilated, and authentically American all the way.

My brother did the follow-up show and had me come on as a guest. The shooting day stretched to twelve hours, filming in an unair-conditioned room somewhere in the Ukrainian boondocks, with no union rules and no lunch breaks. It was already evening when we finally finished up, just in time to hit the after-party.

My brother and I and one of the *Holostyak* producers rode to the nightclub and climbed out of the limo. Immediately we were gang rushed by a horde of female fans. I remember the moment well, with them tottering toward us on stiletto heels, managing to look silly and dangerous at the same time.

"Omigod, omigod," they called out. "Can we have a picture?"

People started to pour out from the front doors of the club. In an instant, the scene spiraled out of control. One of the female fans wrapped herself around my brother, something like a tongue around a lollipop. In the background I saw a big dude rumble forward, summoned from inside by the bouncers. He turned out to be the tongue's boyfriend.

As if it were going down in cinematic slow-motion, I witnessed the confrontation happen. The boyfriend steamed up to Maks, said, "I know you" in Russian, then—*boom!*—punched my brother in the face.

I reacted on pure impulse, before I could think. *Bam!* I slugged the dude with a right hook I'd been perfecting in Brooklyn boxing gyms since I was a teenager. He crumpled to the ground.

By the time my brother recovered and turned around, his assailant was already laid out, with me on top of him. My adrenaline spiked into the stratosphere and the hand I had punched him with was already swelling up like a balloon. I didn't want to continue the battle, because instinct told me to put a quick end to the whole situation. The fight had gone down like nothing in the movies. Nobody won.

"Don't hit him again," Maks hissed.

Then the cameras swooped in, with the Kiev equivalent of paparazzi exploding flashbulbs in our faces. The next day, a picture of me pinning the boyfriend down was splashed all over the

Ukrainian newspapers. The caption read, "The Chmerkovskiy brothers, just over from America for a day, in a brawl."

In the spirit of my habitual Val-ian overanalysis, I'd say my relationship with Maks shifted right there, at least in my own mind. *Now we're even*, I remember thinking. You've looked out for me and had my back my whole life. Now, when the shit hit the fan, I did not hesitate, I did not think twice. It was as if I was at last ready to say to Maks, "Yo, I'm never going to stop caring about you or loving you or doing things for you, but it will never again come from a place of owing you, or of 'look how much my brother's done for me.' Now I've done just as much for you as you've done for me."

And that was a proud moment.

I grew up around people who were hustling all the time to provide for me, and I felt an overwhelming urge to return the favor, to give back as good as I had received. Maks had been such an immense force in my life. I was a product of his teaching, so my return on his investment in me was my winning dance competitions. I might have been the racehorse, but I wouldn't have a stable, I wouldn't have food, I wouldn't have anything if it weren't for his teaching.

Somewhere in my brain I had formulated the definition of the alpha man as someone who paid his debt to whoever helped him along on the road of life. If he can't pay them back personally, he pays it forward in his attitude toward others. I always felt the impulse to even up the scales.

That single episode, with me coming in and protecting Maks for a change, might have been the moment when he finally understood an essential truth. He could hear himself say the same words that I have always had running through my own mind: *I have a brother who would go to the mat for me, I have a brother who's looking out for me, I have a brother who will be there.*

Put it on my tab, Maks.

LEAVING

I can nail down the exact moment it happened, when I decided to leave the competitive dance world, where for over a decade I had found my home, my inspiration, and really my whole reason for being. I was in Blackpool, England, in 2011, for the British Open Latin Dance Championship, right in the middle of a samba. The field had been winnowed from hundreds down to the top forty-eight, with my partner Daria "Dasha" Chesnokova and me cruising toward the finals.

We had danced a couple of rounds now, and I was getting into my groove. At that point in my career, I was no longer the dark horse, the up-and-comer. Instead, I was a recognized favorite. The scorekeepers—called "scrutineers"—had tallied the points for each round, and the standings were already clear.

In a huge competition such as Blackpool, the judges didn't necessarily assess every single couple out on the floor. How could they? Within the space of a few minutes, it would be impossible to focus on every dancer. No, what happened was the team of judges understood which favorites were likely to pass through to the next round. Dasha and I knew that when the round of forty-eight couples was judged and the number of couples halved to the top twenty-four, we would be among those still standing.

I was dancing and we were killing it. In the samba, a moving dance, dancers travel counterclockwise and the traffic on the floor just flows. By contrast, the paso doble is more of a march, while the cha-cha and the jive are more stationary—we would choose our position and remain in a fairly limited area.

In movement dances like the samba or the waltz the dancers are like the cars in a NASCAR race, with couples constantly maneuvering around in a crowd. We were on the inside track and covered up, hidden from the judges and spectators by a screen of other dancers. No one except the other dancers could really see us, but it didn't matter, because Dasha and I had probably been marked as favorites before we even started dancing.

But then my pride kicked in. Favorite or not, I didn't want to be lost in the crowd. I wanted to connect to the audience and feel the inspiration flow from them to me. I'd been in the same position before, traffic-wise. The situation can lend an airless feeling to the proceedings. If I wasn't creating beautiful art for the audience to see and the judges to mark, why was I there?

I was dancing a promenade run into a volta, another volta and then a slow volta, whereby my partner and I would wind up facing each other. And during that precise combination I remember thinking "promenade run," and then, immediately, came a second thought. "What the fuck am I doing?" That was the question posed in my mind. "What is this movement and why am I doing it?" It suddenly occurred to me that I had been performing the same movement for more than fifteen years, fine tuning this same step, and beyond that dancing the same five Latin dances, in the same order, chachasambarumbapasodoblejive.

It was odd and at the same time meaningful to me that I would manage to have a conversation with myself while in the middle of a competition. It meant that I wasn't in the moment, wasn't connect-

ing with my partner, and wasn't connected to the opportunity—
the Blackpool Dance Festival! The dance world's most celebrated
event! In the grandest terms, I wasn't connecting to the universe. I
was only connecting with myself.

"What are you doing?" my interior voice asked. "Why are you
doing this again? Why?"

The question "Why?" hung in my mind and wouldn't go away.

My answer? "I'm pursuing this for reasons of pride only."

Then my pride spoke up. "Yo, we're good."

It sounded crazy but that was how it played out in my head.

"We're good here," said pride. "I'm so proud of you." At that
moment pride had taken on a Mister Rogers kind of tone.

"But you've got this other shit to do. You know, go do it, bro!
Stop trying to satisfy me, because I'm proud of you. You've had a
long career, nineteen years all told, almost two decades."

My mind flashed back through my partners, my friends, my
teachers, my mentors, my coaches, Moms and Pops and Maks
and everyone else, the lessons, the competitions, Blackpool, Palm
Beach, Moscow, Italy. I was nothing but a dead-broke dancer. How
could I have hit all these wonderful places? Some wealthy dude I'd
run into would be nattering on about spending time in Capri, and
I could say, "Oh, yeah, dope, I've spent time in Ischia." What? How
did you possibly manage that?

During my competitive career I always kept three responsibilities firmly in mind: to myself, to others, and to the art of dancing
itself. That was my holy trinity. I never wanted to be a part of something where I wasn't giving my everything to all three. If I didn't
take care of my responsibility to myself, then I was destined to fail
with the other two. And at that precise moment during the samba
at Blackpool, I knew I wasn't being true to number one. It was the
oxygen mask situation on an airplane: be sure to put your own
mask on before you try to help anyone else. You can't do anyone
any good if you pass out.

For the first time in my entire life, I had been taking dance for granted. I knew I would be marked to advance to the next round, so I was just going through the motions. But without heart, my dance was empty. It was nothing.

Finally, my pride gave me permission to let go.

All this happened in a frozen second, in the midst of that one volta.

Dasha and I took third at Blackpool that year. But I thought that we should have been fifth, and the guy who was twelfth should have been third, and the couple who was first should have been thirteenth. But I understood that wasn't how things worked. "Don't hate the player, hate the game." As I left Blackpool I remember feeling such love and affection for every single person on the floor, really for everyone in the world of competitive dance, doubling down on the emotion because I knew I would be leaving them.

A thousand thoughts whirled around in my head. I was writing a lot of rap and poetry at the time, and I had fantasies of pouring all my energies into a music career. I really thought I could do it, and I still think I could—I just, um, haven't found my sound yet. Or maybe I'll make one last desperation run at a career in the NBA . . .

And if I missed competitive dance? I hadn't burned any bridges or slammed shut any doors. I was younger than most of the current champions. I could take off for three years and still come back in my prime. Right at the moment, though, I simply didn't want to haul that train anymore.

I texted Maks. "Bro, I think I'm done competing."

My dear brother, bless his heart. I had told him the same thing many times, six years before, five years, three years, out of frustration with this or that situation, and he had always responded with encouragement to keep at it. Well, this time lo and behold Maks replied simply and differently.

"Bro, it's about time."

The *Dancing with the Stars* folks had been contacting me off and on over the years, peppering me with invitations, either through Maks or face-to-face whenever I was in L.A., wanting me to join the show. With my focus on the competition world, I always politely put them off. The show was Maks's thing, I thought. My thing was Blackpool, the German Open, international champion-ships. Of course, since my brother had been my first and by far my most influential teacher, my thing was Maks's thing, too. I was proof positive of his genius as a mentor.

"Do you think they're still interested in me at *DWTS*?" I texted.

"I dunno," he texted back. "Let me text them and ask."

"*Text* them??!!!"

"Okay, all right, let me call them."

I still had to break the news to my partner. We were already committed to a competition in Shenzhen, China, outside of Hong Kong. I couldn't refuse to go to that, but otherwise, I had to tell her we were finished.

The whole business was complicated by the fact that my family had basically rescued Dasha from a shitty, going-nowhere situa-tion in Ukraine. I had reached out and asked her to dance as my partner, and the next day she was on a plane to the States. It was as if she jumped from high school and got drafted straight into the NBA. Plus she quite literally found a new home with us, moving in with my parents in New Jersey. Now our run was ending.

"Dasha, I think I'm done competing," I said. "I think China's going to be it."

She was heartbroken. She started crying. Her life as a competi-tive dancer was just beginning, but her first thought wasn't even about that. She needed parents. She needed family.

"Can I still live with you guys?"

"Jesus, of course, yes!" I said, heartbroken myself by the ques-tion. I stumbled trying to reassure her, but the words tumbled out. "Yes, yes, you are not— You know, this isn't a breakup. We don't have a business arrangement, okay? We have a people arrangement. We're still people and we love you and will still love you and no way we're ever going to turn our backs on you."

The tears kept coming. *Sniffle, sniffle, weep, weep.* Much more of this and I was going to start crying, too.

"Competing together or not, I still want to see you succeed."

Sniffle, sniffle.

"Hey, do you want to maybe come with me to *Dancing with the Stars*? Maybe you want to do that?" Dasha's English wasn't that good, so the producers probably weren't going to consider her for a position as a pro and give her a celebrity partner, but there was always the show's dance troupe. And she did later join the show as a troupe dancer, which kind of put a Band-Aid on the wound of me leaving her as a partner.

Eventually, Dasha also went back to competition. But she lived with my parents in Jersey for about a year and a half after that, until she got her bearings and was ready to make a go of it on her own. She went on to be ranked number two in the world.

Beyond my partner, I still had one more person to tell of my decision to leave competition, and this was a conversation I dreaded most of all. I had to inform my dad.

I went to him like a man and we had something of a heart-to-heart about it. By the expression on his face I could read the heart-break he was feeling. More than anyone else, even more than Maks or my mother, my father lived that whole competition life through me. He had been at my side throughout. The image of him proudly waving the Stars and Stripes at the 2001 Junior Worlds remained fresh in my mind.

The conversation we had marked the beginning of a transformation in our relationship. It was the Chmerkovskiy family equivalent of the moment many kids have at eighteen or nineteen, when they leave the nest to head off to college. Just like most parents in that situation, my dad was sad and proud at the same time.

"Well," he said, "finally you're sticking up for yourself." At that moment, I loved his response more than anything in the world. It was as if his words made me realize the door of the cage had been left open and I was free to fly.

Ashley Edens and Joe Sungkur, two producers on *Dancing with the Stars*, called me, both of them on the phone at once.

"We'd love to have you!" Ashley said. In Hollywood everyone talks in exclamation points.

"It'll be an incredible season!" Joe added.

"Cool!" I said. Now I was doing it, too. "When do I come in?"

"In August—August eighteenth," they replied, talking over each other.

My whole life has been an audition. But this time I didn't have to try out or show my chops or impress the gatekeepers. I didn't have to find an agent. I didn't hire a manager. I didn't even have to kiss too much ass. My victories on the ballroom circuit spoke for me.

I was twenty-five, and I was going to Hollywood.

LEAVING THE FIELD OF COMPETITION USUALLY INVOLVES AN announcement at a dancer's final event, an opportunity to be feted, petted, and praised. You get on the mic and say your thank-yous. My last competition was off the usual circuit, in China, so any sort of formal leave-taking wasn't in the cards. Dasha and I won and were invited to perform the last unjudged "honor dance" that was traditionally awarded to champions.

I danced my final dance without anybody in the audience realizing that it was my final dance. It was a special moment. The only ones present who understood what was happening were three couples in the competition who were my friends. They knew, and they were all bawling.

Still, the occasion wasn't the ceremonial public goodbye that retiring dancers customarily made. Instead, that summer I sent a semiofficial letter to *DanceBeat* magazine, then the leading media outlet for the ballroom world. I needed closure. I wasn't just going to bounce and not say my thank-yous.

I tried to use the announcement as a lever for change in the world of ballroom competition, which was then tangled in bureaucracy and red tape. As in boxing, where there are no undisputed champions anymore, with separate belts awarded by the WBO, WBA, WBC, and IBF, ballroom had split into competing federations. I bemoaned the impact the split had upon the lives of dancers.

I emphasized how hard it was to be a ballroom dancer on the competition circuit. For years, my inspiration arose from the community, from the opportunity to be able to compete against the best in the world. None of us were doing it for the money, because there wasn't any. Now with the flurry of sanctions and the competing organizations, the only incentive we ever had was being diminished. A stupid bureaucratic clause meant that I could not compete against Nino Langella, for example. My letter was a plea from the ranks.

Within the small, cloistered community of ballroom dancing, the news broke huge and the buzz was crazy. I fielded dozens of calls from all over the world. A few dance blogs that were popping at the time reposted the letter, and suddenly it was all over the internet, translated into six languages. It was as though I had offered myself up as a martyr to the cause—the fight to make life easier for the poor, beleaguered dancers competing in the thankless, moneyless competition world. The activist call for change actually ignited a movement, resulting in a realignment of the competitive circuit.

In the final paragraph, I sounded a valedictory note:

I am who I am because of dance, music, and self-expression. I will continue on my journey of self-enlightenment through dance, music, and self-expression, but it will be through different avenues. I will forever champion the principles I

*acquired through the world of Ballroom Dancing. I will
forever be grateful for the memories I was so fortunate to
have. I walk away from competition a humbled man, a
grateful man, but most importantly an inspired man. I am
inspired to reach new heights and pinnacles in my future
endeavors; however, I will never forget the world that raised
me and shaped me into the man I am today.*

Nuff said.

IN AUGUST 2011, I MOVED INTO A RENTED HOUSE IN THE HILLS
of West Hollywood, sharing it with Maks, Dasha, and Teddy Volynets, Jhanna's kid, who was also a member of the *Dancing with the
Stars* troupe for Season 13. We lived just a couple of blocks up from
the Viper Room, Whisky a Go Go, and the rest of the clubs that
made Sunset Strip the most crowded stretch of crazy in L.A. I didn't
"go Hollywood" so much as I jammed locally on the Strip. For a
hot second that summer, I seized the opportunity to be a rock star.

Los Angeles has the most beautiful people in the world, at least
aesthetically. Intellectually, not always. They're like the weather:
gorgeous and warm and just a tad bit boring. Every once in a while
I would feel myself missing the street life in Brooklyn, remembering
the lines from one of Neil Simon's plays: "When it's 100 degrees
in New York, it's 72 in Los Angeles. When it's 30 degrees in New
York, in Los Angeles it's still 72. However, there are 6 million interesting people in New York, and only 72 in Los Angeles."

When there was fantasy involved, reality got suspended. People
in L.A. were caught up in a dream world. There was nothing more
addicting than the Hollywood fantasy, because in a fantasy anything
was possible. During those first days in Los Angeles I indulged in
frantic waves of partying, letting myself go because I was experiencing such a sense of release on leaving the world of competition.

But in the back of my mind I heard a whisper. *Don't make the fantasy your whole world.* Stay present. Stay focused. I was on a mission. I had just made a big statement, retiring from competition and presenting the ballroom world with all my righteous shit in the *DanceBeat* letter. Now it was time to put my money where my mouth was. Okay, okay, big shot with the big ideas. You've sold us all on your big-deal vision. Now let's see how it plays out.

When the time came, I brushed the party cobwebs from my brain and headed down the hill to a soundstage on Beverly Boulevard, where I would take my place as a professional dancer on *Dancing with the Stars*.

PART 5

A JOURNEY IN
DANCE

TWO PAIR

Eleven seasons in as a professional dancer, now I was finally going into *Dancing with the Stars* not as a rookie, not as a newbie. After my triumph with Rumer, I was the reigning champion, a status I never had before. For my partner first meeting on Season 21, I drove north out of L.A. to the fancy suburb of Calabasas. The casting director gave me an address, but of course didn't inform me whose house I was headed toward. The gated community featured yellow hillsides of parched grass and a collection of huge, very fancy residences.

It was a neighborhood I had no business being in, but I felt not too out of place because I was driving a BMW 6 Series. Maks had challenged me to buy it.

"I don't need anything like that, bro," I told him, as we scoped out the awesome vehicle online.

"Don't be such a little bitch," he said. "You've got the money now, go ahead and get something of value. You'd rather be hauling your ass around in an economy compact?"

In the back of my mind, the answer was a resounding yes, but I caved in anyway. I have to say I didn't get much more pleasure from driving a luxury vehicle than I did from the clunker Hondas and Fords that I had owned in the past. The car mania of California, where it was really important to people what car you drove, was totally lost on me.

I passed Kim Kardashian's house, one of them, anyway, Dr. Dre's place, then a series of monster real-deal mansions that looked like fortresses. At the very top of one of the hills was the fanciest house in the community, just a beautiful, beautiful home.

But I was only the help come to call, so I wasn't ushered into the main house. Instead, I was directed to one of the two guesthouses on the property, which were large residences on their own terms. There I met Tamar Braxton, the singer, TV personality, actress—a one-woman force of nature, vibrant, loud, and dynamic. She was the kind of person who becomes your friend as soon as you shake her hand.

We hit it off immediately, starting a comfortable, back-and-forth banter that stuck with us the whole time we were together. She called me "Pal." Maybe she misheard my name. She repeated personal catchphrases such as, "You tried it! You tried it!" She quickly realized that I wasn't the ballroom-dancing white boy she had expected. She found out that I had more soul and more hip-hop in me than her little privileged ass had ever experienced on the planet. But she's still fucking Tamar Braxton, she's still the youngest sibling of the fabulous Braxton family, and that's where she had it all over me.

She was also stretched way too thin. I kept a mental tab as we spoke, and I counted five gigs she was juggling in addition to *Dancing with the Stars*: hosting a Fox network talk show called *The Real*; starring in a reality show about her personal life, *Tamar & Vince;* promoting a new album, *Calling All Lovers;* releasing another album, of Christmas-themed songs, that she was doing with her sisters, Toni, Traci, Trina, and Towanda; plus random singles, music videos, and guest appearances. I felt dizzy trying to keep track of it all.

She'd been on the show-business map a long time, and I don't think she'd ever been broke. But she met her match in me and we had the best time that season. Odd couple that we were, on some deep-down level we were identical twins. She had a lot of potential, a lot of talent, a lot of sass, and she was a star, which meant she could carry off pretty much any performance and make it look effortless. Every time we got together she gave me everything she had.

Unfortunately, there were times when she just didn't have anything left to give. Our schedule was insane even by early twenty-first-century standards, when multitasking turned crazy. She was promoting singles from her new album, and I was always flying all over the country to meet her at this venue or that. The rehearsal process was difficult for her, and we never had enough time. We had to catch dance sessions when we could, in hotel lobbies, on hallway carpets (like dancing in mud when compared to parquet), or green rooms of concert halls. In the course of working with her I became a professional lobby rehearser.

In a car, a warning light tells you that you need gas. You ignore it and the gauge falls down to empty, but you still ignore it and ride on fumes for another ten miles. Sooner or later, though, there's going to be nothing left in the tank. Tamar's low-gas warning light had been on for a long time.

During our *Dancing with the Stars* appearances, we had a series of great moments. The highlight of the season came in week six, when we scored a perfect 30 on a Janet Jackson routine centered around the album *Rhythm Nation*. Since Janet was Tamar's idol in a lot of ways, the tribute had a deeply personal meaning for her.

Tamar was definitely one of the more vocal contestants on the show. I was able to handle it, but I'm not sure the audience could.

A lot of times, people react to strong characters with their strong, outspoken comments, especially on social media.

We made the quarterfinals on the show, then flew to Vegas, where Tamar had a concert. Next she went to Atlanta, and I met her there. She was clearly exhausted when we headed to the set the following Monday and taped from six in the morning until eleven that night. We finished our dance early at the dress rehearsal, and I could see she was about to pass out. Her eyes were just swimming around in her head like marbles.

"Oh, man, Tamar—you don't look so good!"

"You tried it!" she responded automatically. But her husband, Vince, noticed her condition, too. He jumped up to take command of the situation.

"I've got to take her to the hospital!"

At Cedars–Sinai Medical Center, doctors hooked her up to an IV and began running different blood tests, but the results weren't instantly available. She wasn't an athlete, and she wasn't in her twenties, and in the end her health just caught up with her. She hadn't had a stroke, we knew that fairly quickly, but certain other conditions that could still be life-threatening hadn't been ruled out. It was an extraordinary situation, like nothing I had ever experienced before. As difficult as the process can be, none of what happened was the show's fault, because none of it could have been predicted.

Dancing with the Stars was set to go live at five o'clock (it aired at eight on the East Coast, but in L.A. we were live at five). We had two dances for that week-nine episode, a solo contemporary to Chris Isaak's "Wicked Game" and then a group dance to "Hey Jude."

The episode ran through the other couples and then came to our slot. With me standing there alone like an idiot, host Tom Bergeron conducted an interview on camera. "Where's your partner?"

"My partner's in the hospital because she almost passed out during dress rehearsal."

"The judges will stay tuned to what is happening at the hospital," Tom announced. "But here's footage of Tamar and Val from dress rehearsal today."

The rule was that if you couldn't dance in the actual show because of an injury, the producers would play rehearsal footage, and the couple got judged on that. I could see from the dress rehearsal recording that Tamar had been close to fainting the entire time she was dancing. The footage sucked, but I didn't care anymore about what was happening on the show. As competitive as I was and as serious and committed as I was to my craft, her health was my number one priority. Maybe I had changed, maybe I had grown up a little, or maybe my Mirrorball win had taken the edge off, but for once I didn't care about the competition. I just wanted to make sure my partner was all right.

Across town at the hospital, though, Tamar had been battling it out with her husband and doctors, insisting she was well enough to hit a TV dance contest being shot a dozen blocks away. This wasn't the Grammys, this was a ballroom dance competition with a partner she met two months ago. She probably thought she would never be this invested into this process. She had joined the show to have a good time and learn a little something. But she had grown into her commitment, until now here she was, literally putting her life on the line. How far she was willing to go was absolutely incredible to me. There was no rehearsal footage of our second routine. If she didn't make it back to the set that day, we would be eliminated.

"I'm not going to let Val down, not after all we've been through." She finally decided to go against doctors' orders, got into her car, and headed the mile down Beverly Boulevard to the studio.

Our scheduled second number was coming up, and the clock was still ticking. She quickly slipped into a dress, slapped on some makeup, and tied her hair back, all the while barely seeing what was in front of her. She wobbled out toward the parquet as the stage manager counted down the seconds.

"Five . . . four . . . three . . ."

And suddenly there she was, much the worse for wear, maybe, but present nonetheless. Part of me was saying "This is stupid and ridiculous," but another part of me was so proud that here was a true teammate and a friend for life.

We did the rumba number, one that she hadn't even had time to fully learn yet. I led her through the entire routine and she just followed, as if she had been doing it for years. We finished and she took her seat, where fellow celebrity contestant Nick Carter, formerly of the Backstreet Boys, sat next to her, holding her upright. Nick's pro partner, Sharna Burgess, and I stood behind them, all of us in shock about what we had just witnessed. Tamar's eyes were rolling around in her head again, and she was about to pass out on live television.

"The marks are in, Tamar!" Tom announced. "The results are in and both you and Nick are in the semifinals!"

The audience erupted in cheers. The whole place went nuts.

"What just happened?" Tamar whispered.

I gave her a hug. She murmured, "I don't understand. I'm still about to pass out."

The show went into a commercial break and Tamar went straight back to the hospital. There doctors discovered she had a burst of blood clots, a very serious condition. The dance we had just done featured jumps, lifts, and runs, moves which could have had serious consequences for Tamar's health.

"If just one clot gets into your heart, it could be a wrap for you," the doctor informed her, telling it like it was. "What don't you understand about this? You cannot continue in this competition!"

I remember when she broke the news to me. I came to visit while she was still in the hospital. "You tried it!" I said, and we both laughed. But we were so proud—I was proud of her, and most importantly she was proud of herself.

What a trouper. In fact, Tamar Braxton proved herself that day to be what I consider a great teammate.

DANCING WITH THE STARS WAS AN ABC SHOW, SO WE NATU-
rally did all of our premieres, cast reveals, and finale events on the network's hit flagship show, *Good Morning America*, which everyone knew as *GMA*.

From the very start, I wanted to fit in on the *GMA* set, wanted it to be like home to me the same way it was for my brother. When he showed up at the show's production facilities in Times Square, he was treated like an old friend. I loved the fact that host Robin Roberts would greet him with a "Damn, Maks! You look *good!*"

It was actually through Robin that I became a member of the *GMA* family. Our friendship began the year before I became a pro on *Dancing with the Stars*. As part of the celebration of her fiftieth birthday in 2010, Robin made a running riff out of ticking off items on her bucket list—things she wanted to do before she kicked the bucket. "Dance with Maks Chmerkovskiy" was one of the entries, a fantasy she had evidently nursed for a long time.

My brother was of course game, but Robin didn't consider herself a natural dancer, so she felt she needed to take a few lessons beforehand. I was the obvious candidate for a dance teacher, because I was nearby, on the East Coast, and working as a coach and instructor at our Dance With Me social dance studio in Soho.

It was nothing much, just a half-dozen sessions, but Robin proved such a warm and engaging person that we bonded instantly. Back then, I wasn't by any means a known entity, having made only a few appearances on *Dancing with the Stars* for dance-offs or routines with my brother. I wasn't a fan favorite. And no one gravitated to me because of my TV popularity.

During the in-between period before I signed on as a pro, I found the whole *Dancing with the Stars* scene difficult to navigate.

That world was very well stocked with really flashy go-getter personalities, people who had aggressive ways of establishing their spheres of influence. At times the show's set in West Hollywood seemed to me to be where a pack of wild dogs peed to mark their territory. I thought that kind of shit was foul, and wanted to tell people to go pee in their own corners, not in the commons where we all were supposed to coexist. Even beyond that, they also all knew each other, and here I was a newbie, with a "kid-brother" reputation to live down.

Maks flew to New York to dance on *GMA* with the birthday girl. The routine they did was nothing fancy—she wore a leopard-print dress and Maks wore jeans—but the other hosts gathered around to act as "judges" and a fun, goofy time was had by all. The paddles that the judges held up offered only one possible score: 10.

The time spent rehearsing with Robin allowed me to feel a little more like an insider than I had before—both in the world of *GMA,* but also in the TV community that existed around it. So I got to know Robin, but I wanted more. With *GMA* I always had this fantasy of me coming into the Times Square studio and being recognized and welcomed. The image floating in my head had me glad-handing my way through the staff. "Hey, what's up, Lara? Hey, George, how are you?" Being from New York, the Times Square *GMA* studio was like a landmark to me. This wasn't some soundstage in Hollywood—though those were pretty cool, too—this was like holy ground, a studio right next to the Dow ticker, the news zipper, where they held the biggest New Year's Eve celebration in the world. This was Robin Roberts and George Papadopulous, faces of every single one of my mornings growing up. They were interesting people, and like always, I just wanted to connect and have conversations with people who I respected on a very high level.

Fast-forward to the spring of 2016, when I finally had a chance to realize my fantasies. In March of that year the cast of the upcoming Season 22 of *Dancing with the Stars* was announced on

GMA. The audience and staffers went crazy with applause when it was revealed that I had been matched with a *GMA* favorite, Ginger Zee, the show's in-house meteorologist. Through that alliance I not only made a friend for life, but was granted the keys to the inner sanctum at *GMA.* I got to know the sound techs and the grips, the camera operators and the other hosts. That's the level of friendship I have with *GMA* now, after my *Dancing with the Stars* season with Ginger.

And an awesome season it was. I was just coming off a show that ended with my partner checked into a hospital. Thankfully the situation sorted itself out without serious repercussions, but it still served as something like a reality check for me. After my season with Tamar I had to step my game up to another level. I realized that not every dance partner would be a twenty-five-year-old Rumer Willis, someone whom I could push physically, mentally, and emotionally to be all that she could be. Going forward, I would have to learn to make accommodations for partners who were mothers, wives, and other adult women who had a lot going on in their lives beyond *Dancing with the Stars.*

Husbands were part of the equation now, and I had to consider the natural, instinctive reaction a husband might have, seeing another man fully in his wife's business. I was never physically disrespectful, always mindful and classy, but that didn't mask the fact that I would be holding another man's wife five hours a day every day for three months.

My partners and I sweated blood during rehearsal in order to create art every Monday night. That sort of experience brings people together at a very tight level. When my partner happened to be a twentysomething girl from Hollywood, she'd fall in love. But with a grown-up mother and wife, the relationship had to be compartmentalized. She might fall a little, but she had to go back to her real home and real love afterward.

The situation itself tended to bring out the green-eyed monster of jealousy. A husband might ask his wife, "What are you so in love with? I'm right here, and you're in love with your tango? Are you in love with your tango or are you in love with your dance partner?"

That's the dynamic I had to keep firmly in mind, that no, this grown-up woman next to me, who had her own adult life and loves and family—she wasn't falling in love with me. She was in love with the process, with the prospect of winning the Mirrorball, with the whole intense circus of *Dancing with the Stars*.

So before every rehearsal period I asked myself what kind of season this was going to be, what kind of dance instructor I would become. I needed to be a little bit more mindful, adjust my methods a bit more carefully, and fit my style into the lifestyle of my partner.

The old distinction between lessons at Rising Stars Dance Academy and those at our Dance With Me studios served me well. One was a boot-camp-style affair where we prepared young souls for the world of competition, and the teaching was very much hard-core and authoritarian. Do this, don't do this, shut up about it. The other was a grown-up social affair, softer, warmer, more a case of "What would you like to do?" One was tailored to children, the other to adults.

With Ginger Zee, I knew immediately that I had a partner who was very much an adult. She was a mother of a newborn son, just six weeks old. She had joined the show a month and a half after giving birth. It was as if her placenta had just dropped and the umbilical cord was still pretty much intact.

She was one of the coolest people I had ever met, and if we had met ten years earlier, in a different life and in different circumstances, I would have probably married her. As it was, we developed a great friendship that never once strayed into the romantic. I got a contact high seeing this young couple, Ginger and her husband Ben Aaron, still practically newlyweds, riding the euphoria of having their first child. I became the really cool fifth wheel on their baby stroller.

Ginger did *Dancing with the Stars* to help her rebuild her body after the atom-bomb impact of pregnancy. But I had to ask myself, Was it too soon? The physical part of the process was hard for her, and meanwhile she was still working as a meteorologist on *GMA*. For all that, I was overjoyed to once again be able to spend a rehearsal period in my city, the first time since I was paired with Sherri Shepherd during Season 13.

It was spring, and if there is any place better to be in springtime than Manhattan I don't know about it. Keep your Aprils in Paris, I'll take a day in May strolling down a street in the Village. New York had become even more of my town during that period, because the family had opened a Dance With Me studio in Soho, the trendiest and high-endiest of all high-end neighborhoods in Manhattan. It served as a signal the Chmerkovskiy ambition had fully realized its American dream.

I could walk on a sidewalk crowded with thousands of interesting people, head into the rehearsal studio, hit the parquet, and teach an incredibly fun woman how to dance. I was working, but I was living my life at the same time, and that allowed me to be a little looser than I'd been lately, not take things so seriously. It's that feeling you have when you genuinely want to come to work. After we finished our rehearsals I became that most enviable creature in all the world, a free man in Manhattan.

"See you later, Ginger," I'd say, already halfway out the door. "Good rehearsal, girl, practice your steps, okay?" Then I would hop right on the phone with my homies. "Hey, whatup? Whatcha doing? Wanna grab some snackage? Fuck, yeah, let's go!" It was my dream life, being surrounded by my friends and family working at my dream job.

Yes, there were challenges. Could she dance? No. Was she physically fit? Not really. But Ginger Zee was the perfect teammate because she was intelligent as fuck, which for me was everything. We talked about every subject under the sun. I learned a lot from her, and got to vent to her about situations large and small. She always gave me a measured, interesting response. As a teacher, I've only ever been as smart as my student.

We developed a great, easy banter. When I first met her, I said, "Oh, we've got a little generation gap here."

"Fuck you!" Ginger returned. "I'm only six years older than you!" I teased her about being a meteorologist, meanwhile secretly thinking, How dope is that?

"You're a weather girl," I teased her.

"I'm a meteorologist!" she said, pretending to be offended. "There's a difference. I am a *scientist*."

"Listen, I'm just saying that you could pass *aesthetically* for a weather girl, because weather girls are hot and you're hot. If you're a scientist, too, good for you."

Forget the physical process, because physicality was the least complicated part, since I could act the dictator and simply order Ginger to get it done. I pushed her to her physical new-mom edge.

I remember at the first rehearsal we were working out some basic stuff when she put up her hand and called a halt.

"Hey, listen, I need to pause for a second," she said. "Do you mind if I take a ten-minute break?"

"Of course," I said. "Go ahead."

We were in a studio right next to the Empire State Building. She crossed over to the side of the space where we'd been dancing, sat on the couch, and unpacked an apparatus, all tubes and buttons and motors. Then she undid some buttons, slapped the apparatus aboard, and started pumping.

"I'm still breastfeeding," she said, explaining the obvious.

I recorded a little video of her pumping and put a soundtrack over it: Technotronic's "Pump Up the Jam." Ginger had a good laugh about it. I realized that we had become family. I always put forth my willingness to connect, and whenever it was reciprocated, the other person and I reached some sort of family status. I was happier than I had ever been working with a partner.

Because I had been able to remain in New York during the rehearsal period, I got to celebrate my birthday surrounded by old friends, new friends, and all my family members. It was a milestone, my thirtieth.

"What do you want to do?" everyone asked.

"What do I want to do?" I knew exactly. "I want to go back to Brooklyn, to Brighton Beach, to the most Russian club in the city—that's where I want to go! And I want to bring all of my Hollywood friends to that bitch!"

Rasputin, the place was called, closed now. Rasputin, named for the mad Russian monk who mesmerized the czarina. Rasputin, on Coney Island Avenue near Avenue X, just blocks down from my old grade school.

The Russian community of Brighton Beach by then wasn't what it once had been. But Rasputin represented the nearest thing to the old clubs where I used to dance with my brother and our partners on Friday and Saturday nights. Even though they were now more than a decade in the past, I always held those gigs close to my heart. No one could have been happier than I was then.

South Brooklyn, Gravesend, Brighton Beach: the essence of where I came from. At some point early in the night at the Rasputin, I managed a toast—I know it was early because I was still able to speak.

"This is me," I said, sweeping my arm around at the garishly decorated surroundings. "This is where we came from and this is how we celebrate thirty years! From dancing at the Paradise, to the paparazzi flashing photos, showing love for the kid from the five boroughs, I couldn't be more proud to come back to my roots with the new friends I've made throughout my years. Now I got fancy friends in this city who are club owners and promoters and athletes and celebrities and actresses and . . . and . . . *meteorologists*! And whoever else is in the room! But I'm coming back as a little gangster with my own family and we're celebrating. Let's get this party lit! Raise a glass to mother Brooklyn!"

Uh-huh. Well, I told you I was drunk.

The food was incredible, the drinks were too many, and the Hollywood imports were jaw-droppingly obsessed with the whole scene. They had never seen anything like it before. I was so excited that I took shots with everybody, to the point where I blacked out three hours into the party and woke up the next morning in bed at home in Manhattan. I had a little trouble recalling specifics of the night before, but I knew I had spent it in the one city I loved most, surrounded by people I adored, people I'd taught, and people I'd learned from. Happy thirtieth birthday, Valya!

GINGER AND I WENT ON TO HAVE AN AWESOME SEASON ON *Dancing with the Stars.* I saw her blossom as a dancer, but more than that she changed physically, coming out of her post-pregnancy softness to get toned and fit. It was hard work for a young mother with her first child, especially for someone on television all the time.

Every day Ginger appeared on a morning show in front of millions of people, and that could feel intimidating if she was insecure about how she looked. But she had that new-mother glow, and she was actually more beautiful now than she'd ever been.

On *Dancing with the Stars*, I put her all in lace for an Argentine tango that was just about the sexiest thing she had ever done. The effect was not merely about the aesthetic, but about the confidence she had gained on the show, with the sultry moves of the tango showcasing her newfound poise. Across the course of the season the audience witnessed Ginger's growth and progression, step by step, episode by episode, dance by dance.

I wanted more than anything to give Ginger the best possible experience on *Dancing with the Stars*. Of course, with a new baby she was already having the best time of her life. So I asked myself how I could celebrate her recent motherhood. How could I enhance her peak moment through dance?

For "Most Memorable Year" theme night, I did a contemporary with her that told the story of her most memorable year—the year that she met Ben. Her husband, by the way, was excited and supportive throughout Ginger's season. I tried to involve him whenever possible, because when he was comfortable she could relax and concentrate on the performance. I choreographed a dance that symbolized their meeting and his proposal. We finished with her standing in front of me, both of us reaching around to lock fingers over her belly. The camera zoomed in, the symbolism was obvious and tight, and the routine turned out to be as beautiful as Ginger and Ben's love story.

"At the end of the day, the most important thing to me is family," she said in the preroutine video package, sounding much like me. "My son, my husband, everything that I've come to know as home. When I do this dance, it will absolutely be a career highlight, because now it's like my career and my personal life are coming together. To be able to tell the story through dance—it's going to be the most beautiful moment of the season for me."

The soundtrack was "Home," by Phillip Phillips, a favorite of Ginger's. Ben had once given her the framed sheet music as a present. "We hung it in our first home," Ginger said. To set the scene, I put my hair up in a top-knot, and we both danced barefoot, wearing casual, lounging-around-the-house clothes.

Baby Adrian was in the audience, all of three months old at this point, wearing little headphone-like ear protectors to shield his tender ears from the noise. After the routine, I had him brought up to the Skybox, where dancers assembled for the comment session from the judges. A production assistant surprised Ginger by giving her the infant, in a scene straight out of *The Lion King*: "Here. Is. Your. Baby!"

The poor kid started crying hysterically. No one could get him to stop. I was making faces at Adrian to distract him, but he kept wailing, and I started laughing.

"Oh my God," Ginger muttered to me. "The show is going to kill me for suggesting this!"

The producers in the control booth were frantic. "How do we get this #$%@& baby to stop crying?"

It was a special moment, so authentic, so genuine, so light-hearted. That season with Ginger was the first time in a long time that I didn't have any romance drama, any husband drama, any drama at all. In terms of my partner it was the most stress-free time I'd ever had.

Ginger and I made it to the finals on *Dancing with the Stars* that season, winding up in third place. We had a lot of injuries. The process was hard, but it was also beautiful, both for her and for me.

What could be better? In fact, I knew very well what could be better: winning a Mirrorball for dear Ginger Zee, and knocking down a second trophy for myself just for the sake of self-validation. Could I do it again, or was it a fluke?

LAURIE

I realize that I left you hanging somewhat, introducing you to my Season 23 dance partner, Laurie Hernandez, but never really detailing what happened to us on the show. Heading in to tape our first meeting segment, I walked through the entrance into the gym where she trained, and I remember I had to take my shoes off to head out onto the mats. She turned around and saw me, her face lighting up as she pranced—there was no other word for it—up to me.

The expression she wore made me understand why her nickname was "the Human Emoji." She didn't just smile, she beamed. She appeared to be a miniature powerhouse, an atomic bomb stuffed into a U.S.A. leotard.

We embraced, a big-brother-little-sister hug that set the tone for our whole subsequent relationship. Her mother, Wanda, was there, and her manager, Sheryl Shade, and the whole atmosphere was one of warmth and family, a vibe I was very familiar with growing up in my own household.

"Hi! How you doing? I'm Val."

"I know who you are. I'm Laurie Hernandez."

"Nice to meet you, Laurie," I said. "I know who you are, too."

"Well," she said, looking me straight in the eye, "are you ready to win this thing?"

"Eeey!" I laughed. "I love your ambition. We're going to do our best."

My close-but-no-cigar experience with Zendaya flashed through my mind. The small sting of regret from not being able to bring home a win that season still remained with me two years later. We had come in second, within a hairsbreadth of the championship. I felt like I had failed Zendaya as a mentor. This time, I vowed, it would be different. I had to be at the top of my game, because the stakes weren't just the Mirrorball Trophy. They were bigger than that. Laurie Hernandez was at an age where each little influence could have an enormous impact.

Why couldn't I work to create more avenues for her? Why not inspire her to give back even more than she had already given? If I did that, I thought, this young woman could change the world. Helping others should be everybody's foremost responsibility in life, and I realized it was what made me the happiest, was where I found my place.

I looked at Laurie, and told myself, this season I would be better. I was there to guide her, to help her, to lift her up where she belonged—so she could hold up that Mirrorball Trophy.

That day at the gym, I gained another small insight into the life of Laurie Hernandez, courtesy of a scene that I was not sure I was supposed to witness. I passed by the office of Laurie's long-time gymnastics coach, Maggie, and caught a glimpse of her in tears. She wept in the privacy of her office, but I saw her and understood immediately.

My arrival on the scene represented a rite of passage. One phase of Laurie's life was ending and another, more adult one, was beginning. This woman had been by Laurie's side for years, and perhaps she felt someone was taking away a precious diamond of a child.

The end of an era can be wrenching. I respectfully tried to keep my distance, but I knew the heartache she was probably feeling. I knew the transition wasn't going to be easy for Laurie, either, despite what she said about loving the show and dreaming about being a contestant.

"I started watching it from the very first season, when I was five," she told me, making me feel every minute of my age.

"Damn, I'm old," I said. "And, damn, the show is old, too."

Just as her coach's life may have been changing, so too, of course, was Laurie's. She was leaving the world that she knew behind, a kind of upheaval that I was familiar with, having left the competition world to do *Dancing with the Stars*. Laurie was coming off the biggest result of her career, an incredible achievement for her and her coach. She came home from the Olympics and immediately went into rehearsal with me. Her commitment to *Dancing with the Stars* would be only for three months, but its symbolism made the time frame feel more extreme than that.

The afternoon opened the door to an incredible partnership and a lasting friendship. I felt something of a mysterious transition, a passing of the torch. My time wasn't up for sure, not by any stretch of the imagination. But even though I was only a few years older—okay, I was fourteen years older—Laurie seemed to me like an avatar of a new generation.

I would get a chance to teach somebody, someone ready to learn how to dance correctly, who knew how to take guidance and coaching. I could teach her the things that were taught to me. I never had the chance to be an older brother, but I would get to be one with her. All the experience that I had gained over the course of my thirty years I would now get to share with this sixteen-year-old standing before me, a vision of awesomeness bottled up in a gymnastic outfit.

What I saw in her was not just an athlete, which was what the world saw in her, but a superstar. When I spoke to Laurie I came to understand the depth of her intellect and even wisdom. Not many sixteen-year-old girls thought like her, and her maturity served as a testament to her parents and the way they raised her. I saw an opportunity for me to bring out the best in what already was a pretty awesome kid.

But I never did treat her like a kid. I knew there was a difference between being young and being a child. I wanted her to make sure that she knew the difference, too, that just because she was sixteen didn't mean she couldn't have the ambition to change the world. She didn't have to wait. She could do it now, today, at sixteen, not when she grew up. She didn't have the excuse some kids use—"When I grow up, I'm going to do this and I'm going to do that." You don't have to wait to grow up to do any of those things. You could do them right now.

Our backgrounds served as a kind of common denominator, and I was able to relate to her right off the bat. My experience as a national and a world champion in competitive dance, and my pedigree as a high-caliber dance coach, gave my voice authority for her. If I was just another Hollywood kid teaching her how to dance, we probably wouldn't have had the same relationship.

That first day at the gym she quite literally showed me the ropes. We had a little race up the climbing rope, and I wasn't even close—she was up and back down while I was still barely halfway up.

"I'm going to blame it on the age difference," I told her, laughing as I sheepishly dropped back to the floor.

I called Deena Katz immediately. "Thank you so much," I said. "She's incredible. I'm grateful for the opportunity and very grateful that you trust me with her."

At the moment Laurie was a priceless American jewel. My teaching and mentorship style had matured since my Zendaya days, to the point that I was confident I could do Laurie justice.

That day Wanda Hernandez invited me to their house for dinner. I met Laurie's father and her siblings. The Hernandez family did not live in a fancy house, nor the kind of huge mansion that you see in some Jersey communities. They were a blue-collar family from the suburbs.

I recognized the atmosphere right away. It felt familiar. I was a Chmerkovskiy in a Hernandez household, but it felt like I was home, eating not the most lavish five-star dinner, but a meal that was indescribably finer, because it was so clearly served with love. By the time we were finished and sitting contentedly over our *cafés con leche*, they knew they had the right guy, and I knew I had just completely lucked out with my partner.

One of my first events with Laurie was a promo shoot the next day at a high-end photography studio in Manhattan. The single aspect of *Dancing with the Stars* that floored all of my partners was the costumes. It didn't matter what kind of celebrity they were, the costumes got them every time. When the stars see that stuffed-full rack from *Dancing with the Stars*, oh, man, the glittery stuff and the rhinestone dresses, they got a hint of what they were in for.

I could just imagine what the moment was like for a sixteen-year-old girl, one who had deprived herself of a normal life for the last decade, chasing the single-minded dream of an Olympic gold medal. The friendships she didn't get to develop, the movies she didn't go to, all the cake and candy she didn't eat—every awesome childhood thing under the sun, Laurie had sacrificed for her goal. She broke her wrists and legs. She was constantly sore all over and in pain, just to be able to earn the reward of standing up straight and proud as her national anthem was played for the world to hear.

So for her, that costume rack was the first tiny taste of those rewards that she had labored for over the course of eleven years. It was a beautiful moment. She was a kid in a candy store. I helped her choose the dress that would be appropriate for the photo shoot, made sure the shoes fit, cut off the excess material to make sure the soles would be slick for the picture. I ran around like a butler in a palace. I knew first impressions were vital, and I always felt like

I was a kind of ambassador for the show. I wanted the family to understand that their daughter was in the best of hands.

"Do you want some food?" I asked, then turned to Wanda. "Are you okay? Would you like something to drink?" I told her about my mom carting me around to rehearsals and lessons, knowing the stories would sound familiar. They were getting to know me now.

I spoke to the stylists. "What about the makeup? Can we make it a little brighter, a little younger?"

I was there every step of the way. When we entered into our rehearsal period, Laurie was on a national gymnastics tour, so I would fly around the country to meet her and grab a few minutes of practice time. Once again, I was immersed in the old routine of rehearsing in hallways, green rooms, the wings of an auditorium.

Remember what I told you about the *Dancing with the Stars* audience being tuned in to the dancers' growth across a season, rather than their expertise? It was that way with Laurie. We started out on the first episode with a cha-cha to "American Girl," the perfect song for who she was at that moment in her life. Although we tied for first on that premiere episode, for the first three weeks the judges never marked us higher than a score of 8.

The fourth week had a Cirque du Soleil theme, and Laurie and I did a jazz dance to Michael Jackson's "The Way You Make Me Feel," with acrobats performing around and behind us. The effect was spectacular, and that show was a turning point. The judges gave us perfect 10s, the highest score for any couple on the show. Laurie had always been a favorite to win the season—coming off her Olympic gold, how could she not be?—but from that routine onward she and I took our place as the front-runners. We never looked back.

I was sad for her, though, because Olympic swimmer Ryan Lochte was in the cast that season, and the scandal about his behavior in Rio swirled in the media. The season featured other strange moments, such as rapper Vanilla Ice doing a number MC'd by Texas governor Rick Perry. We had it all on *Dancing with the Stars*.

It didn't matter, none of it mattered, because nothing could stop Laurie and me. For the last four episodes—from "Halloween Night" and "Showstoppers Night," to the semifinals and the finals—we were marked with perfect scores twenty-four times and earned only two 9s. Laurie had to find room on her shelves for a Mirrorball Trophy to go along with all the Olympic medals and gymnastic awards.

I wound up with much more than a second trophy. In that wonderful whirlwind of a season, Laurie taught me that like love, inspiration was a two-way street. Sometimes experience can batter you into changing, but sometimes it can lift you up and transform you with a sense of joy, rather than agony.

"I just want to thank everyone for their support and riding along this crazy roller coaster of my life," Laurie said after winning. Then she continued, with words after my own heart: "My goal is just to inspire others as I go on with my journey."

Laurie and I took our place among couples with the highest averages on *Dancing with the Stars*, and were ranked in the top twenty at least, behind my brother, who led the pack in his championship season with Meryl Davis.

But who's counting?

HARMONY

In the spring of 2017, leading up to Season 24 of *Dancing with the Stars*, I felt for the first time that a case of burnout was sneaking up on me. For one thing, I had done eleven seasons in a row and was now committed to doing a twelfth.

Like college students who "step out" for a year in the midst of their educations, pros on the show take seasons off all the time. Sometimes they're just not hired that year, and sometimes they step out by their own choice. When you don't see the best of the professionals on our show, most likely they've been asked to participate but decided they needed a season off, because they were burned out or just wanted to pursue other opportunities.

That wasn't me. Over the course of the six years since I had signed on as a pro dancer, I had never stopped out. I pursued my other opportunities during the midseason breaks while still banging out the shows, simply because I loved it.

But like they say, when you're broke you have the time, and when you finally have some money, you ain't got the time. My schedule had been relentless. I was coming off five straight midseason tours, both my own and ones with the *Dancing with the Stars* cast. The 2016–2017 off-season *Dancing with the Stars* tour was the best-attended yet, selling something like 130,000 tickets. That was more than ticket sales for the first two arena tours combined, back in the good old days when the show tours had just begun.

Screw the good old days—*these* were the good old days, and I was living them in the moment. My status as one of the leading pro dancers on *Dancing with the Stars* was hard-won. I had just made it to the top with Laurie Hernandez. I had managed to solidify my position as the new sheriff in town. I had always wanted to be "the Guy," and now that I had realized my goal and had become the Guy—one of them, anyway—I should have felt happy and fulfilled.

"Hey, by the way," I would humble-brag, "have you heard that I just took home my second Mirrorball Trophy?"

So I was living the life. Out on the road with the *Dancing with the Stars* tour, I got to witness the reaction of the fans, see the country, and become familiar with every nook and cranny of the United States of America. What could be better?

But somehow a tiny element of doubt crept into my mind. Was I personally being fulfilled? I felt like an ungrateful little shit, but if I was honest with myself, I had to admit that, no, I wasn't fulfilled. It drove me crazy, because I was facing what's called a first world problem, you know? Get everything you want, live the high life, pin on your new sheriff star. What the hell? You are still not satisfied?

I could not dodge the feeling. The basic question I posed to myself was the same as it always was: Was I growing? Financially, yes, indeed, my bank account was growing. But was that all there is? Was I growing as a person?

My true wealth came from an inner sense of growth, of transformation, of connection. Way back at those meet and greets during my first season on the show, I had realized that connection was important to me. I needed to learn about other people, and to do that, I needed to experience other cultures. I learned through travel and learned through immersing myself in history. That kind of activity was just incredibly fulfilling for me, and that's what I was missing.

I spent most of my younger years traveling overseas to competitions. All the family money went into that air ticket to Berlin for me to dance in the German Open, or to Prague, Turin, Moscow, London. Without really being aware of it, I became bit by bit a true cosmopolitan, a citizen of the world. By my early twenties, I found myself having worldly conversations with older adults, discussing, say, the intricacies of the architecture by Gaudí in Barcelona, how impressed I was by its impact on public space in the city.

"Gaudí's genius of cutting all the corners off his structures creates little squares throughout the city, and that allows more opportunity, spatially, to erect monuments or install pieces of art."

Huh? Had those words really come out of little Valya's mouth? I was twenty-four, and still a kid, but I had been all over the world. I could speak confidently about my architectural impressions, or about how I thought the South of France was overrated, or about the time I spent at Blackpool or on the island of Capri.

"Hey, I just stayed in Naples with my boy Nino Langella for a couple weeks," I'd find myself saying. "Tough as nails environment, but a really picturesque place."

But all that travel had taken place before my tenure on *Dancing with the Stars*. In the years since, my international forays had been cut off, and through tours and appearances I'd been instead immersed in an exhaustive—and exhausting—exploration of America. It was the best thing ever, because I got to know the greatest country in the world, inside and out. But for a five-year stretch, I had essentially been landlocked in the States.

Thinking it over, I decided that I was missing my old vagabond days of globe-trotting. I mean, maybe I had been a little fucking nuts to have gone on five straight off-season tours. I lived onstage and I thought that was all that mattered to me. Talk about the Grateful Dead—me and the rest of the pros on the tours were like the grateful dancing dead. I used to have dreams about being on a tour bus while I was actually asleep on the *Dancing with the Stars* tour bus. Living out of a suitcase became more comfortable to me than having a home. I felt less anxiety, just having a suitcase, because there were fewer decisions to be made every morning.

Question to myself on the road: "Aw, man, which shirt am I gonna wear today?"

Answer: "The same motherfucking shirt you wore yesterday, bro."

Our super-successful off-season tour was over, and that spring I was headed into my next appearance as a pro on *Dancing with the Stars*. There were other elements contributing to my unease, like the breakup of a four-month relationship. In the week-long stretch between the end of the tour and the start of the season, I took my nagging little doubts to a four-day yoga retreat in Arizona, trying to sort everything out.

I was coming up on my thirty-first birthday and for the first time in my life had some respectable digits in my bank account. I wasn't exactly Bill Gates, but at least I could buy my mom a gift, help my family, help my friends. I finally got to be the man of my little tribe. That had been the motivating goal of my life for as long as I could remember. I always sent out the same message to whomever supported me.

"Wait 'til I make it, I'll give you way more than what you've given me. I'll give back to you tenfold on this shit. I'm the best investment you guys ever made."

So I was able to fulfill those promises, but while I was out there doing a downward-facing dog in the desert air of Arizona, the question still remained. What about me? What did I want for myself? I was blessed to have work, but at some point, to be effective in my work, I had to mandate a moment for myself as a human being, to recharge my batteries.

I had to travel. Not just in America, either, but in the wide world of Europe, Asia, fucking Oceania if I wanted to. I had a contract for another season on *Dancing with the Stars*, and I would do what I signed up for. But I decided I would not commit to another off-season tour. My brother was getting married that July, and I couldn't just take a couple of days off from a tour for that. After five and a half years of ping-ponging between nonstop tours and seasons on prime-time TV, I promised myself a breather. I was going to live my life.

Extricating myself from the lotus position, I left Arizona and returned to L.A. to find out who I'd be matched with for Season 25.

"Your new partner's going to be doing this event at a rodeo in Houston," the producer told me. "We want you to do the first meeting segment with her there."

We ended up shooting the footage in front of 70,000 people at NRG Stadium, normally where the Houston Texans played their home games in the NFL. The biggest rodeo in the world was happening at the venue that night, with girl-group megastars Fifth Harmony as featured entertainers.

I went along mainly because later in life I would be able to say that trademark line, "This is not my first rodeo." The scene in the stadium totally blew my mind. I'd never been to a rodeo before, and I had never been around so much horse shit outside of Hollywood. I waited in the wings as Fifth Harmony took the stage.

"Normani Kordei is about to do *Dancing with the Stars*," the MC called out, naming one of the group's singers. "Surprise, folks! Here is her new dance partner!"

I came onstage and the audience cheered like crazy. It made for an epic moment, definitely in keeping with my new partner's celebrity status. I was shocked at first, in the same way I had been shocked that Rumer Willis had wanted to do the show. Normani Kordei was a huge star, a member of the biggest-selling all-female pop group since the Spice Girls. I was stunned that somebody of her stature would sign on. *Dancing with the Stars* was a hard project to do, a pretty intense gig. When you're busy with your own career, why in the world would you want to embark on the super difficult journey of doing the show?

Oddly enough, Normani had joined Fifth Harmony courtesy of an another reality TV talent show, *X Factor*, where she tried out as a solo singer and hadn't made the cut. However, producer Simon Cowell saw something in her, recruited four other singers who had also tried out and failed as *X Factor* solo acts, and put them together to create Fifth Harmony.

Even though some pop stars tended to be a little bit diva-ish, I immediately felt quite an opposite vibe from Normani. I got a peek behind the pop-star curtain and saw an unpretentious, fairly insecure twenty-year-old girl who struck me as being really down. "Down" was, of course, one of Fifth Harmony's big hit songs. Normani came across as somewhat lost and at the same time excited, but with no real idea what the upcoming experience would be like. The only reference point she had was *X Factor*, an experience that for her had been all anxiety and intimidation.

"We're going to be working real hard," I told her. "Are you ready for that? What are you doing in the meantime? Do you even have time for this show?"

"I'm a huge fan of *Dancing with the Stars*," Normani said, dodging the question. "I've watched nearly every season with my grandma. Grandma Barbara is an expert. She loves you. She keeps a catalog of everyone who's been on."

For myself, I was excited to have Normani as a partner, because she was a performer, so at least we had that element in place. But I had seen Fifth Harmony in concert, and I wondered how much her experience in the group was going to transfer. She was expected to look pretty onstage, with minimal movement, including some shallow—no offense—commercial type of choreo.

"Look in the camera, smile, touch your boobs and keep it moving." I knew the *Dancing with the Stars* process had a lot more to it than that.

Houston was Normani's home turf. She was born in New Orleans and lived there for years before Katrina hit. Her parents had just moved into the house of their dreams when the hurricane came and swept their whole life away. As did many other Katrina refugees, the family relocated to Houston, where Normani's dance teacher became a second mother to her. Just as it had been for me when my family relocated, dance became Normani's escape, and the dance studio served as a safe haven from all the craziness going on in her world.

I GUESS SOMEONE WAS LISTENING WHEN I WISHED THAT I could travel the world again, since Season 25 turned out to be the most outrageously elaborate, multileg, frequent-flyer, jet-set trek I ever accomplished in my life.

For the first three weeks of the show, Normani was on a multistop tour of Asia with her group. I went along to rehearse with her, feeling as though I had been sucked into the pop-star whirlwind. Our schedule turned insane. We ended up doing *Dancing with the Stars* live as usual on Monday night, going straight from the show to LAX, getting on a flight to Asia that night, crossing the date line, and landing on Wednesday morning. The Fifth Harmony tour started with Okinawa, then moved on to Tokyo, Hong Kong, Philippines, Malaysia, and Singapore.

One week, because of the schedule crunch, Normani wound up flying a red-eye back to L.A. to arrive on Monday morning, with only minutes to spare for the car ride to Television City. If there had been a cyclone over the Pacific, which happens all the time during that season, she would never have made the live show.

I pictured myself trying to explain to America that, believe it or not, this was actual live television, where shit happens, and, obviously, shit felt like it always happened to me. Normani was a girl who traveled with a lot of bags, and she was flying internationally, where there were so many factors that could cause delays.

What made the whole business easier was having a field producer along from *Dancing with the Stars* who really knew his craft—Adam, from Staten Island, New York City. We meshed perfectly and shared a lot of common experiences. He was a diehard basketball fan with a New York Knicks tat. We were cut from the same cloth. I had grown up making fun of losers from Staten Island all my life, and when we were together the trash talk flowed both ways.

Plus he was the absolute best cameraperson in terms of getting shots in the middle of crazy, exotic settings. One way or another, Adam would figure it out, because he had that confident, not to say cocky, attitude of a native New Yorker. He didn't need release signatures because he knew how to duck the camera in order to get the shot with no bystanders involved. He understood what it took to put a package together without having to shoot hours of footage for a one-minute spot.

With Adam operating the camera and the girls of Fifth Harmony as willing participants, we fucking killed it. Far from being a grind, going on tour with Normani actually wound up being the best time—in fact, one of the best times I've ever had on the show. I know you've heard that from me before, but it's true and it's actually how it should be. I always want my last season to be the best one.

The accepted wisdom on music tours has advised stars to stay cool and not get involved with the locals. "Sit in the hotel and just chill."

I wasn't having any of that. "We're in Malaysia. Let's go!" Or "I've been to Hong Kong before, and you've gotta see this!" Or "This is Tokyo, and I know a great place in the Ginza area."

We ended up celebrating my thirty-first birthday in Tokyo. I took out Fifth fucking Harmony to the *Kill Bill* restaurant, the one re-created for the movie. All of a sudden, I'm at a hibachi dinner preaching to them about how great they are and how, individually, they will do everything they want to do, but together, they have the opportunity not just to provide for each other, but to inspire and

entertain and make so many people happy. If I hadn't been dancing on the show, they would have hired me as their manager right
there and then.

While I had my usual understanding that I had to make allies
of Normani's parents, I knew it was equally important to build a
partnership with her group, because that was her second family.
If the members of Fifth Harmony felt invited to be a part of her
journey on the show, they'd be a lot more supportive of me taking
her away every ten minutes to work on our cha-cha, and Normani
herself would be more likely to open up to me and to the whole
Dancing with the Stars experience.

I wanted Normani Kordei to be able to communicate her truth
to the audience. To do that, she had to come from a point of safety
and comfort. "I'm actually not all about that onstage sass. I'm a
young girl, and I have insecurities just like you do." That was a
message that I knew she wanted to convey to the world, and for the
first time in her life she had the opportunity to do so.

After dinner, we hit a club where a friend of mine from New
York was deejaying.

We hung out, they danced, and everyone bonded. I sat next to
their long-time tour manager, Will Bracey, somebody who would
become a solid friend.

"Bro, I've been touring with these girls for years now," Will
told me. "I mean, they've appeared everywhere, seen it all, done
it all, and I've never seen them have this much fun together
before."

Part of the reason was that in that little Tokyo club, the members of Fifth Harmony were anonymous. The place wasn't packed,
but instead resembled a private refuge of our own, with good
people, the best vibes, and a sense that we were all in it together.
The night changed the group's dynamics, which can get pretty
claustrophobic in a pop act, as the Beatles and the Stones and
Oasis have demonstrated. It actually did them good to celebrate

someone else, to sing "Happy Birthday" to me at the airport, and to focus on someone outside of the group.

That all happened in week one of the season—*Dancing with the Stars* premiered on March 20 and my birthday fell four days later. I could gauge how Normani's spirits rose, despite the frantic back-and-forth shuttling across the Pacific. We'd fly nonstop from the Asian tour whirlwind, only to dive into another whirlwind in L.A. It was an insane schedule, but somehow it wound up fueling our mutual excitement.

For the first time in a long time, she was able to find her purpose as an individual, not just as a member of Fifth Harmony. Just like this book gives me my own voice outside of a television show, Normani found the experience of creating art outside the group to be life-changing. She was better in Fifth Harmony because of it, and I'm better on *Dancing with the Stars* because I have writing as an outlet.

One of the highlights of the season for me was getting to know Normani's grandmother, Barbara, a super sassy lady. In fact, if Normani had half the sass that her grandma had, it would have made surviving in show business much easier for her. Barbara ended up being the guiding spirit behind Normani doing the show, which became a shared experience for them. A long-time *Dancing with the Stars* fan, she would put together costumes for Normani based on what she saw on the set.

But I found out Barbara's secret: she wasn't on Team Val after all. She was on Team Maks. From the moment he showed up on Season 2, my brother had been her boy. Humble old me, who had usually sat first chair with my violin whenever I was in youth orchestras, had to play second fiddle with Barbara.

To be successful on *Dancing with the Stars*, a celebrity has to connect to the audience. How could people relate to a pop phenom who sells out arenas and is a fancy, supersexy twenty-year-old? Where's the average human experience in that? The cameos that Normani's grandma made on the show helped, but in the end, we were able to bring out the human connection in the most spectacular manner. That accomplishment was the true Mirrorball Trophy—which she and I didn't wind up winning, by the way. In my mind, we did something better.

It happened in week seven of the season. The producers did a special program, where the pros were allowed to choose music we thought best suited our celebrity partners. This was an awesome opportunity for me to take a chance creatively.

I picked "Freedom," a song by Kelvin Wooten, Anthony Hamilton, and Elayna Boynton from the soundtrack of *Django Unchained*, an intense number that would normally never have been approved for the show. Because of a certain incident that had happened in her recent past, I thought it fit Normani perfectly.

"Look," I said to the producers, "so you're going to okay this song, right? And we're doing it exactly how I set it, right? Because I'm going to talk about it on camera during rehearsal and that's how it has to go."

Eight months before, in the summer of 2016, Normani had been swept up in a nasty case of cyberbullying that showed just how ugly the internet can be. The incident got triggered by a Facebook Live interview, when she was asked to say nice things about each one of her Fifth Harmony bandmates. Normani seemed to hesitate in describing a member who had just left the group.

"She is—let's see. Very quirky. Yeah, very quirky. Cute."

No big thing, right? But fans went berserk on social media, reacting way over the top to an offhand comment that they somehow construed as disrespectful. She hadn't gone all gushy the way she was apparently supposed to do. The trolls came out in force. An image showed up online of Normani's face pasted over a historical image of a lynching.

So, boo hoo, right? Happens every day. To a certain audience, the reality of cyberbullying doesn't seem like a big deal. Brush it off, go on with your life, and if you can't stand the heat, blah blah blah. But life is different for kids born around the turn of the millennium. Because social media is such an integral part of their world, the nastiness of the internet has become a huge mental health issue for them.

Parents used to worry about kids getting bullied on the school playground, back when children were on the playground for an hour a day, the playground was in the neighborhood, and kids knew exactly who the bully was. Nowadays social media is a 24/7 phenomenon, an endless universe that features some very dark psychological matter. It's a fake world that has become a generation's reality. I'm a product of it as well, as we all are now to some degree.

"Hey, let me get this person," says some rancid little troll staring at a computer screen. "What can I do to her? Oh, look, she's black, let me pick on that!"

For the family, it is painful to see a child go through trauma that they can do nothing about. When my brother was robbed of his Rollerblades when we first moved to America, at least my dad could come out in his socks, and the punks knew that at some point somebody was going to show up. Nobody could come to Normani's rescue on the internet. How many of the trolls can any single person respond to? How many people could her mom answer? It wasn't happening.

Normani grew up in Houston and was Texas through and through. She was an American girl. She's wholesome, goes to church, loves God, and was one of the kindest people I had ever met. Now race was being thrust forward in her life in a very public, very direct way. She wound up being hounded off Twitter because of the bullying.

We came up with a piece that worked as an answer to the bullies, but also served as a sort of therapy for Normani's posttraumatic stress. "Freedom" was a song that seemed to address the whole situation perfectly.

Felt like the weight of the world was on my shoulders
Should I break or retreat and then return . . .
But I've come too far to go back now

I am looking for freedom, looking for freedom
And to find it cost me everything I have

I choreographed a routine that opened with Normani stranded in the middle of a mob who were all pointing their fingers at her. She was surrounded, and you could feel the heaviness in the air as I put myself into the circle and pulled her out of that reality. We danced a contemporary that symbolized the quest for freedom from all the shitty things in the world, all the repercussions of angry, vile group-think. My character pushed her to find her strength, find her freedom, help her defeat this mob mentality that had been holding her down.

Not giving up has always been hard, so hard
But if I do the things the easy way I won't get far

Life hasn't been very kind to me lately
But I suppose it's a push for moving on, oh yeah
In time the sun's gonna shine on me nicely
Somethin' tells me good things are coming . . .
I'm looking for freedom, looking for freedom

We went all in. Normani actually cut her hair for the routine. I dressed her in rags, stripping away the pop-star persona she was normally dressed in. As she emerged from the circle of negativity and oppression and we danced, I began screaming at her to break free.

"Go! Go! Go!"

On television, viewers could not hear me yelling, but the live audience could. On camera everyone sensed my energy. In replays the shots of the audience showed stunned faces all around. At that moment *Dancing with the Stars* ceased to be a pop show and became something else, a testament to the endurance of the human soul. Anybody can be exposed to the nasty side of life, not just the glitz but the shit of life, and how we react makes all the difference.

In the routine Normani came off as so strong, so honest, so undeniably vulnerable and human. We ended up in the middle of the circle, fingers pointing at her once again, but with us looping around and knocking their hands down one by one. They peeled off and we wound up embracing in the center of the floor, where she collapsed exhausted into my arms. What I wanted to show with the piece wasn't all negative. I wanted to demonstrate that with the help of maybe just one other person, no matter what situation you're in, you can find the light.

It was one of the most important pieces of choreography I've ever done in my life, easily the best dancing I had ever done on the show. All of a sudden I felt fulfilled. I decided I didn't need to travel to Rome or Barcelona in order to feel that I'd grown, that I'd made a connection. That I made a difference. I could cry right now, writing about it.

With the help of the show, we had re-created some of the most important moments of Normani's life. Forget her entertainment life, her professional life—this gave her validation as a person, as an individual. It brought her family closer. On the surface, the whole world, including me, believed the girl had it all. But deep down, she didn't believe she was talented, didn't think she was "worth it," to pun on the title of another Fifth Harmony hit song.

I watched her change. She ended the season filled to the brim with overflowing inspiration. She was no longer what the cyberbullies made her out to be, "the black girl from that pop group." She had broken free as Normani Kordei, as a dignified human, as an artist. Her smile shined brighter than ever and her voice had more bass to it now. She came of age, and her family was there to witness the transformation. To see her take her life back on her own terms was an incredible thing, and I was a small part of that.

FINAL THOUGHTS

I know it's more than slightly ridiculous, a thirty-one-year-old writing a memoir. Also comical, arrogant, and bizarre, all those things. Shouldn't I have actually lived a life before putting mine down on paper?

But I hope this book will be the first of many from yours truly. What you've read is an account of me growing through a quarter century as a dancer, at times in ballroom competitions, but mostly on a reality show called *Dancing with the Stars*. And as I said from the get-go, I'm not just a dancer, and I'm not just the *Dancing with the Stars* guy. Like my fellow Brooklyn homeboy Walt Whitman, I contain multitudes—and yeah, I just compared myself to one of the world's greatest poets. I look forward to a future where I can trot out all my multitudes and dance them around the floor. Next up, *I'll Never Change My Layup*, a thrilling book about my battles on the hardwood.

Looking over these pages I can see that I wasn't doing my own memoir at all—I was writing a double autobiography of me and my brother. He was and always will be so much a part of me that the phrase "my life" is meaningless without him being part of it. At least up until this point in time, it's been more like "our life."

What I'm most happy about, reading over what I wrote, is that I can see our relationship has never stood still, it has always evolved, and that it has finally settled into a very good place.

We are better friends now, better allies, better people.

When Maks married in the summer of 2017, taking for his wife the incredible artist, standout *Dancing with the Stars* pro, two-time Mirrorball winner, and all-around hottie Peta Murgatroyd, he didn't have far to look for a best man. For the occasion I had to really reflect on our relationship, feeling a great deal of responsibility to try to voice what my brother means to me as best I could. It was before this book was written, and my thoughts back then represented a pretty accurate portrait of our love and commitment to each other. I would like to present you with the speech I made that day, which I'm really proud of but which you should forgive because I was more than slightly intoxicated at the time.

Ahem.

Ladies and gentlemen, my name is Val Chmerkovskiy. I am the best man, and, well, I couldn't have thought of a better title. Given the competitive nature of the groomsmen I will indeed flaunt this one for as long as I can.

Jokes aside, the best title I've ever had wasn't necessarily the two world championships that I won, the fifteen national titles, or the German Open win. It wasn't the Blackpool title, or being named concertmaster of a youth orchestra at age fifteen, or being high school valedictorian, or a two-time Mirrorball winner. And no, not the rock-paper-scissors victories, the in-house Ping-Pong championship, or the three-on-three recreational basketball wins, or that one time they gave me a trophy for smiling the most in second grade.

Now, if you're thinking, "Wow, he's certainly not the most humble . . ." you are correct. That is one title that has evaded me for all these years. Nor was I ever a valedictorian, by the way—I just kind of threw that in there for effect.

Anyway, I digress. I was pinned with many titles in my life and some were more dear to me than others. Being a son to the greatest parents of all is up there with hopefully being a decent friend to some. My newly acquired title of being an uncle—boy, was this a special one, life changing—it even made it to my Instagram bio.

But out of all these titles the one that has the most presence in my life, the one that is tied to pretty much every important moment I've ever experienced (including the ones I just named), the one I'm most unapologetically proud of . . . is the title of Maks's little brother.

Yes, believe it or not, he's older, even though today after shaving it certainly doesn't look like it.

"Hey, wait a minute . . . are you?!"

"Yes! I am Maks Chmerkovskiy's little brother!"

That's the reply I've played on repeat to the world that has gotten to know us in the last ten years.

"You look like that guy from . . ."

"Yeah? You mean that brash, emotionally irresponsible, aesthetically exceptional Russian dude from that reality dance show?" Yeah, I know. He's my brother.

But our life began a long time before the glitz and glamour of Hollywood tried to overproduce a brotherly rivalry that just never existed. My brother and I shared everything together, from growing pains to personal triumphs. Nothing was ever personal between us, it was always shared. When I hurt, he suffered. And when I won, he celebrated. When life wouldn't even give us lemons, we rallied and planted our own trees.

We worked together, sharing the stage at Russian restaurants in Brighton Beach as teenagers, enduring ego *checks nightly as the odor of intoxication and herring filled the air. Nonetheless we gave it our all, trying to perform the best hip action east of the Hudson River.*

We lived and slept in the same room together, sharing everything from conversations, to bunk beds, to the adult magazines we used to hide underneath them. From the little apartment in Odessa, to the even smaller apartments in New York, we shared it all.

I remember Maks coming with me to Blackpool one year, when we shared a room so small that we had to rest our legs on our suitcases, because only our upper bodies fit on the bed. I remember lying there thinking, "Wow, this is the greatest shit ever!" since I never felt poor, I never felt small, I never felt unhappy with you by my side.

I once wrote:

You are the roof
that kept me dry
and when I asked to fly
You took me underneath your wing
And flew against the wind,
so high

I wrote that years ago, and I mean it more today than I ever did.

We shared it all and continue to do so. Being your brother has by far been the greatest gift the world has ever given me.

I am so grateful. Especially for that one time when Igor, Alex, and I got arrested for truancy in ninth grade and we all had to call our homes. An ass whooping was inevitable, but not for me. They didn't have an older brother to pretend to be their dad, and I did.

They didn't have an older brother to bulldoze through life's disappointments and heartaches, as I walked behind enjoying the wisdom of hindsight. It's hard to explain our bond to people, why my sense of loyalty and camaraderie is the way it is. Why, as grown men we still cuddle—yes, we cuddle sometimes when Peta's not looking.

Very few will understand what pickles and milk means, or stolen Rollerblades, or being a breadwinner at age seventeen, what it's like to be an example to not just me but to all my friends. I struggled vicariously through you and you enjoyed life vicariously through me.

I love you, bro, and it is absolutely incredible for me to see someone next to you who loves you even more than I do.

Peta Chmerkovskiy, aka "Murgasnitch," aka "Lamborghini Mercy," aka "Turn-up Extraordinaire"—I love you.

I love you more than you love the E channel and Keeping Up with the Kardashians. I couldn't have imagined my brother sharing the rest of his life with anyone else. You have given him a greater purpose and a greater focus. You truly made him into a man. I've never seen him more in love or more driven than when he's around you. You are his true love, his muse, his wife, his teammate, the point guard to his team. And when ball is life—trust me, that's a huge compliment.

I wrote once:

Maks, realize that
Love is really blind
Brother, if you stay true to you
In time true love will find you

Looking at you now, as man and wife, I can confidently say you both have found true love. I wish the two of you a

*life of camaraderie, respect, health, and happiness. I hope you
two continue to inspire each other, continue to grow together,
and continue to be the incredible parents that you are.*

*To a few more kids, a lot more smiles, and a lifetime of
memories . . .*

I love you both dearly!

The simple message of the first tattoo I got, "Family Over
Everything," still holds true above all. At first, it was just those
simple three words, along with "keep it moving," that represented
my personal motto. But over time I went back to the studio for more
ink, adding to the design until it took over my whole bicep—my
extremely large (I wish), hard as steel (not likely), often shirtless
(yup) bicep.

I think of the tat now as telling the story of my life, starting
out with the core value of family, then getting enlarged with more
experiences, more embellishes, more design.

In the Chmerkovskiy family, we always stay true to our
roots. Three of the guests at Maks's wedding were among those
original seven kids who showed up at the Rising Stars open
house, two decades before. Many of my friends are Rising Stars
alumni, and many of them have been on *Dancing with the Stars* as
members of the dance troupe. I'm in touch with almost all my
competition partners from the past, and I count as close friends
the celebrity partners I've worked with, as well as many of their
families.

This book is a testament to the friendships and relationships
I've cherished over the years. Their support is another sign for me
that what I've written is not just an ego-stroke, but a validation
of real ties I've made, friendships that weren't just for show and
weren't one-sided either, but two-way streets that we built together.
Without the friends, allies, mentors, and partners I've had in my
life, I would just be a fool dancing alone in a solo spot.

My moms and pops, my grandmother in Far Rockaway—we all maintain strong bonds even though we are usually a continent apart. I see them often, and always feel the urge to communicate to my mother and father the gratitude I feel. I want to tell them how grateful I am for all the sacrifices they made for me, for all the tools they've given me, and to assure them their youngest son is fine and thriving in the world because of the opportunities they provided.

Thanks, Maks. Thanks, Moms and Pops. I love you more than words can say—even though I've just used 300 pages of words to communicate that fact as best I can.

I'VE ALWAYS BELIEVED THAT YOU'RE ONLY AS GOOD AS YOUR last performance, and whatever *Dancing with the Stars* season I just completed always seems to be my best one yet. It might be a question of me improving all the time, not so much as a teacher, dancer, or choreographer, but simply getting better at living life altogether.

As I write this, I am in the middle of, yup, my best season ever. That has nothing to do with me, and everything to do with the incredible individual that I lucked out getting as a partner.

Victoria Arlen is a Paralympic gold medalist from New England with an incredibly inspiring story. She grew up very active and sporty, but when she was eleven years old she came down with transverse myelitis and acute disseminated encephalomyelitis, rare infections that made her brain and spine swell. She gradually lost feeling in her extremities, and then her speech went as well. One morning she woke up and found she couldn't move at all. She was "locked in," aware, able to hear and think, but incapable of expressing herself.

At eleven and a half years old, she heard a doctor inform her parents that recovery was impossible.

"She's not going to make it," said the so-called expert. "You just have to accept the fact that your child is going to die."

Imagine Victoria hearing and understanding those chilling words, but being unable to call out, react, or object. The doctors didn't really have a prognosis. They had no idea how to address her condition, and when physicians don't see a clear path to a cure, their reaction can be to throw up their latex-gloved hands in defeat.

But her mom and dad were very stubborn people. As parents they never stopped believing and never stopped loving their daughter. They took her out of the hospital and cared for her at home, keeping faith that Victoria would somehow pull through. She was stuck, her body totally nonresponsive. Her thoughts grew darker and more blurry and then just faded to black.

Two years passed. Victoria was in her midteens when she emerged from the coma, and her mind came back, too. One day her mom locked eyes with Victoria and realized that something had changed. *Oh my God*, her mother thought, *she's here! There's a consciousness there!*

"Blink twice if you can hear me," her mother said, overcome with emotion.

Victoria started blinking, and that's all that was necessary to move forward with her recovery. She and her family began communicating, she began exercising, and with enough faith and hope they embarked on a grueling five-year recuperation just to get Victoria into a wheelchair. Two years later, she won three medals swimming in the summer 2012 Paralympics. She eventually began working as a commentator at ESPN. In 2016, after being paralyzed from the waist down for nearly a decade, she took her first step.

A year after that, still with no feeling in her legs, she joined the cast of *Dancing with the Stars* as a celebrity contestant.

The timing of this book, with me reflecting on my life, meditating on all the different blessings that came into fruition, and my desire to pass those blessings forward—I think it all culminated perfectly in my partnership with Victoria.

Victoria is not just an American hero for winning medals in the Paralympics. She's a human hero for triumphing over something that universally unites us: our mortality and fight for life. There's no greater example of the human spirit, and no better demonstration of strength in family.

Ultimately, that's what this book is about. We all have different challenges and we all have different paths in life. We all have trip-ups along the way, and some of us have bigger trip-ups than others—some of us can't even feel our legs. But we gotta keep it moving.

I began this book by talking about being put into boxes. Racism, anti-Semitism, anti-immigrant bigotry, prejudice against the disabled are all examples of the most deadly kind of labeling. They drain the humanity from individuals and reduce them to stick figures.

Oh, that's the black girl from that singing group.
Oh, that's the Hispanic chick who thinks she can be a
gymnast.
That's the new mother, that's the gay guy, that's the Muslim,
that's the Christian, that's the Jew, that's the foreigner,
that's the liberal, that's the conservative, that's the
outsider, that's the other.
That's the girl in the wheelchair who wants to dance.
That's the immigrant, that's the Russian kid who can't speak
English, that's the geek with the stupid kicks whose mom
always makes him tuck in his shirt.

They don't belong, those people. They can't do it. They, they, they.

I don't want any part of it. How many roads do we need to walk down before we realize that there is no "they"? There's only us.

Closed-minded attitudes have killed millions over the centuries and are still killing people today. Beyond that, they place a heavy weight on the human imagination, on possibility and self-image. We lose so much when we obsess over differences and ignore our common humanity.

But that shouldn't discourage us. It shouldn't discourage all those people moving forward with open-minded attitudes, who are seeking to inspire others with their own joy and happiness, sharing the beauty they see in this world. As much as this book deals with negativity, it doesn't dwell on it, either. I've been very fortunate that I've felt the wind beneath my wings from my family and mentors, and I hope this book can be that for others as well. Meet adversity with a smile and keep it moving.

Take a look at the cast members of *Dancing with the Stars*. They're like poster children for diversity, for the idea that no single attribute can ever define a creature as complex as a human being. Athletes come on the show and magically transform into dancers. All flavors, colors, and backgrounds are welcome, with the only qualification being a willingness to learn, grow, and work hard toward a shared goal.

I've come to see *Dancing with the Stars* as a microcosm of the American dream. Over twenty-five seasons, what's been reflected in the countless mirrors of the Mirrorball Trophy tells the real truth of what's out there in the world.

My experience, as chronicled in this book, is likewise a symbol of what America is all about. I have a fierce allegiance and a wild kind of gratitude toward the country that has given me a wonderful home, and I try to live up to its ideals every day of my life. I've seen America, I've met her by the thousands while out on tour, we've hugged, shook hands, and inspired each other, and I know the goodness that resides in the hearts of her people. We only need to tap into it to make this world a better place.

That's the message I've tried to convey in everything I do. Keep the positive, optimistic beat. You can do it. Don't let the naysayers—or the judges—get you down. With love in our hearts, rhythm in our souls, and a little shimmy in our hips, we can achieve miracles. Be kind. Be great.

VALENTIN CHMERKOVSKIY: COMPETITIVE BALLROOM DANCE RECORD

Fourteen-time U.S. National Latin Dance Champion

Two-time World Latin Dance Champion

Blackpool Dance Festival Champion

U.S. Open Champion

German Open Champion

Asian-Pacific Champion

UK Open Latin Champion

North American Championships, First Place

La Classique du Quebec, First Place

GRATITUDES

I call it gratitudes because acknowledgments sounds so formal. So clichéd. My appreciation for my mentors, my friends, my family, and everyone that gave me their time, their hearts, I'm most proud of those ties. Those that have shared their most precious gift with me, their time. But more than that, they gave me their effort, their knowledge, and their wisdom. These are folks for whom I'm genuinely grateful. In their own way of course, I have an individual story and tie with each person, but the authenticity with which I appreciate them is across the board one hundred percent.

To my brother Maks for really *really* being that guy. The Foreword speaks for itself, but growing up, he always had to speak for himself plus one. The plus one was the flyest little brother in the universe but was always a plus one, minus six years, and a whole lot of inches. In height. Maks was always proud of me, always concerned, and always there. For me to truly be able to have a book of stories to write about, is because of Maks. And as I said after the final bow of *Our Way,* "It's nice to say 'I did it,' but it's even better to say that 'we did.'"

And to my parents, y'all the shit. The best. The absolute best, and I reap the fruits of your labor. Mom literally, Pops literally. And God, to see you sacrifice so much so often for your kids growing up was and still is the most inspirational energy I have ever been around. You have shaped me into the mind, the man, and the person that I am today. I love you, and thank you so much.

To my friends, y'all the village that gave me everything I ever needed. My pride lies in the friendships that I keep. Alex, my oldest friend. We've had twenty-three years of friendship, competition, growth, laughs, basketball, arguments, durak, cee-lo, being dumb and ambitious, and way too smart for our own good. I love you, my brother, for holding me to a standard that never lets me breathe, but always makes me the best version of myself. I appreciate you. Nicole Volynets, who, if Martha Stewart and Coco Chanel had an offspring, she would be it. Thank you for always being there, and for always being excited and supportive of all the crazy ideas I have. The entire Volynets family, for being my second family for fifteen years now. You have loved and supported me like I was your own and I'll always be so grateful for that. Eugene Livshits, Igor Drobyazko, Ted Volynets, Serge Onik, Mervin Samuels, Yaron Abraham, thank you for being my brothers, my teammates, who always inspired me to be my best. At least that's how I justify all the trash talk from y'all in my mind.

Thank you to all my dance partners that I have ever had the honor to dance with. Being able to create with you, compete with you, teach and learn from you, and have the time of my life doing so has been absolutely incredible. Anyone catch the inadvertent *Dirty Dancing* reference? The truth is, I am only as good as my partner and I believe that and apply that thought to this day. Thank you all for sharing the stage with me all these years.

Special thank you to Deena Katz for being the Hollywood mother that, even though she has literally a million phone calls to take in a minute, always picked up the phone on me. Anytime I called to talk, to vent, to share the "next big Hollywood show" idea, you always made time to hear me out. To Ashley Edens, Joe Sankur, Rob Wade, Mandy Moore for believing in me all those seasons of bad haircuts, terrible bites, and questionable choreography choices. You all stuck with me and gave me a chance on *Dancing with the Stars*—to not just change my own life, but also the lives of so many around me. Everyone in my *DWTS* family, thank you for being the hardest workers in the business, there is definitely a reason why we're going into our 26th season.

Thank you to Guy Phillips, for being wise and cool headed, from believing in me and giving me a shot with our own tour, to becoming a dear friend I can call any time for advice. Kathy Shapiro for having my back and always being there. Marina Kenigstain for being the best. Peter Grant, major gratitude for being my lawyer for the last seven years now, and for always looking out and telling me exactly how it is. I want to thank the most excellent team that worked with me to create this book, leading with Sheryl Shade, who found a home for the project at HarperCollins, where Alieza Schvimer and Lisa Sharkey proved to be expert and enthusiastic guides through the publishing process. Thanks also to the entire publishing team at HarperCollins, including Anna Montague, Lynn Grady, Ben Steinberg, Kell Wilson, and Maria Silva. I'd like to thank Dave Levisohn, Jerry Metellus, and Maarten De Boer for their photography.

To Gil Reavill, who helped me shape my words into stories and form those stories into a book. Besides becoming dear friends in the process of working together, I am forever grateful for the passion you displayed for this book throughout. You quickly understood this wasn't going to be the usual process. That there was a crazy passionate, meticulous, and highly particular person on the other side that is allergic to mediocrity and is really anal about every nuance, flow, and thought that would be written down in this book. Thank you for your patience, guidance, and, at the end of the day, your honest friendship.

Lastly, I want to thank Jenna Johnson. I love you dearly, and this book would never have been made without your love and support. You've been the rock that I needed for years now, way before the book or before anyone would have been interested in reading it. You've heard these stories, and these lectures, and my nonsense every day for years, and your words of encouragement for my crazy thoughts were all I ever needed to make them come alive. You've helped me create so much magic becoming my partner, not just in dance or choreography, but more importantly at home, in life. What's mine is yours, my love.

Thank you to every reader, every fan, and every single person that gave me their time to connect. I hope you got something out of the thoughts in this book and are inspired to go out and live a life worth writing about. Till next time . . .